Dialogues of the Word attempts
contemporary literary-critical sen
received text of the Bible as it has been
essentially fixed for most of the last two
thousand years. Drawing on the theory of
language developed by the Soviet critic
Mikhail Bakhtin, Reed argues that the historically diverse writings of the Bible have
been organized according to a concept of
dialogue. The overriding concern with an
ongoing communication between God and
his people has been formally embodied,
Reed shows, in the continuous conversation between one part of the Bible and
another.

This unique study looks beyond the
close readings of recent accounts of the
Bible as literature to larger paradigms of
communication in the Hebrew Bible and
the Christian New Testament. Reed considers the Bible in its different canonical
states, distinguishing the genres of law,
prophecy, and wisdom in the Hebrew
Bible and describing how these earlier
forms of divine and human communication
are appropriated and answered by the New
Testament genre of gospel. The dialogic
character of the Bible is also revealed
within individual books: patriarchal
answers to primeval failures in Genesis,
cross-talk between justice and providence
in Job, and orchestration of judgment and
worship in Revelation.

Throughout this wide-ranging study,
Reed demonstrates the surprising relevance
of Bakhtin's ideas of literature and language to the biblical writings as they
assume formal coherence within the canon.
Positioning itself between the fragmenting
referentiality of the historical view and the
consolidating authority of the theological
view, this literary reading of the Bible will
interest both literary and historical critics

DIALOGUES OF THE WORD

DIALOGUES
OF THE WORD

The Bible as Literature
According to Bakhtin

WALTER L. REED

New York   Oxford
OXFORD UNIVERSITY PRESS
1993

Wingate College Library

Oxford University Press

Oxford New York Toronto
Delhi Bombay Calcutta Madras Karachi
Kuala Lumpur Singapore Hong Kong Tokyo
Nairobi Dar es Salaam Cape Town
Melbourne Auckland Madrid

and associated companies in
Berlin Ibadan

Copyright © 1993 by Oxford University Press, Inc.

Published by Oxford University Press, Inc.,
200 Madison Avenue, New York, New York 10016

Oxford is a registered trademark of Oxford University Press

All rights reserved. No part of this publication may be reproduced,
stored in a retrieval system, or transmitted, in any form or by any means,
electronic, mechanical, photocopying, recording, or otherwise,
without the prior permission of Oxford University Press.

Library of Congress Cataloging-in-Publication Data
Reed, Walter L.
Dialogues of the Word : the Bible as literature according
to Bakhtin / Walter L. Reed.
p. cm. Includes bibliographical references.
ISBN 0-19-507997-3
1. Bible as literature. 2. Bakhtin, M. M. (Mikhail Mikhaïlovich),
1895–1975. I. Title.
BS535.R39 1993
220.6'6—dc20   92-36420

1 3 5 7 9 8 6 4 2
Printed in the United States of America
on acid-free paper

*For Loree, Seth,
Melissa, and Catherine*

Preface

"The Bible . . . according to Bakhtin?" readers may well ask in disbelief. Literary readers may recall the story by Jorge Luis Borges, "Pierre Menard, Author of the *Quixote*," in which a French Symbolist poet of the late nineteenth century undertakes to write the Spanish novel of the early seventeenth century already written by Cervantes. Although he only manages to produce a few chapters of his own *Quixote* (verbally identical but "infinitely richer" in their alien setting), we are assured by Borges's narrator that Menard has enriched the art of reading by means of a new technique: "the deliberate anachronism and the erroneous attribution."[1]

It is the intention of this study to enrich the art of reading the Bible, although not by re-creating it in the whimsically demiurgic manner of Pierre Menard. My aim is rather to apply a particular, twentieth-century conception of literature and language to an ancient text, in order to understand and appreciate the way this text has organized its various verbal parts into meaningful wholes. In saying that the Bible has organized itself, I am revealing a bias toward literary formalism. I am not primarily concerned with identifying the manifold sources of the Bible, in the manner of historical criticism. Nor am I particularly concerned in this book with specifying its regulative authority within subsequent communities of interpretation, which I take to be the task of theological interpretation. Rather I am interested in making contemporary literary-critical sense of the received and translated text of the Bible, more or less fixed—though in somewhat different versions—for most of the last two thousand years.

The contemporary sense that I make in this book is of course a meaningfulness of my own construction. It is the sense that the Bible makes to a literary critic trained in the twilight of the New Criticism and seeking, like a great many of his colleagues today, to move "beyond formalism" in a way that will not simply consign to the scrap pile the many advances that such formalist criticism has made in techniques of literary interpretation. The great appeal of Bakhtin for an increasing number of literary critics in the Anglo-American tradition comes from the way he himself began to move beyond formalism—beyond Russian Formalism—more than sixty years earlier, into the wider reaches of philosophical reflection and cultural history.

In my own case, and quite by coincidence, I became interested in Bakhtin about the same time that I became interested in the Bible itself. It was only in the mid-1970s that I began to read, to teach, and then to write about the Bible in the context of my study of literature. And it was in 1977, at the urging of my friend and then-colleague Michael Holquist and with the aid of his and his students' translations from the Russian, that I began to read in a more than casual way the literary theory of this powerful and long-unknown Soviet thinker. For some time these interests ran on separate tracks. But as I read more widely in the vast archives of biblical criticism and as I read more deeply in the growing volume of Bakhtin's writing being translated into English, I began to see that the questions I was asking in the one area were finding answers, or at least more searching formulations, in the other.

I am aware that there will be readers of this book who will want more explication, perhaps more critique, of Bakhtin's theories themselves and less attention to the Bible. They are referred first and foremost to several excellent books by Holquist and others who have worked with him: the biography *Mikhail Bakhtin* (Cambridge: Harvard University Press, 1984) by Holquist and Katerina Clark; *Rethinking Bakhtin: Extensions and Challenges* (Evanston: Northwestern University Press, 1989) by Gary Saul Morson and Caryl Emerson; *Dialogism: Bakhtin and His World* (London: Routledge, 1990) by Holquist; and *Mikhail Bakhtin: Creation of a Prosaics* (Stanford: Stanford University Press, 1990) by Morson and Emerson. My desire in this book is to apply a theory of verbal communication rather than to explain it in terms of other theoretical (or commonsense) approaches.

There may also be readers who would prefer a less peculiarly mediated presentation of the Bible. They may feel, not without reason, that to read the Bible in the light of Bakhtin is to hold a candle in sunshine. Such readers (if they have made it beyond the subtitle) are asked to reflect for a moment on their own theoretical assumptions and consider whether it is possible to read any text without someone's guidance, somewhere along the way. As I can testify from my own experience as a student and a teacher of literature over the last thirty years, the Bible is often simply not read at all these days in American higher education, which is to be regretted on many counts. Whether the guidance Bakhtin offers to reading the Bible ("perhaps without wanting to," as Borges says of Pierre Menard's enriching the art of reading) is appropriate, enlightening, or in some sense true to the text is a question that can only be answered by those who read on and give the dialogue of this book a hearing.

In the Afterword, I reflect more generally on the assumptions that govern a literary reading of the Bible as distinct from those that inform a historical reading on the one hand and a theological reading on the other. One of the things Bakhtin's theory of language and literature suggests is that a literary reading positions itself between the fragmenting referentiality of the historical view and the consolidating authority of the theological perspective. Historians tend to regard the Bible as merely a part of a much larger archive of documents and other cultural evidence of human expression; theologians tend to consider it as a set of scriptures of intrinsic and essentially self-contained authority proceeding, in some manner, from God. Literary critics inevitably treat the biblical writings as an anthology selected according to various criteria of aesthetic value and gathered into coherence according to ideas of literary genre, even as they realize (or should realize) that these criteria and ideas are not the primary concern of the authors of the text. Readers who desire more preliminary orientation about the assumptions behind this and other treatments of "the Bible as literature" are advised to read the last part of the book first.

One last apologetic and explanatory note. I have written with "small Greek and less Hebrew" on writings originally composed in these ancient languages, not from the misguided conviction that knowledge of these languages is unimportant for understanding the text, but with a lively appreciation for the many translations, commentaries, and analytic tools that have been provided for unprofessional readers of the Bible by biblical scholars of all persuasions over the centuries. This is a book by a biblical amateur, though I confess to being an "amateur" of the Bible in more than one sense of that word.

Atlanta   W. L. R.
October 1992

Acknowledgments

This book has been long in the works and has benefited from the advice of many friends and colleagues. Michael Holquist has been an invaluable source of inspiration and instruction about the writings of Bakhtin. Vern McGee has combined counsel about Bakhtin with advice about biblical matters. John Cogdell and Ken Frieden asked hard questions that led to more adequate answers than I would have been capable of otherwise. Encouragement and more suggestions than I have been able or willing to take have come from Bracht Branham, Leslie Brisman, Martin Buss, Dan Davis, Robert Detweiler, Harold Fisch, Alan Gregory, James Nohrnberg, Stephen Prickett, Vernon Robbins, Gray Temple, Jr., and Leonard Thompson. None of them, of course, is responsible for any of the errors of judgment or infelicities of argument that may remain.

Research leave provided by the University Research Institute of the University of Texas at Austin allowed me to begin the writing of the book, and leave granted by Dean David Minter of Emory College and the University Research Committee of Emory University allowed me to complete it. I am grateful to both institutions and their representatives for this support. A preliminary version of part of Chapter 1 appeared as "A Poetics of the Bible: Problems and Possibilities" in *Literature and Theology*, 1, no. 2 (September 1987): 154–66, published by Oxford University Press; a shorter version of Chapter 4 appeared as "Dimensions of Dialogue in the Book of Job: A Topology According to Bakhtin" in *Texas Studies in Literature and Language*, 34, no. 2 (Summer 1992): 177–96, published by the University of Texas Press. I appreciate permission from both presses to republish this material. Unless otherwise indicated, the Bible quotations in this book are from the Revised Standard Version of the Bible, copyright 1946, 1952, 1971 by the Division of Christian Education of the National Council of Churches of Christ in the U.S.A., and are used by permission.

My greatest debt in writing this book is to my wife, Loree, who first challenged me to read beyond the safe lowlands of literature in the risky high places of the Bible and sustained me in my explorations of this terrain in more ways than I can acknowledge here. It is to her and to our children, also supportive of my scholarly preoccupation, that the book is dedicated.

Abbreviations

The following abbreviations for editions of the Bible are used throughout the text:

KJV   King James Version
NIV   New International Version
RSV   Revised Standard Version

Contents

DIALOGUES OF THE WORD

1

In the Beginning:
Dialogue in Genesis
and the Gospels

"Literary criticism, long thought to be peripheral or even irrelevant to biblical studies, has emerged since the mid-1970s as a new major focus of academic biblical scholarship in North America, England, and Israel." In *The Literary Guide to the Bible*, Robert Alter and Frank Kermode thus take note of a recent shift in the scholarly study of the Bible, a shift to which they have both made major contributions.[1] This movement can be observed among staunch biblicists as well as theological liberals; it has taken place in the ranks of the most contemporary of literary theorists as well as among traditionalists in literary criticism.[2] It is true that the concept of literature is often different in many of these studies; it may be a matter of recurrent images, of traditional genres, or radical indeterminacy between competing tropes. It is also true that such studies vary in their conception of the Bible itself. Some critics treat the Hebrew Bible of Judaism, others the Christian Bible with Old and New Testaments; among those who deal with the Christian Old Testament some treat the more restricted Protestant canon and some the expanded Catholic list of books. Nevertheless, in spite of these differences, a striking convergence has been taking place between biblical scholarship, traditionally cast in historical and theological frameworks, and literary criticism, traditionally concerned with secular texts.

The single most important precursor of this recent revival or renaissance of literary interpretations of the Bible, as Alter and Kermode also note in their *Literary Guide*, was Erich Auerbach's classic study *Mimesis: The Representation of Reality in Western Literature*, first published in German in 1946 and translated into English in 1953. In the first two chapters of this magisterial and still much-admired survey of Western culture, Auerbach juxtaposes episodes, first from the *Odyssey* and Genesis, then from Petronius, Tacitus, and the Gospel of Mark, to show the way the biblical text in particular influenced and prefigured the representation of reality in subsequent European literature. Other scholars have paid more extensive tribute to the enduring value of Auerbach's initiative. Hans Frei has singled out Auerbach's treatment of the "history-like" qualities of the Bible as an important alternative to an excessive concern with referential truth or falsehood in biblical studies.[3] And Geoffrey Hartman has rehearsed in more theoretically sophisticated terms Auerbach's most telling observations about the Bible's imperious claims to truth and its demands upon the reader.[4] I will begin my own study of the Bible as literature according to Bakhtin by looking at Auerbach's discussion of the sacrifice of Isaac in Genesis 22.

I

One of the distinctive features of Auerbach's approach to both the Old and the New Testaments was to shift the discussion of the literary features of the Bible away from the idea of poetry and the poetic to the idea of narrative and historical realism. Like Robert Lowth's *Lectures on the Sacred Poetry of the Hebrews* two centuries earlier, which organized more casual analogies from previous literary theory and practice into a "complete compendium of critical science," as the English translator of his Latin text put it, most literary approaches to the Bible from the later eighteenth century through the early twentieth treated the Bible as poetry.[5] They considered ways in which the biblical writings resembled poetry or embodied, whether in the medium of verse or prose, poetry's imaginative, pre-logical essence.[6] Since the publication of *Mimesis*, and especially in the last fifteen years, most studies of the literary dimensions of the Bible have concentrated on the idea of narrative, on the narrative rather than poetic parts of the Bible, and on explicit comparisons between the Bible and the modern art of the novel. Frank Kermode goes as far as to speak of "John the novelist" in a reading of the Gospel of John; Gabriel Josipovici writes of resemblances between the Hebrew Bible and Proust's *À la recherche du temps perdu*.[7] Until Auerbach's analysis, the notion of historical realism had been the province of historical critics concerned with the factual truth or historical origins of the biblical writings. These were scholars who regarded literature, especially novels, as lacking the kind of truth value, historical or theological, that the idea of the Bible seemed to demand.

The first thing to notice about *Mimesis* is Auerbach's critical orientation. As a scholar trained in the German discipline known as "Romance philology," he is particularly concerned with the question of style, with a particular level of the literary "code" in which the message is conveyed, to invoke Roman Jakobson's well-known model of the primary constituents of verbal communication.[8] In speaking of the *Odyssey*, for example, Auerbach considers various ways of accounting for the "retarding effect" in Homer's leisurely digression telling how Odysseus got the scar by which he is about to be recognized in the dangerous and emotional scene with his old nurse Euryclea.[9] He dismisses the argument that the effect is determined by the intended impact on the audience, a rhetorical explanation advanced by earlier commentators. "The true cause of the impression," he argues, lies "in the need of the Homeric style to leave nothing which it mentions half in darkness and unexternalized" (5). Thus "the Homeric style" is personified as an agent, in order to account for a formal property of the poem. It is not a question of the poet or author expressing something of his personality or his social views. Nor is it a question of the poem's reflecting the reality or external world to which it seems to refer; the "mimesis" which Auerbach invokes in his title is not conceived according to a mimetic theory of art.

The singularity of Auerbach's critical orientation toward stylistics or "poetics" as a motivation for the form of the text is less clear-cut when he turns his attention from Odysseus's scar to the sacrifice of Isaac. In treating the Bible, he is willing to consider the greater "depths of time, fate and consciousness" (12) in the characters of Abraham, God, and Isaac, emphasizing the immediate suspense and the ultimate mystery of all the characters' motives. In probing the ambiguities of the biblical text, Auerbach acknowledges the expressive concerns of the author ("the Biblical narrator, the Elohist, had to believe in the objective truth of the story" [14]); he describes the pragmatic, rhetorical effect on the reader ("the Scripture stories . . . seek to subject us, and if we refuse to be subjected we are rebels" [15]). He even allows that there are mimetic demands proceeding from the represented world ("It is clear that a large part of the life of David as given in the Bible contains history and not legend" [20]). Nevertheless, as the argument develops, these secondary determinants or motivations of the particular form the narrative takes—a narrative "fraught with background," in Auerbach's famous phrase (12)—are seen as deriving primarily from the literary or semiotic code, the set of stylistic and generic conventions upon which the biblical text, in chapter 22 of Genesis and beyond, is drawing.

Here Auerbach shifts his discussion from the level of style to the level of genre. Although he initially calls both the *Odyssey* and Genesis "epic" (7), he goes on to distinguish them (using episodes in the life of David recounted in 1 and 2 Samuel to bolster his biblical example) as "legend" and "history," respectively. This is not simply a matter of the referential accuracy or the reliability of evidence in the two types of narrative, according to Auerbach. It is a matter of form: "their structure is different" (19). The structure of legend is smooth and repetitive; the structure of history is various, contradictory, even confusing. Where legend is static and tends to unfold from a single perspective, history is dynamic and dramatizes multiple points of view.

Auerbach has been criticized for ignoring the question of literary genre. William Whallon has noted that the poetry of the Old Testament—in Job, the Psalms, and the classical prophets, for example—has much more in common with Homeric epics than the historical narratives of Genesis, 1 and 2 Samuel, and other "historical books" do.[10] One could take this argument further and note that even in the case of the Bible's prose history, there are some sections that are rather similar to the repetitive patterning of "legend" in Homer: the Book of Judges, for examples, with its recurrent cycles of apostasy and deliverance, or the celebratory, idealizing story of David in 1 Chronicles as opposed to the more critical, historical account in 2 Samuel. But Auerbach's overgeneralization of the evidence from his core sample to the stylistically various Old Testament as a whole has been mitigated by most of those who have followed his lead in emphasizing the history-likeness of the narrative in the Hebrew Bible or Old Testament. Robert Alter has gone on to write an *Art of Biblical Poetry*, analyzing parts of the Bible not covered in his *Art of Biblical Narrative*. What is more problematic and influential in Auerbach's reading of the episode is the way the appeal to the literary

code of the Bible, to the "poetics of biblical narrative," in Meir
Sternberg's theoretical rendering of this critical approach, jumps
from the quite specific level of style to the highly general level of
history (a supra-generic genre, in Auerbach's scheme of literary
development). This quantum jump gives rise to a two-story conception of literary form, one that stresses gaps in syntax and inde-
terminacies of information on the level of style while emphasizing ideological unity and coherence on the level of the text as a
formal whole. Such analysis overlooks the many levels of formal-
ization in between style and the dominant genre. What Auerbach
ignores in particular is the local generic resemblances among the
various episodes and incidents that the Bible has singled out for
scenic elaboration. An episode strikingly similar to the sacrifice
or near-sacrifice of Isaac, for example, lies close at hand in Genesis: the sacrifice or abandonment of Ishmael recounted in the
chapter immediately preceding.

In the narrative of Abraham's sacrifice of Ishmael in chapter
21, there are numerous parallels with the succeeding episode in
chapter 22, in wording and in action. Abraham is ordered, initially
by Sarah but subsequently by God, to "cast out" his elder son along
with Hagar, the son's mother. We are told that Abraham "rose early
in the morning" (as in his journey to Mount Moriah with Isaac) to
send the victims forth. Hagar places Ishmael under a bush when
he seems about to die, anticipating the "thicket" in which the ram
appears in the next chapter, whereupon God addresses Hagar by
name and assures her that the child will live. The promise is
extended of a "great nation" coming from Ishmael, akin to the
numerous descendants promised to Isaac, and a well is revealed
to Hagar for their sustenance in the desert. Ishmael is even provided by his parent with a wife afterwards, as Isaac is, at much
greater length, in chapter 24.

The play of similarities and differences between the two episodes is striking and seems a significant feature of the literary structure of this stretch of narrative in Genesis. A notable difference
between the two episodes, in Auerbach's own terms, is the noticeably less spare and mysterious quality of the account of the crisis
over Ishmael. It is a natural jealousy on Sarah's part that requires
the sacrifice rather than an inexplicable will of God. Indeed, Sarah's
jealousy has already been described, with a similar though only
temporary exile of Hagar into the wilderness, in chapter 16. Abraham's emotions, so laconically passed over in the sacrifice of Isaac,
are given an adequate description—"the thing was very displeas-

ing to Abraham on account of his son"—and Hagar's grief is more
fully dramatized, even though in the Hebrew text, not preferred
by the RSV, it says oddly that Hagar wept and God responded to
the voice of the child.[11] God also confides in Abraham, revealing
in the earlier episode his providential purpose in advance. Thus in
this previous near-sacrifice of a son (a product of the same "Elohist"
source, according to the classic form of the Documentary Hypothesis), there is a good deal of the well-lit "foreground" that Auerbach
held to be such a distinctive feature of the epic style of the *Odyssey*. Indeed, in commenting on the parallel between the two
episodes, Robert Alter uses the term "type-scene" from Homeric
scholarship to describe the generic relationship between them.[12]

What is a literary interpretation to make of this extended
though relatively local resemblance? Who is responsible for it and
what does it mean? Two additional observations might be added
to this question. As already indicated in the allusion to the "sacrifice of Hagar" in chapter 16, the set of episodic resemblances
appears to be a good deal more extensive in Genesis. Both chapters 21 and 22 are reminiscent of an earlier episode of jealousy,
sibling rivalry, and sacrifice in the story of Cain and Abel in Genesis 4. There God prefers the sacrifice offered by the younger
brother, which leads the older brother to sacrifice the younger to
his own jealousy. It is almost as if Sarah is thinking of Abel's fate
when she sees Ishmael "playing with her son Isaac" (21:9) and is
determined to prevent its recurrence. There is also the later rivalry,
developed at much greater length and with greater psychological
complication, between Esau and Jacob for divine and parental
favor, and the rivalry, complete with the averted sacrifice of a
younger child, between Joseph and his jealous brothers in the next
generation. The lonely sacrifice of Isaac turns out to be part of a
much larger pattern in Genesis.

On the other hand, the scene of Odysseus's scar in the *Odyssey* recalls any number of scenes in the poem involving dangerous
hospitality extended by a woman, accompanied by the sacrifice of
animals. Euryclea's recognition of Odysseus by means of the scar
left by the wild boar is a milder, more realistic version of Circe's
legendlike welcome of Odysseus in the forest, where the hero is
in danger of being turned permanently into a wild pig. The episode also recalls Calypso's welcome of Odysseus on her island,
where he is in danger of becoming an immortal consort and los-
ing his humanity in another direction. The *Odyssey* as a whole
can be read, arguably, as an elaborate set of variations on the scene

of perilous guest-host relations, where being welcomed by a faithful wife is the promise, being killed like a sacrificial animal is the threat, that Odysseus faces throughout. In the fabulous first part of his journey, the hero prepares himself for the realistic difficulties he will face from Penelope's suitors once he has landed back on Ithaca. In an irony that escapes Auerbach's distinction between a uniformly legendary *Odyssey* and a uniformly historical Book of Genesis, the *lies* Odysseus tells people when he appears incognito back on his own island are much more realistic than the legendary adventures with giants, witches, and ghosts he recounts to the Phaiacians, adventures which we, like this first audience within the poem, are apparently meant to accept as the true account.

This more explicit, more pervasive, and more homogeneous typology of the *Odyssey* may be explained, relatively uncontroversially, by appealing to the artistic genius of the poet (whether or not he is the same as the poet of the *Iliad)*, or to the mnemonic requirements of oral epic, the literary genre of which the poem has been long considered a prime example. The multiple variations on a primary scene might also be explained, following Eric Havelock's theory of the *Iliad* and the *Odyssey* as a "tribal encyclopedia" of Greek oral culture, as a form specially adapted to information retrieval, organizing accounts of disparate activities into memorable shape.[13] There is no reason, in fact, that all three motivations, or some other version of each of them, might not be invoked in concert with one another to account for the intricate formal patterning of the received text. With the more sparing, apparently ad hoc parallelism of episodes we have noted in Genesis, such explanations would have to be modified to take account of the different character of the Hebrew Bible as it has been perceived by the different communities of interpretation that have concerned themselves with it. Initially, however, it seems that plausible interpretations might be offered along similar lines. One might claim it is the author of the source document (E) (or the redactor of the various sources) who is responsible for the similarities between Genesis 21 and 22, that he takes care to express through the parallelism his notion that there is a providential design in the otherwise scattered set of stories and legends he had inherited, through oral tradition or scribal documents. Or one might argue from the perspective of the audience, as Regina Schwartz does in a perceptive discussion of these episodes, that the similarities and differences between the two stories are intended to reinforce a particular theological and ethical paradox about free will and determinism that the Hebrew Bible repeatedly impresses on its readers. This is an argument from rhetorical impact.[14]

It is more difficult to imagine a mimetic argument, a claim that the resemblance between the two episodes is occasioned by the external world or the context to which the Genesis narrative refers. Nevertheless, a structural anthropologist might deduce a particular conflict between patrilineal and matrilineal descent that was being represented in the pair of sacrifices involving a mother's and then a father's will. A hermeneutic theologian might triangulate from the two examples of averted sacrifice to a higher-level concept of divine mercy underlying divine judgment. A traditional Christian typologist might claim that the two sacrifices actually occurred in this contrastive fashion, in the historical happening beyond the text as well as in the salvation-historical narrative of the Old Testament, in order to sharpen a prefiguration of the sacrifice of God's only begotten Son, Jesus Christ. The sacrifice of Isaac would be the true prefiguration, with Ishmael's fate representing a false, pagan alternative, a sacrifice according to the flesh.[15] As Auerbach explains in another influential essay, "Figura," concerned with Christian typology, this would count as a mimetic interpretation because the Old Testament prefiguration or type was held to have as much historical reality as the New Testament fulfillment or antitype, even though such a reading could also be said to reinscribe God as author, a planner of historical happenings for instructive effect.

As my last three examples, admittedly contrived, indicate, the perception of patterns or correspondences on the level of action or plot raises questions about the status and motivation of the biblical text that are less easily resolved than those raised by the similar perception of form in Homeric epic. The kind of world or truth the Bible conveys, the context within which it has referential meaning, remains a contested issue: is it sociohistorical or theological, rational or contrary to rationality, patriarchal or gender-inclusive? The question of the Bible's authorship is similarly controversial, even among literary critics. Is it a text composed by human initiative alone or is there some higher inspiration behind it? The question of the rightful or intended audience of the Bible—whether secular or religious, ecumenical or sectarian, Christian or Jewish—is similarly fraught. It may be argued that this "conflict of interpretations," to borrow a phrase from Paul Ricoeur, is essentially extrinsic, read back into the text by the two or three millenia of passionate readerships that have embraced its story as their own.

Or it may be that a "sacred discontent," as Herbert Schneidau terms the Bible's destabilizing authority, is intrinsically encoded in the received text, inscribed by the conflicted interpreters who assembled the Bible in the first place.[16] In any case, it should be clear to the most irenic of literary critics that a reading which tries to assign responsibility for the Bible's heterogeneous and shifting formality to any single determinant, or even a reading which tries to correlate the claims of all quarters from a detached aesthetic distance, will not be capable of responding to the full range of meanings invested, from whatever quarter, in the text. It will simply introduce a new, single-minded determinant or source of significance, such as "style" or "genre," "structure" or "text," in the manner of Auerbach's persuasive but, in the final analysis, narrowly focused reading in *Mimesis*. James Kugel has complained that many of the recent approaches to the Bible as literature simply substitute a notion of textuality for the idea of divine inspiration, that they are therefore unable to "hear the Bible with, as it were, biblical ears" as they attend to its imperative, but also variously inflected, articulations.[17] A more comprehensive version of a literary approach to the Bible seems to be needed, one that is responsive to the concentrations of authority but also to the dispersions of power that are reenacted in the long past and broad present of its ongoing communication.

II

I return once more to the example of the doubled sacrifice of Abraham's sons, in order to give a more preliminary and open-ended reading, one that emphasizes an initial comprehension of the formal pattern without assigning an original cause or ultimate significance to it. The story of the sacrifice of Isaac, read by Auerbach as a prefiguration of Western European historicism, I am claiming, is given a much more immediate, though rather less definite, context of meaning by the story of Ishmael that precedes it. Through repetition with differences, an interplay of significant variations is established in the text: a jealous triangle of parents, a pair of sons, and a mercifully intervening God are succeeded by a single, tormented parent (Sarah is not mentioned in chapter 22), a single son, and a God who himself plays two radically opposite roles. In the first episode, God works out for Ishmael's good what Sarah means for his harm. Abraham is instructed by God to cooperate with Sarah, but is promised in advance that God will make a nation out of Ishmael's descendants. Hagar, a woman, a servant, and a foreigner, suffers the anguish of leading her child toward death; she experiences the relief of God's provision for his needs (and hers) but she herself receives no promise about his descendants. In the second version of this story of apparent child sacrifice, a version more dramatically intense, God initially announces evil toward Isaac, then provides an animal victim in place of his original demand. Abraham, the original patriarch of Israel, suffers the anguish previously felt by the slave woman from Egypt, although neither the parent nor the child in this second episode, in contrast to the first, expresses any emotion directly. Now at the end of the ordeal rather than in the beginning (and through his angel rather than in direct address), God promises anew not just a multitude of descendants to Isaac but a blessing to all the nations of the earth through his line. At the beginning and at the end of this episode it is made clear, first to the reader and then to Abraham himself, that this has been a test of Abraham's loyalty to God and that the blessing is passed on in response to his obedience, not just because of his powers of procreation.

A description such as this is not innocent of assigning meaning to details of both stories, of attributing value to some elements and not to others. Nevertheless, it proceeds on the assumption that the parallelism itself generates meanings and values for both episodes together. The immediate context of the narrative, in other words, provides the initial frame of reference for understanding a constituent part.

Nevertheless, the term *narrative*, although it currently dominates literary approaches to the Bible, is misleading. In its traditional conception, it implies a univocal structure—a single authorial consciousness presiding over the text. It also implies the presence of a plot with a definite beginning, middle, and end, of characters whose individual fates, realistic or symbolic, freely chosen or predetermined, are the primary determinants of the action of the text as a whole. Unless one has in mind the experimental and alienated anti-narratives of European literary modernism and postmodern fiction—as indeed some critics now argue we should[18]—it is more accurate to say that the Bible contains examples of narrative than to say that the category of narrative contains the Bible. Particularly when one gets beyond Genesis and the first nineteen chapters of Exodus in the Pentateuch, beyond Samuel and Kings in the Historical Books or the Former Prophets, and beyond the Book of Acts in the New Testament, the narrative character of the Bible diminishes rapidly. Even in the case of the parallel stories in Genesis 21 and 22, I would now like to propose, it is the dialogue between stories rather than any narrative structure in which they are embedded, that is the most prominent formal feature of the text. The model of narrative is well suited to a stylistically and narratively homogenous text like the *Odyssey*, as Aristotle's remarks on Homer in the *Poetics* demonstrate, but the heterogeneous textuality of the Bible, where narrative segments are juxtaposed with one another and interspersed with other verbal forms like genealogies, laws, oracles, proverbs, and songs, is better served by a model of *dialogue*, of question and answer, of story and counterstory, of statement and response.

As those familiar with literary criticism and literary theory will realize and as the subtitle of this book makes clear, such a model of dialogue has been developed in the writings of the Soviet critic Mikhail Bakhtin. Born three years after Auerbach and influenced by the Neo-Kantian philosophy of the University of Marburg where Auerbach was later a professor, Bakhtin evolved a theory of literature and philosophy of language opposed to the stylistics of Romance philology of the kind practiced by Auerbach. Bakhtin's theory was also conceived in opposition to the structural linguistics of the Swiss linguist Saussure and those critics and schools that elaborated his "abstract objectivism," as Bakhtin called it, into later kinds of structuralism concerned with the logic of narrative.[19]

In his various books and essays, written between 1919 and 1974, Bakhtin argues that both of these approaches to verbal communication are one-sided, incapable of grasping the radically dialogic nature of all human "utterances," from brief oral exclamations to long written texts. Both stylistics and structural linguistics (or narratology, in its literary form), even though they appear to proceed from opposite epistemological extremes, are symptomatic in Bakhtin's view of "monologic" forces in the human use of language, forces that seek to deny or repress the fundamentally "dialogic" nature of all verbal messages. Dialogue for Bakhtin is not merely the phenomenon of two people speaking back and forth to one another; it is the linguistic precondition for all communication whatsoever, and its interactive awareness of the utterances of others, before and after, is inscribed in every utterance a person makes. In "Discourse in the Novel" he describes the situation as follows:

> Indeed, any concrete discourse (utterance) finds the object at which it was directed already as it were overlain with qualifications, open to dispute, charged with value, already enveloped in an obscuring mist—

or, on the contrary, by the "light" of alien words that have already been spoken about it. It is entangled, shot through with shared thoughts, points of view, alien value judgments and accents. . . . The word . . . weaves in and out of complex interrelationships, merges with some, recoils from others, intersects with yet a third group: and all this may crucially shape discourse, may leave a trace in all its semantic layers, may complicate its expression and influence its entire stylistic profile.[20]

Of course not all utterances or types of utterance are attuned to the dialogic character of language in action. Here Bakhtin singles out the novel as that genre which brings the dialogism of speech and writing to its fullest realization. The novelist "elevates the social heteroglossia surrounding objects into an image that has finished contours, an image completely shot through with dialogized overtones" (278–79). Bakhtin characterizes epic, in contrast, as monologic, in a manner not unlike Auerbach in *Mimesis*. Epic, he explains in his essay "Epic and Novel," is the literary genre in which dialogism is the most repressed, subjected to an "absolute past" and thus sealed off from linguistic diversity and historical becoming (17).

On the face of it, Bakhtin's theory seems ill-suited to the Bible, an ancient and in many respects authoritarian text. In contrast to his voluminous references to Greek and Roman literature, he says very little about the biblical writings; when he does mention the Bible, Bakhtin tends to treat it as offical, single-voiced discourse, stressing its public, institutional role in dominantly Christian cultures and periods. Nevertheless, Bakhtin's theory has a religious dimension to it, derived "not so much from traditional Orthodox thinking within the church," as his biographers put it, "as from the religious revival in the early twentieth century among Russian intellectuals who sought to break new ground in theological thought."[21] Although the evidence is scant and the relevant texts ambiguous, his own adherence to Christianity seems to have been persistent.[22] In any case, as Bakhtin's writings have become more widely known through translation into English in the last ten years (many of the essays first appeared in Russian only in the 1970s), a few critics have begun to notice the striking relevance of Bakhtin's philosophy and aesthetics of dialogue to the peculiarly polyform nature of the Bible. Stephen Prickett is particularly forthright: simply on the level of the diversity of its languages, "the Bible not only illustrates Bakhtin's thesis, but actually provides one of the supreme examples of the way in which discourse arises and takes its meaning from the intersecting of contextual and linguistic boundaries."[23]

The advantages of approaching the Bible on the basis of Bakhtin's "dialogics," as distinct from the concepts of "narrative," "narrative poetics," or "narratology" currently dominating the field, are
many.[24] First and foremost is the attention Bakhtin gives to the
issue of authority in the use of language. This issue lies behind
the debate over the motivation of the various forms or resemblances that a critic may perceive (observed in our discussion of
how to account for the parallel sacrifices of Ishmael and Isaac) and
the related debate over whether these forms are indications of unity
or diversity in the canonical or received text. (It is an axiom of
the Documentary Hypothesis, according to Martin Noth, that repetitions of similar narrative materials must be assigned to different
sources.)[25] Instead of forcing the critic to choose one position or
another in both these debates (authorial motivation of the text and
maximum unity of the form, for example), Bakhtin's approach situates such controversies, at least initially, within the sphere of
the utterance itself. It is not just that the different voices, styles,
dialects, accents, or genres rest inertly juxtaposed within a text,
according to Bakhtin. Rather there is a struggle for dominance
among them, symptomatic of a pervasive struggle between "two
embattled tendencies in the life of language." One of these tendencies is centripetal, asserting unity and central control of the
utterance; the other is centrifugal, dramatizing diversity and the
leverage of the margin. "Every concrete utterance of a speaking
subject serves as a point where centrifugal as well as centripetal
forces are brought to bear. The processes of centralization and
decentralization, of unification and disunification, intersect in the
utterance; the utterance not only answers the requirements of its
own language as an individualized embodiment of a speech act,
but it answers the requirements of heteroglossia as well; it is in
fact an active participant in such speech diversity" (272). Thus the
conflict of interpretations that the critic of the Bible faces may be
understood as a symptom of struggles acted out within the text.

A second major advantage that Bakhtin's dialogism offers to
the interpretation of the Bible is that it encourages the perception
of more than one kind of formal ordering and more than one level
of significant shaping in the canonical text. By acknowledging different historical "layers" within any utterance, semantic and rhetorical, Bakhtin allows the literary critic to attend to the final form
of the Bible without complete disregard for the analysis of intermediate stages of the Bible's formation—or to attend to an intermediate stage without ignoring the final form of the text. Indeed,
the concept of dialogism allows one to see that the process of can-

onization is never truly finished, as new communities of interpretation inevitably subject even a fixed list of books to different constructions of relatedness and to new distributions of authority among and within them.

The last advantage that I would mention of a Bakhtinian approach to the Bible in general and to the question of the Bible as literature in particular is that it allows for a greater rapprochement between the form of the Bible and one of its major themes. Both the Hebrew Bible and the Christian Bible that incorporates a version of the Jewish Scriptures within itself are overwhelmingly and persistently concerned with one thing: the relationship of a single God to a particular subset of humanity designated as his people. The particular names of this God and the way he manifests himself in action and in speech are various. And the composition and character of his people are subject to considerable change. But it is the ongoing dialogue between God and people to which the whole of the biblical text and a great majority of its parts are supposed to testify. Bakhtin's theory of dialogism reveals much about many different kinds of literature, but as far as the Bible itself is concerned, it brings the Bible's most pronounced theme and its most pervasive formal characteristic together under the same conceptual roof. Literary critics who adopt such an interpretive approach need not submit in their own persons to the Bible's command "to monotheize" human experience, as James Sanders puts it.[26] But they can claim, even as they listen from a literary distance, to be hearing the monotheizing *and* humanizing text with "biblical ears."

The thematic concern with dialogue is readily apparent and is affirmed by critics of many different persuasions. As Leonard L. Thompson puts it in his own literary approach, "a dialogue between the Lord God and a people . . . is the crucial relationship in the biblical world, in light of which every other relationship and all other actions are judged."[27] The formal expressions of this dialogue have also been widely noted, though they have not always been thought of as such. They occur at all levels of the text, from the *Leitwörter* described by Buber and Rosenzweig, the subtly but significantly reiterated words and phrases, to the massive renarration of Genesis through 2 Kings presented at the conclusion of the Hebrew Bible in 1 and 2 Chronicles, the most extended version of the phenomenon that Michael Fishbane has termed "inner biblical exegesis."[28] Such large-scale dialogic revoicing, of course, reaches beyond the Hebrew Bible, into the "Oral Torah" of rabbinic Judaism, as well as into the oral sayings and stories of Jesus that became the New Testament of Christianity. It includes the typological redeployment of the Exodus story in some of the Psalms, in some of the prophets (especially in Hosea and Second Isaiah), in the Letter to the Hebrews (via Psalm 78), and in the Book of Revelation, to mention only one of the recurrent "types" deployed within the boundaries of the Jewish and Christian canons. And it includes the many repetitions-with-a-difference in the New Testament itself—the four-fold life of Jesus presented in the four different narrative Gospels or the contrasting images of the apostle Paul that emerge from the Book of Acts and Paul's letters to particular churches.

Bakhtin's model of dialogue also allows one to correlate the "poetical books" of the Old Testament with the "techniques of repetition," as Alter calls them, in biblical narrative.[29] The essentially rhetorical device termed "parallelism of members" by Robert Lowth in the eighteenth-century and controversially assimilated to "biblical poetry" since then is best seen not as something sharply distinguished from biblical prose, but as a conventional, economical, and flexible form for linking paratactic clauses together in heightened and mutually animating relationships. In the words of one of its best recent interpreters, parallelism juxtaposes the two parts of a verse in such a way that "the lines, by virtue of their contiguity, are perceived as connected while the exact relationship between them is left unspecified."[30] Another critic speaks of an "elementary drama" in the tension between expectation and fulfillment created by the two (or occasionally three) members of the verse.[31] Later versions of this Hebraic (and more broadly Near Eastern) rhetorical convention can be seen in the New Testament in the parables of Jesus, with their play of similitude between the kingdom of heaven and the things of earth, and the "staircase parallelisms," as they are called, of repetitive rhetoric in the Fourth Gospel and the Letters of John.

Thus a dialogics of the Bible can make use of much existing scholarship, correlating more localized descriptions and reformulating interpetations that are oriented in different directions. The model of dialogic interplay can also take account of literatures beyond the Bible itself, of the influence of ancient Near Eastern and later Greco-Roman genres on the biblical writings, or the Bible's "transformation" of these genres, as the case is sometimes put in recent studies.[32] And it can deal with the impact of the canonical writings on later literatures, religious and secular. Nevertheless, reading the Bible in the light of Bakhtin's theory of dialogue is not simply a matter of rebottling old wine, as I shall demonstrate in the remainder of this chapter with two dialogic readings, one of the Book of Genesis as a whole, the other of the incident of Peter's denial of Christ as presented in Mark and the other New Testament Gospels.

III

It is a commonplace of commentary on Genesis that there are two major sections of the book, the "primeval prologue" of chapters 1–11 and the "patriarchal prologue" of chapters 12–50. In Auerbach's terms, one might say that the primeval prologue is more "legendary," with elements like a talking snake, giants, and a worldwide flood. Similar stories, even similar sequences of stories, have been noted in earlier Mesopotamian epics and chronicles.[33] The patriarchal prologue is more "historical," lacking supernatural elements, apart from God and an occasional angel, and giving considerable attention to human responses to the divine initiatives.

Beyond this widespread agreement, there is a considerable body of opinion that there are smaller divisions of the book signaled by the phrase "These are the generations of" (as the King James Version faithfully renders the Hebrew *toledot*), yielding five narrative units interspersed with five genealogical lists.[34] This idea of an overarching structure has led critics to emphasize different analogies between one story segment and another—between the story of Adam and the story of Noah, for example, or among the stories of Adam, Noah, and Abraham.[35] More intricate schemes involving concentric or envelope structures or the recurrence of certain type scenes or archetypes have been proposed as well, although some of these are less concerned with the overall form of Genesis than with the articulation of its smaller parts and their relationship to later books of the Bible.[36]

Without denying the validity of any of these perceptions of narrative form—in fact, building on the insights of several of them —a dialogic interpretation proceeds in a different fashion. It begins by observing three different types of verbal exchange between God and humanity in Genesis, three different kinds of situation in which God communicates with the major human characters in this first book of the Bible. In the story of Adam and Eve (beginning in the second creation account), God enters into a joint agreement with a husband and wife. In the story of Cain and Abel, God chooses between two brothers who compete for his favor. In the story of Noah, God commissions a single "righteous" man to preserve a larger community of his creatures, animal and human, from destruction. These three different types of verbal encounter between God and human beings in the primeval prologue recur in expanded and modified form in the ensuing patriarchal section of the narrative. God enters into another agreement with a husband and wife with Abram and Sarai, issuing a new set of requirements and promises. He chooses again between two brothers, Jacob and Esau, this time with less disastrous results to the favorite. And he commissions again in Joseph a single righteous man to preserve and provide for a larger community in the midst of a threatened destruction, not just Joseph's own family but people of Egypt and from "all the earth" (Gen. 41:57) who are saved from starvation. In this repetition of similar verbal encounters between God and people, a sequence of dialogic situations takes shape.

The general significance of this recurrence is not hard to fathom. In the first sequence of situations, the dialogues involving Adam and Eve, Cain and Abel, and Noah, the human characters disobey God and take things disastrously into their own hands. This is not completely true of Noah, who is chosen because of his prior righteousness. But Noah is chosen against the background of the depravity of everyone else in the world; the success of his mission is limited, not only because his is the only human family left alive after the Flood, but also because in the final episode of Noah's drunkenness, Ham's observation of him naked, and Noah's cursing of Ham, this family seems to be reproducing the failures of Adam and Eve and their offspring. The rainbow is there to remind God of his promise not to destroy the earth again, but the problem of human weakness and destructiveness remains. Thus in the primeval phase of the dialogue between God and people and in the universal, cosmic sphere of their interaction, human resistance to God's announced intentions is pronounced.

In the second sequence of these same dialogic situations—with Abraham and Sarah, Jacob and Esau, and Joseph—human cooperation is more evident. Within the narrower sphere of ethnic or tribal history, the sphere of the "nations" produced by the break-up of the Tower of Babel, God meets with a more positive human response: first and foremost from Abram and Sarai, renamed Abraham and Sarah as they establish a history of obedience in successive encounters with him; then from Jacob, whose initial trickery in dealing with a jealous older brother enables him to survive where his prototype Abel met a bad end, but who also learns obedience of his own and appears to earn the blessing he stole earlier from Esau when he endures hard labor in his exile under Laban. Finally, God receives almost total cooperation in the phenomenal righteousness of Joseph. Here God does not even have to say anything directly to his chosen agent to get him to do his providential business. As Robert L. Cohn points out, God's explicit verbal direction of human affairs diminishes as the dialogues of the patriarchal history succeed the dialogues of the primeval history and as the latter dialogues succeed one another.[37] But the response and responsibility of the human characters singled out for narrative attention from the emerging chosen people are also increasingly successful in accomplishing God's higher purposes.

This developing dialogue of dialogues in Genesis is not stylized or stereotyped; it is not signaled by a recurrence of sharply defined type scenes or by obviously repeated key words. Rather it is suggested by a shaping of discrete episodes into generalized patterns of coherence. Nevertheless, the way in which each major patriarchal encounter with God *answers* the corresponding situation in the primeval narrative has important thematic implications. It works out, in the limited partnership of God and the patriarchs, the idea of redemption that will be negotiated, through Moses, in the much more extensive covenant between God and Israel, the family now become a multitude in Israel's exodus from Egypt and wandering in the Wilderness. The brief disobedience of Adam and Eve is answered by the extended faithfulness of Abraham and Sarah, a long-term obedience with its full share of local failings and hesitations. The violent jealousy of Cain and the terminal helplessness of Abel are answered by prolonged rivalry between the impetuous but ineffective Esau and the preemptively manipulating Jacob. In a further twist or reversal of roles, Jacob's scheming is answered by the counterscheming of Laban before Jacob is renamed Israel and effects a wary reconciliation with Esau. The obedient righteousness of Noah, which enables representative creatures to survive the Flood but which does not avert the catastrophe itself, is answered by the resourceful righteousness of Joseph, which is able to preserve all kinds of people and animals as well from the impending famine. Further, Joseph is able to engineer the repentance of his brothers and represent to them the ultimate theological lesson of Genesis as a whole: "As for you, you meant evil against me; but God meant it for good, to bring it about that many people should be kept alive, as they are today" (50:20). The initial commandment of God to man and woman in the first chapter of Genesis to be fruitful and multiply and have dominion over the earth, reiterated in God's blessing of Noah after the Flood, has been fulfilled in Joseph's Egyptian administration. It will of course have to be fulfilled on a broader scale in the Exodus, in a later historical age, against specific opposition to Israel from a Pharaoh who has forgotten about Joseph.

I have emphasized the resemblances in these two sets of dialogic encounters between God and people—people still in the process of becoming *his* people. There are of course many differences as well, not all of them significant. The biblical writers and redactors do not seem to have considered it necessary to bind all the elements of these stories tightly and neatly together, certainly not so tightly and neatly as in the Homeric epics. Either they took for granted a dialogic ethos, believing that one passage spoke to another with sufficient clarity, or they worked to promote it in the loose weave of episodes, assembled from different traditions, within the larger text. For the most part, these three types of divine-human communication, which might be called, in theological shorthand, covenant with a couple (Adam and Eve/Abraham and Sarah), election of a younger brother (Abel over Cain/Jacob over Esau), and provision through a righteous individual (Noah/Joseph), seem localized and ad hoc, specific to the editorial arrangement of Genesis itself. There is an intriguing possibility, however, that the sequence of human figures in these dialogues—a man and wife, two brothers, and a single man—is adapted from earlier Mesopotamian epic. David Damrosch has noted that the main character combinations in the *Epic of Gilgamesh*—Enkidu and the temple prostitute (who cohabit in an Eden-like natural setting), Enkidu and Gilgamesh (who are initially rivals but who then enter into a spiritual brotherhood until Enkidu's death) and Utnapishtim, who is warned by a god about a worldwide flood and survives it with his wife an ark he has been instructed to build—resemble Adam and Eve, Cain and Abel, and Noah respectively.[38] Damrosch suggests not that Genesis is directly indebted to *Gilgamesh*, but that the set of stories that make up Genesis 1–11 is a transformation of the Near Eastern genre of the creation-to-flood epic, known from other Mesopotamian texts as well. If this is true, then the initial series of dialogic situations we have been considering (in Genesis 2–10) constitute an Israelite answer to Mesopotamian myth, an answer in which the most dramatic change has been to introduce Israel's "one Lord" into the conversation. It is out of this Mesopotamian matrix, after all, that God calls Abram and Sarai forth to Canaan as alternative progenitors to Adam and Eve. The Israelite "solution" treats the Mesopotamian myth as a "problem," but it presents its own redemptive sequel in the formal language of the problem itself.

This echo of narrative genres beyond the confines of Genesis, however, is less distinct than the resonance between the primary "speech genres," in Bakhtin's phrase, within the biblical book. "Each separate utterance is individual, of course," Bakhtin writes, "but each sphere in which language is used develops its own *relatively stable types* of these utterances. These we may call *speech genres.*"[39] The sphere of the canonical text of Genesis is more immediate than the sphere of ancient Near Eastern literature. Thus God's treaties with Abraham and Sarah amplify his dealings with Adam and Eve in specific elements common to both. The man and wife are addressed together by God, and they respond to him in similar fashion, for example. They are treated as "one flesh" (Gen. 2:24); there is no question of God choosing between them, as he will with the next generation. Eve talks to the serpent and falls for the fruit, but Adam appears to have been standing beside her all along, listening to the conversation.[40] Sarah laughs at the promise of Isaac in Genesis 18 and is called out for this unbelief (in good-humored fashion) by God, but Abraham also has laughed at the idea of Sarah giving birth in the preceding chapter (Gen. 17:17). God's "No, but you did laugh" (Gen. 18:15) applies to them both.

There is also in this initial dialogic situation, present in each of the two parts of Genesis, a good deal of conversation back and forth as agreements, covenants, or treaties are entered into by both parties and subsequently reaffirmed or abrogated. There are ten separate occasions on which God speaks to Abraham and Abraham responds, the most extended of these conversations taking place in Chapter 18, which ends with Abraham boldly pleading for the city of Sodom. (Sarah herself is addressed directly only in this chapter.) But there are also eight separate "words" that God addresses to Adam and/or Eve in the course of their two-plus chapters, and in two of these words, the invitation to name the living creatures and the invitation to name the woman, Adam's verbal response seems tantamount to an act of co-creation.[41] The articulate reciprocity of this initial dialogic situation, explicit in both its versions, is noticeably absent from the dialogues between God and the other characters that succeed it. Finally, there is the common element of God drawing the man and woman forth from a larger geographical space and situating them in a specifically designated territory. Adam is of course literally "formed . . . of dust from the ground" in Genesis 2:7, but he is also taken and placed in the garden in Eden, which God prepares for him and his still-unformed helper, "to till it and keep it" (Gen. 2:15). Abram, already married to Sarai, is called by God to leave his country (Haran or Ur or both) and go to the specially promised land of Canaan. Conversely, the ground is cursed when Adam is expelled from the garden and he is told that it is to the "ground" and "dust" that he will return in death. Abraham's lengthy negotiation with Ephron the Hittite for the field with the cave in Machpelah as a place to bury Sarah in Genesis 23 recapitulates this motif of the promised land turning into a grave. Nevertheless, the fact that Abraham establishes legal title to a piece of real estate in Canaan is a significant answer to Adam's loss of Eden and a significant preview of Israel's later possession of the promised land. References to land, earth, ground, and dust are less frequent in the succeeding dialogic situations in Genesis, which are more concerned with the nature and number of the people to whom the land will eventually belong.

Elements common to the story of Cain and Abel and the story-cycle of Jacob and Esau are the motifs of election (the establishing of a preferred communication between man and God), of vengeance (the problem of preserving any communication between two people when God has given one of them preference) and exile (a strategy for establishing distance between two parties between whom communication has broken down to keep the stronger from destroying the weaker). The simple but unexplained preference of God for the sacrifices of the younger brother in the story of Cain and Abel is succeeded by the more complex but also more comprehensible preferences of Isaac for Esau and of Rebekah for Jacob, superimposed on God's still mysterious election of the younger son, announced in advance to Rebekah. It is interesting that the only times God communicates directly with Jacob, at Bethel and at Peniel, as Jacob commemorates these places, Jacob responds with sacrifical gestures that strike one as more self-serving than worshipful. At Bethel, he promises God a tenth *if* God will be with him in Paddan Aram; at Peniel, he clings to his heavenly antagonist after he has been bested until he gets a blessing from God himself.

Jacob thus seems to have acquired Cain's aggressive initiative along with Abel's favored status. In any case, the vengeance of Cain is widely distributed in the Jacob cycle. Esau contemplates revenge on Jacob; Jacob survives a displaced version of this vengeance at the hands of Laban—the poetic justice of his having to marry the rejected older sister Leah before the preferred younger one, Rachel; Jacob turns the tables on Laban in the breeding contest between the pure white and the speckled flocks. The vengeance of Esau that Jacob fears when he returns to Canaan turns out to have dissolved into brotherly affection in Esau's shorter memory; but it erupts among Jacob's own sons in the revenge that Simeon and Levi take on the Hivites for the rape of their sister Dinah. This last violent episode seems to recapitulate the seventy-seven-fold revenge that Cain's descendant Lamech boasts he has taken for his wounding (Gen. 4:23–24). The permutations of this particular motif make this part of Genesis a structuralist's paradise.

The exile of Cain, which includes a paradoxical mark on him indicating God's qualified favor in spite of his crime, is reenacted by Jacob in his pastoral interlude with Laban. Unlike Cain, Jacob does not make his alienation permanent by building a city. On the other hand, when he returns to the ultimately promised land, he keeps moving restlessly from one promising spot to another and ends his life, thanks to his son Joseph's fortunate advance work, in another exile in Egypt. When his bones are taken back to the cave at Machpelah in Canaan at the very end of Genesis, he seems to combine the fate of Cain, a "wanderer on the earth" (Gen. 4:14) with the fate of Abel lying underneath it. Esau, in the meantime, has moved off into Edom to the east (Gen. 36:6–8). Exile for him, in his unchosen and unenlightened condition, is not an issue, although as Leslie Brisman points out, he is presented with disarming sympathy in his last meeting with Jacob.[42]

In contrast to the other major human figures in Genesis, Noah and Joseph are defined primarily by their ethical virtue. We are told at the beginning that Noah "was a righteous man, blameless in his generation" and that he "walked with God" (Gen. 6:9). Joseph may be irritating in his moral rectitude, to modern readers as well as to his brothers, but we are told repeatedly that "the LORD was with Joseph" and that "the LORD caused all that he did to prosper in his hands" (Gen. 39:2, 3). Both Noah and Joseph are presented as instruments of God's purposes, revealed in advance to Noah and revealed after the fact through Joseph. Although each has discernible human weaknesses—Noah for wine and Joseph for savoring his own preeminence—each of them is a figure who brings divine correction to bear on previous human wrongdoing. Their obedience to God and their election by God are never contested, as these things are with the characters who precede them. Noah cleans up the general moral mess that has led God to bring on the Flood. Joseph cleans up the specific family conflict that has threatened the survival of Israel. As I have argued, Joseph is more effective in providing for the future of mankind than Noah, since he preserves a multitude of people where Noah is merely instructed to multiply new ones, a task which he leaves to the three sons he has already produced. Joseph provides food for generations already in historical existence; Noah merely supplies the genes for generations of the future.

The dialogic answer that Joseph makes to Noah is full of differences as well as similarities. Noah says nothing to God; he simply listens and does what he is told. In contrast, though with the same effect, God says nothing to Joseph. For the first time in Genesis, we have no direct discourse from God to the patriarch. There are Joseph's dreams, but even here he shifts from having dreams of his own to interpreting the dreams of others. The help that he gets from and ascribes to God is something we have to take on faith from Joseph himself; it seems to be a matter of Joseph's wisdom, his innate grasp of spiritual principles, rather than of revelation through a prophetic oracle. In the dialogic situation in which Joseph appears, his divine interlocutor remains in the background.

There are other motifs in which Joseph differs from Noah, usually for the better. Joseph's self-control, over sexual temptation with Potiphar's wife and over temptation to revenge with his brothers, contrasts pointedly with the drunkenness of Noah that leads to the cursing of Ham. Noah is good in the worldwide crisis of the Flood, but lacks the domestic skills for successful peacetime living; Joseph is clearly the master of the private as well as the public sphere. The motif of nakedness reenforces this contrast. Noah's disrobing comes from overindulgence in wine, Joseph's from his trying to steer clear of a dangerous woman. There is prudence as well as moral virtue in his chastity in Potiphar's household. The single mention of Noah's garment becomes a whole language of clothing and unclothing in the story of Joseph: his coat (of uncertain ornamentation) given by his father, stolen by his brothers, and falsely used as a sign of his death; his garment (presumably supplied by Potiphar), stolen by Potiphar's wife, and used as false evidence for his imprisonment; and his "garments of fine linen" (41:42), given by Pharaoh to symbolize his political authority and used by Joseph to conceal his identity from his brothers until he has engineered their repentance. As Robert Alter has shown, this language of clothes even carries over into the interlude of chapter 38, the story of Judah and Tamar, where disguise and material identification play an important role in setting a wrong situation right.[43]

Of course, as the example of Judah and Tamar reveals, the concern with clothing and nakedness is not limited to the stories of Noah and Joseph. It begins with Adam and Eve and recurs in the disguise of Jacob, in Esau's clothes and goatskins, before the blind Isaac. My focus on the three genres of dialogue in Genesis is not intended to deny the significance of these other dialogic connections. There are aspects of Noah's situation that cast him as a second Adam as well as a prefiguration of Joseph. As Allon White has observed about Bakhtin's concept of dialogue, it allows us to dissociate "structure" from "homogeneity."[44] We need not insist, if we become aware of more than one voice making music, that there be a single conductor in control of the chorus. There are other patterns of relatedness in Genesis that cut across, loop around, or speak apart from the dialogic orchestration we have been considering in the book as a whole. There are also episodes and characters simply unrelated to these three repeated types of dialogue between God and his emerging people. Nevertheless, two significant episodes in the narratives of Genesis that might seem to be loose ends—the story of Isaac himself and the story of the Tower of Babel—can be directly related to the overall typology of utterances that I have described thus far.

The episodes devoted primarily to Isaac, where God's dealings with Isaac himself are foremost, turn out to be limited to a single chapter in Genesis, chapter 26, which tells of Isaac taking refuge from a famine with Abimelech, a king in Gerar. In this encounter, where Isaac passes Rebekah off as his sister, however, Isaac is repeating a stratagem that his father Abraham used twice before him, first with Pharaoh in Egypt and later with Abimelech in Gerar. The treaty that Isaac makes with Abimelech over a well later in the chapter is also merely a reaffirmation of a previous treaty between Abimelech and Abraham. As with his marriage to Rebekah, where Abraham's servant makes the choice and the arrangements, Isaac's early career as patriarch is almost completely subordinated to his father's. And the scene of his later patriarchy, the "*story* of Isaac son of Abraham" (as E. A. Speiser renders the Hebrew *toledot* of Gen. 25:19 in the Anchor Bible), is almost completely stolen by Jacob, who moves to center stage as soon as Rebekah conceives the twin brothers. Isaac figures primarily as a son to Abraham and Sarah in the first dialogic situation of the patriarchal narratives and as a father to Jacob and Esau in the second.

Isaac's election over Ishmael, as we have noted earlier, is a recapitulation of God's preference of Abel over Cain and it prefigures God's and Rebekah's preference for Jacob over Esau. It might even be argued that the "sacrifice of Isaac" is itself a condensed or collapsed version of this second dialogic situation, in which Isaac is first "rejected" by God and then "chosen" by him all over again. In such a reading, Isaac would only become the recipient and the channel of God's blessing after he has experienced the absence of this blessing—indeed, after he has experienced something that amounts to a curse. In any case, Isaac's own communication with God is explicitly assimilated to the two dialogic genres on either side of him in the patriarchal prologue of Genesis, even though he is remembered prominently—indeed, more prominently than Joseph—in later recollections of the patriarchs in Exodus, where God identifies himself as "the God of Abraham, the God of Isaac and the God of Jacob" (for example, Exod. 3:15). It is not only Pharaoh who does not remember Joseph in later generations.

The episode of the Tower of Babel is also full of echoes and anticipations of previous and subsequent motifs. It parodies the construction of the ark by Noah in its attention to architectural detail and the problem of survival; it prepares for the calling of Abram out of the paganism of "Ur of the Chaldeans" (11:31); and it sketches out a version of the imperial absolutism that Joseph will encounter, become a part of, and turn to redemptive effect in Egypt. It may even be a didactic parody of the conclusion of the *Epic of Gilgamesh* (more likely of an earlier version of the story), where the hero is consoled in his failed quest for immortality by contemplating the walls of Babylon.[45] Nevertheless, as a number of literary critics and historical commentators have pointed out, the most significant cross-reference of this episode within Genesis is to the creation account at the beginning of the book—not the creation account that zooms in, as it were, on Adam and Eve, but the earlier account, by the Priestly writer, with its orderly, cosmic panorama of the making of the heavens and the earth. Edwin Good describes the Tower of Babel as an "anti-Eden, a humanly constructed paradise from which God is to be excluded."[46] But the specific verbal and narrative echoes that he and other commentators note, particularly the repetition of God's "Let us make man in our image" (Gen. 1:26) in the men's "let us make bricks," "let

us build ourselves a city" and "let us make a name for ourselves,"
followed by God's doubly ironic "let us go down, and there con-
fuse their language" (Gen. 11:3–7), point not to the brief description of Eden but to the longer description of creation of the universe, capped in chapter 1 by the making of man and woman on
the sixth day. The magisterial first-person plural of God frames
and exposes the anxious human attempt at solidarity. As Isaac
Kikawada notes, the parallelism of these two episodes suggests that
it is not just a prideful desire for autonomy that motivates the
builders but an anxiety-ridden resistance to God's command to
human beings to "fill the earth," a command given to the first man
and woman in Genesis 1:28 and reiterated to Noah in Genesis 9:1.
The offensive urban project of Babel grows out of the men's fear
"lest we be scattered abroad upon the face of the whole earth"
(Gen. 11:4).[47] Through David, God will later establish a city of
his own, but this sense of the city as a form of human creativity
directed against the will of the Creator himself runs throughout
the Bible, from Cain's city Enoch, named after his son, to the
demonic, archetypal Babylon of the Book of Revelation.

Recognizing that the building of the Tower of Babel is a parody
of the creation of heaven and earth allows one to see that each of
the threefold sequences of dialogue in Genesis, the primeval
sequence beginning with Adam and Eve and the patriarchal
sequence beginning with Abram and Sarai, comes in response to a
prior act of creation. Furthermore, each of these prior acts of creation is verbal in character and thus a kind of speech act in its
own right. God decrees the heavens and the earth in the beginning—speaks them into obedient being—but then experiences the
defection of the human caretakers he has appointed over this creation from Adam to Noah. After Noah, through whom humans
have been invited to recommence their caretaking, men attempt
to stand God's great speech act on its head. They decree a city and
a tower that will consolidate their control over a small part of the
creation, apart from God. Their notion that the tower will reach
up into the heavens is probably not something that God finds genuinely threatening, though he purports to take their delusions of
grandeur seriously. Nevertheless, it appears as an anti-Creation.
The homogenous "bricks" that the builders use for their tower
collapse the vital separation of opposites God used to construct the
heavens and the earth in Genesis 1. And the "name" that they
try to make for themselves in the form of a tower is the obverse

of the "image" or "likeness" of God in which they have been created.

God therefore bursts the bubble of their pseudocreation and undertakes a new delegation of authority. By breaking up the unity of human language, he divides a previously homogenous human community into different nations. In Bakhtin's terms, particularly appropriate here, God introduces radical "heteroglossia" into humanity's previously "unitary language" and begins a renewed process of dialogue, this time singling one people out of the many nations, in order to bring about another kind of partnership between himself and humanity. As he tells Abraham, this partnership is ultimately for the benefit of all the nations, not just for the chosen people alone. On this reduced, patriarchal scale of operations, God finds a more receptive audience in the people to whom he speaks than in the all-inclusive primeval sphere. The relative success of the patriarchal dialogues, in turn, prepares the way for the vastly greater redemptive project of calling Israel, now greatly multiplied in number, out of Egypt under the even more receptive leadership of Moses.

Thus in terms of the double sequence of three dialogic situations that we have been examining in Genesis—covenant with a couple, election of a younger brother, and provision through a single righteous person—the first creation account and the Tower of Babel function as two beginnings: a positive, sacred beginning to the primeval succession of encounters, in which God orders the physical universe; and a negative, secular beginning to the patriarchal, protohistorical succession, in which men disorder the social world. The ambivalent attitude shown here toward merely human history and social institutions, where God establishes the nations as a punishment for men's rejection of his authority and command but also uses the existence of these nations for his own larger purposes, is reflected later in the Bible in the ambivalent account of the monarchy in Israel in 1 Samuel, when God condemns Israel's motives for wanting a king but declares that he will also use the dubious means they propose to good effect nevertheless. Indeed, historical critics believe that the composition of Genesis was significantly shaped by the political and theological attitudes of the monarchy of David in the first place, when, they think, the larger narrative of the Pentateuch began to be put together. But in terms of the succession of books presented in the canon, in the Christian Old Testament as well as the Hebrew Bible, we perceive this redemptive reversal of human propositions as being established in Genesis in the beginning and as being rehearsed throughout the history of Israel thereafter.

IV

This introduction to a reading of the Bible as literature according to Bakhtin concludes by looking ahead to the New Testament. As in the four chapters following, my movement back and forth from Old Testament to New is a deliberate attempt to focus attention on the Bible in its broad, canonical form, to show that the creation of dialogic genres takes place at the far end of the canonical scriptures as well as at their beginning. There are, of course, different ideas about which scriptures are canonical in the different religious traditions that claim "the Bible" as their own. As we shall see in Chapters 2 and 3, the relationships among the Hebrew Bible, the Greek, Septuagint translation, and the Christian Bible composed of Old and New Testaments are complicated, in literary terms as well as in their historical and religious dimensions. Questions of how the New Testament writings engage the older Jewish scriptures will be addressed in detail in Chapter 3. Here, however, following the example of the literary analysis in Auerbach's *Mimesis*, I shall simply turn my attention to the New Testament Gospel of Mark.

As with Genesis and other books of the Hebrew Bible or Old Testament, so with the New Testament Gospels: the predominant literary approach in recent decades has been through concepts of narrative. Frank Kermode's groundbreaking study of Mark, *The Genesis of Secrecy*, treats this Gospel as a typical example of narrative, particularly in its ambiguities. *Mark as Story* by David Rhoads and Donald Michie subjects Mark to a more normative structural analysis, and has been followed by such narratological analyses as *Matthew's Story of Jesus* by Richard Edwards and *The Narrative Unity of Luke-Acts* by Robert Tannehill. In his recent study *The Book of God*, Gabriel Josipovici assesses the faithfulness of the New Testament writings to the narrative character of the Hebrew Bible, judging the Christian Scriptures according to whether they maintain "the primacy of narrative over interpretation" in recounting the life of Jesus.[48] The more realistic narrative and the less interpretive commentary the better, in Josipovici's scheme of biblical-literary values.

Again, the roots of this literary approach can be traced back to Auerbach, to the second chapter of *Mimesis*, which compares an episode at the end of Mark, Peter's denial of Jesus, with passages in Petronius's *Satyricon* and in Tacitus's *Annals*, passages dealing, as Auerbach argues Mark's episode does, with ordinary people in the midst of the upheavals of contemporary social life. In this chapter, Auerbach places less emphasis on the role of style in the works he is considering and more on the role of genre. But his examples of classical realism from Latin literature complicate the simple contrast between the legendary character of the *Odyssey* and the historical character of Genesis, since the *Annals* of Tacitus belong formally to the genre of written history. Auerbach defines more specifically the kind of modern historiography to which the Gospel narrative belongs, or which it anticipates, in contrast to the classical type. Modern historiography is dynamic and synthetic, dealing with "phenomena in motion" (38), describing social change in categories that are "pliable," and possess "a dialectic mobility . . . which renews them completely" (44–45). The classical Latin history of Tacitus, in contrast, is static, confined by ethical values and by a hierarchy of literary genres correlative to the hierarchy of social classes. These structures also dictate the essentially comic manner in which Petronius recounts the rise in fortune of members of the Roman lower class.

Thus the genre that determines the form of Peter's denial of Christ, according to Auerbach, is a kind of writing that transcends genre, the genre of history-writing included. The paradox we noted earlier in our discussion of the first chapter of *Mimesis* is more pronounced here, and the phenomena Auerbach attributes to this passage from the Gospel of Mark and to the New Testament in general are more clearly being read back into the text from the vantage point of later historical developments.[49] Auerbach claims that in the New Testament the "deep subsurface layers" of history, "which were static for the observers of classical antiquity, began to move" (45). But the evidence for the broadly social character of this movement is supplied largely from outside the episode of Peter's denial, the Gospel of Mark or the New Testament itself. It comes from an "unfolding of historical forces" in the subsequent history of Christianity, which Auerbach reads back into the passage with Hegelian hindsight. Within the text, such historical movement is only evident in the individual psychology of Peter. Auerbach attributes to Peter an "enormous 'pendulation'" of emotions in this scene (42). But where he quotes long passages from Petronius and Tacitus and analyzes particular devices of style, he relies in his discussion of Mark on a sympathetic but largely hypothetical description of the thoughts and feelings that *must* have been going on in Peter during the seven short verses of the spare Marcan account.

Thus Auerbach's description of the form of Peter's denial is less specific than his account of the form of the sacrifice of Isaac, and the movement toward generic transcendence is even more abrupt in his argument. As with the episode in Genesis, a more careful consideration not only of the passage but of the surrounding narrative context in the Gospel of Mark reveals an episode of a similar type—in fact, two episodes, both of which tightly frame Peter's denial of Christ. These adjacent episodes, through a dialogic patterning of words and deeds even more pointed than the dialogic patterns we have just observed at length in Genesis, give Peter's speech and act a concrete and immediate significance. In this case Peter's false testimony to his knowledge of Christ stands in sharp contrast to the true witness Jesus gives to his own identity, first before the Sanhedrin and after that before Pilate.

After Jesus is arrested in the Garden of Gethsemane, in chapter 14 of Mark, he is led before the religious authorities. Peter follows him, "at a distance, right into the courtyard of the high priest," and sits with the guards, warming himself at a fire (14:54). The focus then shifts to Jesus before the chief priests and the Sanhedrin and to the variety of false "testimony" that is offered against him. (The Greek word *marturion* and its derivatives are used seven times in the passage.) Jesus remains silent before these witnesses, until the high priest asks him directly, "Are you the Christ, the Son of the Blessed?" Jesus then testifies to his own identity—"And Jesus said 'I am,'"—and adds a scriptural *testimonium* combining phrases from Daniel 7 and Psalm 110 about his subsequent appearance as the Son of Man "coming with the clouds of heaven." For the high priest, this means that no further witnesses are needed. The gathering condemns Jesus for blasphemy and pronounces him worthy of death.

Against this cloud of witnessing, false and true, Peter's self-protective claims that he does not know Jesus are particularly shocking. It is not the emotional turmoil within Peter but the dialogic contradiction between his testimony and the preceding testimony of Jesus that Mark's narrative montage brings to the fore. Kermode shrewdly compares this juxtaposition of scenes to the ironic interplay in the famous country-fair chapter in Flaubert's *Madame Bovary* between Rodolphe's eloquent professions of love to Emma and the stolid agricultural oratory of the public officials.[50] Peter's three denials are increasingly emphatic. First he says he was not "with" Jesus, then that he is not "of them," and finally "I do not know this man of whom you speak." The cock then crows a second time, making its first appearance in the narrative. The sound reminds Peter of the specific prophecy that Jesus gave earlier in the evening of Peter's threefold denial of his master; it also provides a further, ironic example of a faithful testimony, the bird's instinctual witness to a new day. Peter's weeping, which Mark describes as immediate and oblivious of those around him, is Peter's own testimony, instinctive and remorseful, to his deeper knowledge of the one he has been following.

In a characteristic pattern dubbed by scholars the "Marcan sandwich," the focus of attention then returns to Jesus himself, this time before the secular authorities in the person of Pilate. The false witness of Peter, in which he says less or other than he knows, is succeeded by the true witness of the Roman governor, who finds himself saying more than he knows when he asks if Jesus is "the King of the Jews." In contrast to his direct answer to the question if he is the Christ posed earlier by the high priest, the answer Jesus gives to Pilate's question is ambiguous—literally, "you say"—but it ironically enlists Pilate as a legal witness on his behalf, as we see later in the inscription that is attached to his cross, "The King of the Jews" (15:26). In this particular scene, Pilate is allowed a more personal response as well—he "wonders" or is "amazed" (NIV)—but it is the silence of Jesus before the many accusations brought against him that evokes this response rather than any verbal reply.

The incident of Peter's denial of Christ is thus articulated in terms of a dialogic situation that is prominent in the closing chapters of the Gospel of Mark, a situation of having to give testimony in dangerous circumstances. The witness to Jesus, to his astonishing but also mysterious claim to be "the Christ," can only lead to death in Mark's uncompromising account. But it is only this death that can lead to true life. The "pendulation" that Auerbach correctly observes in Peter in this passage is not simply a psychological or sociological phenomenon as it is presented in this Gospel. It is a function of the paradoxical inversion of religious values, in which to lose one's life is to save it and to save one's life is to lose it—in which the Christ of God is to be rejected and killed with the promise that he will rise from the dead. Throughout the Gospel of Mark the disciples are shown struggling to accept this startling coincidence of power and weakness proclaimed by their leader, and as every reader notices, they fail to "hear" or understand the testimony of Jesus himself again and again.

Peter is the disciple who has come closest to speaking the truth in his pivotal confession of chapter 8, when he answers Jesus' question, "But who do you say that I am?" with "You are the Christ" (8:29). But Peter betrays this testimony—betrays the partial nature of his comprehension of the Messiah—when immediately afterwards he rebukes Jesus for predicting the suffering this identity will entail and is rebuked by Jesus in return. Jesus goes as far as to identify Peter with Satan at this point. As Flannery O'Connor once observed, it is ironically the demons who give the first witness to Christ in the Gospels, a witness that begins in Mark with Jesus' first exorcism in Chapter 1.[51] Thus in the broader perspective of Mark's Gospel as a whole, Peter's denial of Christ and repentance for this denial in chapter 14 constitute a revoicing of his own earlier confession and contradiction of confession in chapter 8, a revoicing in a more hopeful, reversed order. Furthermore, Peter's witnesses, true and false, constitute revoicings of other testimonies to Jesus as the Christ, a distinctive type of dialogue that for Mark begins with the testimonies of Isaiah the prophet, John the Baptist and the voice from heaven saying "Thou art my beloved Son; with thee I am well pleased" (1:11), this last a testimony that echoes two additional Old Testament voices (Ps. 2:7, Isa. 42:1).

The dialogic character of this episode, the way in which it is given significance within a particular, recurrent pattern of speaking between God and people, is, of course, not limited to the Gospel of Mark. Both Matthew and Luke rehearse Mark's account of Peter's denial of Christ while changing the immediate dialogic context. Matthew follows Mark closely in the episode itself, but places after Peter's denial and ensuing remorse the remorse of Judas for his own more calculated and catastrophic betrayal. Judas tries to give back the thirty pieces of silver, and when this restitution is rejected by the religious authorities, he hangs himself. The failure of Judas's legalistic strategy for regaining innocence casts a more favorable light on Peter's spontaneous repentance. Luke brings Jesus himself into the scene; in his Gospel, Jesus turns and looks at Peter after the third denial and the cock's crow. This silent, personal witness of Peter's act of denial by the one he has denied also extends the prospect of forgiveness, leading Peter to go out from the courtyard and weep in private, away from the sight of others.[52]

The most striking reconfiguration of this powerful episode is given in the Gospel of John. Here we find Peter accompanied by "another disciple," presumably "the disciple whom Jesus loved," who, we are told at the end of the gospel, is himself "bearing witness to" and "has written these things" (John 21:24). This apparently authorial witness knows the high priest and is admitted to the court where Jesus is being tried while Peter is made to wait at the door. This other disciple convinces the servant woman, here a doorkeeper, to admit Peter, and it is when she asks Peter if he is one of Jesus' disciples that Peter makes his first denial. After the focus shifts to Jesus—the master's testimony is now sandwiched between the disciple's denials instead of the other way around—Peter is recognized by others and is forced to deny Jesus two more times. The cock crows "at once" (18:27), but Peter's weeping is not mentioned.

In effect, however, John displaces Peter's immediate, emotional response, given in Mark and the other Synoptic Gospels, to a later, more formal encounter with the risen Christ. In the last chapter of the Gospel of John, the resurrected Jesus asks Peter three times, "Simon, son of John, do you love me?" using the strong Greek *agapao*, connoting love as an abiding commitment, the first two times. Peter answers that he does love Jesus, but he only dares to make his profession with the weaker *phileo*, connoting love as an affectional response. The third time Jesus asks his question on Peter's level, using the weaker *phileo* himself. This time they reach a confessional agreement; Peter's triple denial has been ritually unsaid. At each stage of this subtle but moving exchange, Peter is being commissioned to "feed the sheep" of Christ, to take up the role of the "good shepherd" by which Jesus has earlier identified himself (John 10:11) and abandon the role he had played earlier of the "hireling," the one who "sees the wolf coming and leaves the sheep and flees" (10:12). But this metaphorical identification of master and disciple is followed by still another dialogic differentiation when Peter looks over and notices "the disciple whom Jesus loved" (21:20). In a tone of jealousy that recalls the brotherly competitions for God's favor in Genesis, Peter cannot keep from asking, "Lord, what about this man?" Jesus' ambiguous answer—"If it is my will that he remain until I come, what is that to you?" (when he has just told Peter of his own coming martyrdom)—is the final test of Peter's reaffirmed witness to Christ. The prospect of being at one with God continues to tempt God's people to be one up on others.[53]

Literary critics may be forgiven for preferring the human uncertainty of Peter to the divine assurance of "the disciple whom Jesus loved." They may also be expected to prefer the dialogue of contradictory testimonies, hovering around the so-called messianic secret, in the Gospel of Mark, which dramatizes the centrifugal, dispersive force of language described by Bakhtin, to the dialogue of transparent witness in John, dominated by the extended speeches of Jesus himself and more representative of Bakhtin's centripetal or unifying discourse. But it should be clear from this analysis that the dynamic of divine and human dialogue itself, the formation of recurring patterns of verbal exchange to represent the communication between God and his people, is as prominent at the end of one biblical canon as it is at the beginning of both. Put in more historical terms, the ethos of dialogue was as significant in the closing of the Christian canon at the end of the second century c.e., when four narrative gospels were included side by side in the New Testament, as it was in the formation of the Hebrew canon, beginning by most scholarly accounts to be regarded *as* a canon some seven centuries earlier, in the composite coherence given to the different documentary constituents in the Book of Genesis.

The shape of this dialogue in the Bible is various, and it modulates within both canons, as we shall see, between authoritarian and liberationist models of utterance as well as between divine and human speaking. But the dialogic form is a fundamental characteristic of the Jewish and Christian writings as they represent a dramatically interactive communication between remarkably different levels of existence, between a strikingly transcendent God and the notably earthbound people to whom and through whom he speaks. In one of his early essays, "Author and Hero in Aesthetic Activity," Bakhtin uses the term *transgredience*, borrowed from Neo-Kantian philosophy, to describe the all-embracing perspective that an author may have on a character whom he or she has created in a work of literature, a total awareness that no human being can have of another living subject.[54] The concept is peculiarly suited to the absolute authority God has over his people in the Bible along with his intimate knowledge of them. That God is the author of the people who are singled out for attention, that he has such all-encompassing knowledge of them, is made explicit only infrequently in the Bible—in the story of Adam and Eve, in the confession of Psalm 139, and in certain oracles in the prophets, for example—but his creative responsibility for them is everywhere presumed. God is the primordial maker of his people's—of all people's—characters from the beginning and he is the ultimate designer of their plots in the end. But it is also everywhere presumed in the Bible that his characters are allowed, indeed invited, to know something of him in return. Furthermore, they are presumed, paradoxically, to be free agents at the same time, in between their beginning and their end. They are able to talk back to God; they are free to disagree as well as agree with his words about them. People are "characters in search of an author" in the Bible, and like the six truculent characters in Pirandello's play, they are frequently unhappy with the stories they have been assigned. But God is an author in search of characters as well, looking for those who will acknowledge him as "author and finisher" of the drama of their lives, as the author of the Letter to the Hebrews puts it (Heb. 12:2, KJV). Or, as a spokesman for God, a "seer," announces in the last book of the Hebrew Bible, "the eyes of the LORD run to and fro throughout the whole earth, to show his might in behalf of those whose heart is blameless toward him" (2 Chron. 16:9). The people God discovers in such agreement with him, who are said to be men and women "after God's own heart," are often a surprise to those who have been privy to other conversations in the Scriptures.

2

The Law of the Priest,
the Word of the Prophet,
the Counsel of the Wise:
A Poetics of the
Hebrew Bible

In a book of essays published in 1920 entitled *The Art of Reading*, Sir Arthur Quiller-Couch offers an ironic image of "the Bible as literature," one that exposes the frequent cross-purposes of literary and historical study. "Imagine a volume including the great books of our own literature," he invites his readers, "all bound together in some such order as this":

> *Paradise Lost*, Darwin's *Descent of Man*, *The Anglo-Saxon Chronicle*, Walter Map, Mill *On Liberty*, Hooker's *Ecclesiastical Polity*, *The Annual Register*, Froissart, Adam Smith's *Wealth of Nations*, *Domesday Book*, *Le Morte d'Arthur*, Campbell's *Lives of the Lord Chancellors*, Boswell's *Johnson*, Barbour's *The Bruce*, Hakluyt's *Voyages*, Clarendon, Macaulay, the plays of Shakespeare, Shelley's *Prometheus Unbound*, *The Faerie Queene*, Palgrave's *Golden Treasury*, Bacon's *Essays*, Swinburne's *Poems and Ballads*, FitzGerald's *Omar Khayyam*, Wordsworth, Browning, *Sartor Resartus*, Burton's *Anatomy of Melancholy*, Burke's *Letters on a Regicide Peace*, Ossian, *Piers Plowman*, Burke's *Thoughts on the Present Discontents*, Quarles, Newman's *Apologia*, Donne's *Sermons*, Ruskin, Blake, *The Deserted Village*, *Manfred*, Blair's *Grave*, *The Complaint of Deor*, Bailey's *Festus*, Thompson's *Hound of Heaven*.

Quiller-Couch goes on to stipulate "that in this volume most of the authors' names are lost; that, of the few that survive, a number have found their way into wrong places; that Ruskin for example is credited with *Sartor Resartus;* that *Laus Veneris* and *Dolores* are ascribed to Queen Elizabeth, *The Anatomy of Melancholy* to Charles II; and that, as for the titles, these were never invented by the authors, but by a Committee." Still further, the later authors claim that the earlier ones have been predicting their own work in some vague manner, "so that Macaulay and Adam Smith, for example, constantly interrupt the thread of their discourse to affirm that what they tell us must be right because Walter Map or the author of *Piers Plowman* foretold it ages before."[1]

This picture of the biblical canon as a scrambled anthology is, of course, a reductio ad absurdum of the historical criticism that was then at the height of its influence, the centerpiece of which was the Documentary Hypothesis of the composition of the Pentateuch but which extended to all areas of Old and New Testament scholarship. Literary critics before and after Quiller-Couch have gone so far as to try to reassemble the apparent historical hodgepodge of the canonical text into a more logical literary format. Richard Moulton's *Modern Reader's Bible* provides a "structural printing of Scripture" in which formal and generic distinctions are indicated by typography and subtitles. *The Bible Designed to be Read as Living Literature* by Ernest Sutherland Bates offers a more radical rearrangement of the biblical books "in order of their composition" and eliminates apparently duplicate accounts. Deuteronomy, for example, is reduced to three chapters, and the Gospels to "the basic biography of Jesus found in the Gospel according to Mark, . . . supplemented by those incidents and teachings not found in Mark but in the other Gospels." Most recently, David Rosenberg and Harold Bloom have produced *The Book of J,* the literary masterpiece of the Yahwist author (whom Bloom conceives to have been a woman), which they have creatively unstitched from large parts of Genesis, smaller parts of Exodus and Numbers, and a few verses of Deuteronomy.[2]

At the same time, however, especially among biblical scholars no longer persuaded of the absolute authority of the "Documentary fiction, or Source Myth," as one of the disaffected critics in this tradition has termed it,[3] there has been a growing interest in the logic of the canonical or received text of the Bible, as distinct from the chronology of its compositional elements or stages. This interest in the Bible's final form considers larger segments of the canon as well as individual books. It examines the coherence given by editors or redactors to the smaller units, whatever their historical provenance or *Sitz im Leben,* as they were arranged in the relatively fixed canonical texts, first of the Hebrew, then of the Christian Bibles in the first and second centuries C.E., after a centuries-long process of canon formation. Canonical criticism or canon criticism, as it has been called, has been given a strong historical cast by James Sanders and a strong theological emphasis by Brevard Childs, its most prominent practitioners, but as advocates and detractors alike have recognized, it has attended as well to the literary character of the way the compositional parts have been organized into the canonical whole. Canonical criticism describes what might be termed the *Sitz im Lesen* of these parts, their situation in the text as read.[4]

Literary readers, therefore, are not obliged to approach the Bible as an anthology run amok, as Quiller-Couch suggests, nor to limit their investigations of formal coherence, as they have commonly done, to the organization of individual books, episodes, or documentary "sources." Not only biblical scholars, but literary critics in the last two decades have produced systems and schemata— poetics, to use the technical term that comes from Aristotle but that continues to be used by the structuralists—in which the logic of the Bible may be considered on a broader scale. Northrop Frye's *The Great Code* applies a version of the descriptive poetics he developed in his *Anatomy of Criticism* to the Christian Old and New Testaments. Meir Sternberg's *Poetics of Biblical Narrative* offers a comprehensive and normative classification of stylistic and rhetorical strategies found in the earlier half of the Hebrew Bible. And an essay by Edmund Leach in Alter and Kermode's *Literary Guide,* a collection mostly focused on individual books of the Bible, sketches out a structuralist reading of the "mytho-logic" of a particular motif in the Bible, extending from Exodus to the Gospel of Mark. The "biblical coherence," Leach concludes, "is much more radical than most contemporary scholars seem to realize."[5]

Nevertheless, the basis of each of these poetics or literary classifications of the Bible is distinctly modern and pays little or no attention to ancient criteria. Frye uses a visionary symbolism derived from his study of the poetry of Blake, Sternberg deploys a narrative formalism derived from the modern novel, and Leach applies the structural anthropology of Claude Lévi-Strauss in their categorizing of elements in the biblical text. I have analyzed the limitations of Frye's and Sternberg's approaches at greater length in an essay published elsewhere.[6] Here it is sufficient to note the way each of them emphasizes a particular part of the Bible instead of dealing with the canonical whole. Sternberg is concerned with the Hebrew Bible alone, and (like Auerbach) with its most complex historical narratives first and foremost, the narratives of Genesis and Samuel. Frye, in contrast, gives privilege to the canonically marginal genre of apocalypse, a genre only represented by the Book of Daniel in the Old Testament and the Book of Revelation in the New. In his typological poetics, apocalypse is the ultimate fufillment of earlier biblical "phases." Frye also gives weight to postbiblical "legends" like the Harrowing of Hell which he admits are "not mentioned, or [are] only doubtfully referred to, in the Bible."[7] Neither of these generic systems is congruent with the Bible, Hebrew or Christian, in its canonical entirety.

My own approach to this question of a poetics of the Bible, guided as it is by Bakhtin's concept of dialogue, is certainly not immune from the charge of anachronism. Nevertheless, as I shall argue, the dialogism of utterances conceived by Bakhtin allows for a more fully historical poetics than those offered by Sternberg and Frye. A dialogical poetics according to Bakhtin is capable, for example, of treating the Hebrew Bible and the Christian Bible (Old and New Testaments) as distinct canonical entities, even as it describes their close, indeed polemical, relationship to one another. Bakhtin provides a theoretical model for balancing the claims of historicism and the claims of formalism, claims that, as Quiller-Couch's image of a haphazard anthology demonstrates, have pitted the aesthetic and the scientific perceptions of the Bible against one another in exaggerated notions of their incompatibility.

I

That the Hebrew Bible of Judaism is distinct from the Old Testament of Christianity is an ancient truth being newly appreciated in recent scholarship, literary as well as historical. It is marked in Alter and Kermode's *Literary Guide to the Bible*, for example, by the decision of the editors to follow the order of books in the Jewish canon for the "Old Testament" section of their volume, even as they continue to use the Christian term. The distinction is more polemically advanced by a Modern Language Association publication, *Approaches to Teaching the Hebrew Bible as Literature*, and is debated on historical and theological grounds in a recent collection of essays entitled *Hebrew Bible or Old Testament?*[8]

From the vantage point of European and American cultural history, there is ample justification for insisting on this distinction, as there is for Harold Bloom's sardonic reference to "that captive prize of the Gentiles, the Old Testament."[9] The long story of Christian persecution and repression of Judaism, of Christianity's failure to recognize its profound indebtedness to the Judaism of the several centuries before and after the advent of its own Messiah, is not to be minimized. But in the context of those several centuries—perhaps five hundred years, all told—before and into the Common Era in the eastern half of the Mediterranean basin, the relationship between the divergent sects of Christianity and Judaism, with their largely common Scriptures, is less easily moralized. Indeed, due to the paucity of historical evidence, it is much less easily described. Biblical scholars do not agree when to date the beginning and end of the process of canon-formation for the Hebrew Bible of rabbinic Judaism; they are also unsure about when the alternative list, sequence, and classification of books in the Christian Old Testament took definitive shape. The existence of a Greek version of the Hebrew sacred library, the Septuagint, that eventually provided the textual basis for the canonical Old Testament of Christianity, is not in doubt. But the question of whether this constituted a distinct "Alexandrian canon" for Greek-speaking Jews, alternative to the "Palestinian canon" of emerging normative Judaism, has been called into serious question.[10]

What is almost certain is that Jesus of Nazareth, Paul of Tarsus, and the authors of the different writings later canonized as the New Testament regarded the canon ratified by early Judaism as authoritative, even though they may have regarded additional books as inspired and even though Paul and the other New Testament writers had no inhibitions about quoting from the Septuagint text. It is the threefold organization of the Hebrew Bible into the Law, the Prophets, and the Writings that is recognized by first-century Christians, by Hellenistic Jews and by rabbinical Jews, not the fourfold organization of the Old Testament into the Pentateuch, historical books, the poetical books, and the prophets, significantly different in its literary as well as its theological implications. The Septuagint's restructuring of the Hebrew canon according to Hellenistic concepts of genre ("history," "poetry") and its redesignation of the richly significant Hebrew "Torah" as the authorially based "five books" of Moses may well have been initiated by the Jewish community in Alexandria, where the influence of Greek literature was strong. But virtually all the surviving manuscripts of the Greek Bible are of Christian origin, and the Old Testament as such only becomes a meaningful canonical entity with the formation of a

New Testament canon at the end of the second century.[11] This is not to deny that the earliest Christians read the canonical Jewish Scriptures in a different way from the Pharisees of the first century. There were, in fact, many different ways in which these sacred writings were construed, as among the sectarians of the Qumram community or by Hellenizing Jews like Philo of Alexandria. Nor is it to deny that there were important supplementary sacred texts for many of these sects: the "Oral Torah" of normative Judaism, the oral and written collections of "sayings" and "stories" of Jesus in earliest Christianity, or the Dead Sea Scrolls of Qumran. It is simply to say that the different interpetive constructions and the different textual versions of the Hebrew Bible did not produce an alternative *canon* of a significantly different shape and content, one that lasted beyond the destruction of the Second Temple in 70 c.e. for later generations, until the canonization of a whole Christian Bible emerged in the second century from the Church's reaction to Gnostic initiatives to exclude the Jewish Scriptures wholesale from Christian use.[12]

Thus the prologue to the Greek translation of the Book of Ecclesiasticus, a book eventually included in the Christian Old Testament but not in the Hebrew Bible itself, speaks of "the law and the prophets and the other books of our fathers." 2 Maccabees, another "deutero-canonical" book, mentions "the law," "the books about the kings and prophets," and "the writings of David" (2:2, 13). Philo distinguishes the Law, the "Prophets and the Psalms and the other writings"; Josephus, the "five books of Moses," "the Prophets," and "the remaining . . . books." In the New Testament, Luke quotes Jesus referring to "the law of Moses, the prophets, and the psalms" (24:44), while Matthew has him allude to a Hebrew Bible beginning with Genesis and ending (as the overwhelming number of Hebrew manuscripts and listings do) with Chronicles when he speaks of "all the righteous blood shed on earth, from the blood of innocent Abel to the blood of Zechariah the son of Barachiah" (Matt. 23:35). The Book of Psalms, identified with David and usually positioned as the first book of the Writings, seems to stand for the whole canonical division in some of these formulations, although for Philo it may occupy an intermediate position of its own.

Is there any generic basis for these canonical divisions, any literary common denominator to the arrangement of books? According to scholars like Nahum Sarna, there is not. "This tripartite division of the Scriptures is simply a matter of historical development and does not, in essence, represent a classification of the books according to topical or stylistic categories," he writes.[13] It is true that there is a historical, or better, a dispensational, logic in the formation of the Hebrew canon. The Law ends with the death of Moses, the Prophets are supposed to close with the ministry of Ezra, and the Writings are terminated by the historical retrospect of the Book of Chronicles, coming after the more recent histories of Esther, Ezra and Nehemiah. But it is also probable, judging from other biblical allusions to the threefold canon that "topic" and "style," the basic constituents of any genre theory, were at work in the highly complex but essentially circular process of canon formation. In this process, it seems to have been partly on the basis of topic and style that writings from historically subsequent periods were interpolated back into the Law that supposedly ended with Moses, back into the Prophets who supposedly ceased with Ezra, and back into the Writings, which supposedly did not reach beyond the period of the Persian Empire. Thus Jeremiah 18:18 says, in what appears to be a proverb, "the law shall not perish from the priest, nor counsel from the wise, nor the word from the prophet." Ezekiel 7:26 relates, in a prophetic oracle, that the people "seek a vision from the prophet, but the law perishes from the priest, and counsel from the elders." Ecclesiasticus 39:1 praises the piety of the man "who devotes himself to study of the law of the Most High," who "will seek out the wisdom of all the ancients" and who "will be concerned with prophecies." The common denominators here are cultic law, oracular prophecy, and didactic wisdom literature. There are also a number of "canon-conscious redactions" in the Bible, as Gerald Sheppard calls them, prologues or epilogues to individual books that allude to the larger organization of Scripture in similar terms.[14] Deuteronomy 4:1–2 commands Israel not to add or subtract from "the statutes and the ordinances" that Moses delivers from God. Malachi 4:4–5 refers to "the law of my servant Moses" and the advent of "Elijah the prophet" at the conclusion of the division of the Prophets. Psalms 1 and 2 allude to texts of law and oracles of prophecy, respectively, at the beginning of the Writings. Ecclesiastes 12:9–13 correlates the "proverbs" of wisdom with the "commandments" of law.

These suggestions of an implicit or "unwritten" poetics informing the Hebrew Bible in its canonical divisions have been elaborated upon in a considerable scholarly literature analyzing law, prophecy, and wisdom in ancient Israel and early Judaism. Legislative material is clearly most prominent in the division of the Law, forms of prophecy in the Prophets, and types of wisdom literature in many, if not all, the books of the Writings. Some of these studies consider the interaction or opposition between these types of biblical literature; others note elements belonging to one canonical type of religious literature within books that belong to a different canonical division. There is prophetic material in the Writings, there are genres of wisdom literature in the Law. One scholar warns that in some recent studies "the entire Hebrew canon is in danger of being swallowed" by the concept of "wisdom influence."[15] Nevertheless, the basic literary types are generally treated apart from one another, so that the *system* of genres that a poetics characteristically describes is not made evident. Modern studies are guided for the most part by historical or theological determinations—the cultic office or political role of the prophet, the social setting of wisdom, the religious "theme" of the Pentateuch, for example. The literary concept of genre has not been applied to the larger scope of the canon in this scholarship, being reserved for local, highly particular forms like the proverb, the oracle, the messenger speech, the genealogy, the didactic story, the lament, or the hymn of praise. Many of these highly specific genres belong to oral tradition more than to the written stages of the text, and many of them appear in all three of the canonical divisions. More comprehensive generic terms, such as "narrative," "poem," and "saying" proposed by form critics, on the other hand, tend toward purely formal considerations rather than describing, as a literary genre does, a coherent complex of form and theme. Such broad categories, better described by Northrop Frye's term "radical of presentation" or by Claudio Guillen's "universals," characterize a great deal of literature, ancient and modern, not just the Hebrew Bible as a particular collection of sacred writings.[16]

It is here that the understanding of genre developed by Bakhtin is crucial in discerning a specifically biblical poetics. In *The Formal Method in Literary Scholarship* (published under the name of Pavel Medvedev and perhaps with Medvedev as primary author), Bakhtin argues, against a heavy emphasis on literary style and technique among the Russian Formalists before him, that "poetics should really begin with genre, not end with it." But he also stipulates that "genre appraises reality and reality clarifies genre."[17] Individual genres thus articulate the larger configurations of a literary system, but they also look out onto an extraliterary or extratextual world. In *Problems of Dostoevsky's Poetics*, Bakhtin balances the claims of permanence and change in the concept of generic formation. "A literary genre, by its very nature, reflects the most stable, 'eternal' tendencies in literature's development. Always preserved in a genre are the undying elements of the *archaic*," he writes. But he also insists that "the essence of every genre is realized and revealed in all its fullness only in the diverse variations that arise throughout a genre's historical development."[18] Finally, Bakhtin's notion of genre is alert to the contradictory claim of typicality and uniqueness. In "The Problem of Speech Genres," Bakhtin emphasizes the aspect of typicality; even casual, spontaneous oral communication is framed by the formal conventions of a particular culture, he asserts. But in "The Problem of the Text in Linguistics, Philology, and the Human Sciences," he acknowledges the "unrepeatable event of the text" even as it deploys the complex of genres within which it originally aims and subsequently continues to be understood.[19]

These theoretical insights into the dynamic of genre in verbal communication were never put into the systematic form of a poetics by Bakhtin, but in one extended essay written in the late 1930s, he provides a study of generic formations in the history of the novel that is particularly relevant to a literary criticism of the Bible. "Forms of Time and of the Chronotope in the Novel" uses the peculiar term "chronotope," borrowed from Einstein's theory of relativity and meaning a cultural construction of space and time, to present a literary analysis. But as Bakhtin states at the beginning of the essay, "the chronotope in literature has an intrinsic *generic* significance. It can even be said that it is precisely the chronotope that defines genre and generic distinctions."[20]

This essay is particularly suggestive for biblical criticism in that it devotes a good deal of attention to ancient Greek and Roman literature—the various forms of the "adventure novel" (as Bakhtin calls the Greek romance), the Roman comic novel, and classical biography. The discussion eventually extends to modern European examples, but even toward the end of his informal inventory of genres, Bakhtin returns to the idyll, an ancient as well as a modern literary type. Bakhtin also gives considerable attention to chronotopes that invert other genres and that synthesize in textual form oral, "folkloric" genres that have not been part of the official, high-cultural literary system. His primary example here is the "Rabelaisian chronotope" of *Gargantua and Pantagruel*, which he finds anticipated in the strategies of ancient comedy and satire.

The attention Bakhtin gives to the forms of space and time here—especially to time, as the redoubled reference to temporality in the essay's title would suggest—is an extension of his empha-

sis on forms of dialogue among speakers, an emphasis more prominent in his other writings. In adapting Bakhtin's concept of genre
to a consideration of the Hebrew Bible, I shall thus pay attention
to the spatial and temporal definition of the discourse as well as to
the situation of speakers and listeners relative to each other. However, because of the specialized nature of Bakhtin's term "chronotope" on the one hand and because of the vast array of meanings
that have been given to the term "genre," I shall use the term
paradigm of communication instead. In law, prophecy, and wisdom, the Hebrew Bible organizes the historically diverse materials
of Israelite religious expression into three different paradigms of
communication between God and his people. The canon, in this
literary-critical perspective, is simply the way the Bible correlates
these three paradigms of communication with one another. God
and his people are presumed to have worked out their relationship
in geographical space and historical time, and the correlation of
paradigms is intended to provide a "stable, 'eternal'" model for
future generations, as Bakhtin would put it. Nevertheless, since
these paradigms are flexible, the canon also provides future generations with a model that, in James Sanders's phrase, is "adaptable for life."[21]

Recognition of this inner biblical poetics, as it might be called,
need not preclude an awareness of the diverse, even miscellaneous,
historical origin of the various elements, small and large, that have
been absorbed into the final shaping of the canon. But it can enlist
the arguments of various scholars that law, prophecy, and wisdom
are not simply historically successive forms of sacred literature;
rather they are "parallel and persistent modes of knowledge and
education" and they coexist "throughout Israel's literary and religious history."[22] It is certainly the case that the three paradigms
of communication succeed one another within the canon, and that
within later rabbinic Judaism the canonical divisions were considered to have descending degrees of sanctity, with Torah more
authoritative than the Prophets and the Prophets (at least by medieval times) more authoritative than the Writings. It is also evident
that books of the Law were fixed before the books of the Prophets, perhaps as early as the middle of the fifth century B.C.E., and
that the contents of the Writings may not have been settled until
the beginning of the second century C.E.[23] Nevertheless, it has been
argued by scholars in recent years that it was the alternative communication of prophecy that inspired the canonization of the
Law in the first place and the existence of a definitive Torah, in

turn, that caused the Prophets to be given their canonical shape. In both of these processes, the presence of wisdom writings in Israel's sacred literature seems to have acted as an additional catalyst.[24]

The paradigm of communication known as law concerns the cultic constitution of Israel as the people of Yahweh in religious community. Set in the liminal space of the Wilderness, between Israel's slavery in Egypt and its mastery of other peoples in Canaan, the law also exists in a liturgical present that is regularly enacted and that is specifically designed to bind the historical time of Israel's political future to religious observance. The paradigm of prophecy dramatizes the reformation of Israel as a political nation in the historical space and time of their occupation of the "promised land." In prophecy, Israel experiences God's corrective judgment and restorative blessing among the other nations but only within an ongoing temporal future that is still to be realized. The ceremonial nature of law is not condemned as such, but it must be redeemed and renewed by God's sovereign activity in history. The paradigm of wisdom articulates the preservation of Israel, no longer so clearly demarcated from the other peoples by religious or political boundaries and now turned toward a past of tradition and the fathers. In wisdom Israel is domestic rather than political and exists, at least potentially, in a space of exile or foreign domination.

In law, God meets with his people continuously and his verbal initiative is interspersed with their verbal and cultic response, largely and ultimately in agreement. In prophecy, God speaks to his people intermittently, through a series of prophets to a series of kings; the majority of the people are unresponsive to his threats and promises and therefore end up cut off from Israel's new life of the future. In wisdom, the initiative in communication passes to the people. Wisdom begins in an attitude of reverence, "the fear of the Lord," and concerns itself with the order that God has established in nature and human affairs, but it dramatizes communication among men and women as they instruct one another in the way of righteousness that leads to continuing life. In Bakhtin's terms, these paradigms are large-scale utterances, and as such they are "not indifferent to one another, and are not self-sufficient; they are aware of and mutually reflect one another." In the dialogical poetics I shall sketch out in the rest of this chapter, "every utterance must be regarded primarily as a *response* to preceding utter-

ances in a given sphere."[25] Each paradigm of communication, in
other words, is presented in an implicit complementary relationship to the other two forms of divine-human discourse.

II

Law, prophecy, and wisdom are preserved in the Hebrew canon as
genres in relationship to one another, I would argue, much as tragedy and comedy or epic and drama are described in Aristotle's
Poetics. Or to compare them with less explicit systems of genre,
like the "unwritten poetics" of Shakespeare's plays or the assortment of prose fiction from the Spanish Golden Age incorporated
in *Don Quixote*, the biblical paradigms are like the comedies, tragedies, histories, and romances of the Shakespearean canon or the
chivalric romances, pastoral romances, picaresque novels, historical chronicles, and defenses of poetry informally anatomized
by Cervantes's novel.[26] These analogies are not precise, to be sure,
but like the traditional categories deployed by Shakespeare and
Cervantes, the broad generic paradigms of the Hebrew Bible have
been used to frame elements of other literary forms from earlier
periods. The difference is that in the Hebrew Bible, these literary
elements, taken from the culture of Israel and from the culture of
neighboring societies in the ancient Near East, have been gathered
over a much longer period of time and have not been rendered
homogeneous by the style of a single author. The biblical paradigms
have also been more extensively over-written, covered up by the
agendas of later interpreters, theological as well as literary, than
the plays of Shakespeare or the novel of Cervantes. When they have
been noticed in the past, they have usually been read in terms of
their doctrinal content or their social provenance, not in terms of
their generic typicality. The modern literary critic finds himself
in the position of the fictional Averroes in Borges's story "Averroes'
Search," where a medieval Islamic interpreter of Aristotle is imagined attempting to understand Aristotle's literary criticism without any conception of drama. "The night before, two doubtful
words had halted him at the beginning of the *Poetics*. These words
were *tragedy* and *comedy*. He had encountered them years before
in the third book of the *Rhetoric*; no one in the whole world of
Islam could conjecture what they meant."[27]

In the case of the genres or paradigms of communication in
the Hebrew Bible, however, we may gain confidence from recog-

nizing that the still-dominant academic separation of theological and historical interpretation of the Bible from literary criticism is less extreme than the cross-cultural impasse Borges conjures up. The canonical form given to the Bible within Judaism by the beginning of the Common Era is itself radically "interdisciplinary," rooted in a culture that had no inkling of the intellectual divisions of labor and production that theologians, historians, and literary critics work within today. If we have learned anything in the last two decades of intellectual upheaval in modern university culture, it is the socially constructed nature of the disciplines we have inherited and their susceptibility to reconstruction in the cause of understanding better the objects and subjects we investigate.

In the religious literature or sacred library of the Hebrew Bible, therefore—which one should note was not committed to the form of the book or vellum codex by Jews until medieval times, well after the Christians had adopted this technology, and which therefore existed in the form of a collection of separate scrolls[28]—the set of paradigms of law, prophecy, and wisdom is only one of many logics by which these written materials were brought together. Nevertheless, it is a logic that is pervasive and influential within the Hebrew Bible as it has been preserved in its canonical form, and it is a logic that emerged from the earlier centuries of Israel's experience as an embattled but distinctive people in the ancient Near East. It was neither created ex nihilo by God (as later rabbinic legends report of the Torah) nor imposed by a single reader or council after the fact.

In the case of biblical law, there is evidence that the paradigm was adapted for Israelite religious literature from the political form of the international or suzerainty treaty used in other states of the ancient Near East. This literary debt has been established for major parts of the Pentateuch by George Mendenhall and Delbert Hillers, among others, based on the six-part structure of Hittite treaties from the late second millennium, contemporary with the period of the Exodus in Israel's history. Mendenhall and Hillers focus on particular passages, such as the Decalogue in Exodus 20 and the blessings and curses of Deuteronomy 27 and 28, where direct historical influence may be claimed, and they emphasize the quite different form of treaty or covenant that God makes in Genesis with Noah on the one hand and with Abraham on the other. My own proposal is considerably more general: that the paradigm of law in the Pentateuch as a whole is presented in the form of an international treaty writ large, a treaty between Yahweh as divine king and Israel as his vassal state. Within this expanded treaty, Genesis 1–10, from Adam to Noah, functions as the "preamble" or first section of this political form adapted for religious purposes, while Genesis 11–50, from Abram to Joseph, functions as the "historical prologue" or second section.[29]

From this generic perspective, well above the textual particulars, the Pentateuch no longer appears as the "quite bizarre *Gesamtkunstwerk*" perceived by historical criticism, in David Damrosch's witty phrase.[30] It may be seen a large-scale transformation of the international treaty, in which the third section, the "list of stipulations," has been expanded and reduplicated to include a number of different "codes"—the Decalogue (in the two versions of Exodus 20 and Deuteronomy 5), the Covenant Code (Exodus 20–23), the Holiness Code (Leviticus 17–26), and the Deuteronomic Code (Deuteronomy 12–25), to mention only the most clearly distinguishable units. The first nineteen chapters of Exodus, in this generic perspective, repeat the preamble and historical prologue given in Genesis, narrating first the failure of Moses as a self-appointed deliverer of his people (Exodus 1–2), then his success as the deliverer appointed by Yahweh (Exodus 3–19). As James Nohrnberg has persuasively demonstrated, major events in the life of Moses recall in typological fashion major events in the lives of the patriarchs of Genesis.[31] I would only add that Moses reenacts the experience of the three main patriarchs of Genesis in something of a reverse order. He resembles Joseph in his early life as the adopted son of Pharaoh's daughter; he resembles Jacob in his midlife exile and marriage in Midian; and he resembles Abraham in his later verbal encounters with Yahweh as he is called out of the land of Midian back to Egypt, then out of the land of Egypt back toward Canaan. As Nohrnberg notes, the strange episode in Exodus 4:24–26, when God meets Moses and tries to kill him, recalls the opposition Jacob meets at the ford of the Jabbok when God, in the enigmatic form of "a man," wrestles with his chosen servant at the border of his return from exile. There are even reminders in Moses' early life of the "primeval" figures of Genesis: a reminder of Noah in Moses' "ark" of bulrushes (2:3)— as the King James Version translates the Hebrew *tebah* occuring in both episodes—in which he floats to safety on the Nile, and a reminder of Cain in his killing of an Egyptian overseer and his subsequent ineffective attempt to conceal the crime.

These recapitulations in Exodus are less clearly correlated with one another than the dialogues within Genesis itself, but it is evident that Exodus continues to repeat with a difference the earlier exchanges between God and the ancestors of his emerging people. It is only in chapter 20, at Mount Sinai, that God's extended communication of the law to Israel formally begins. Once it does begin, however, this communication continues for some fifty-six chapters, through the remaining twenty-one chapters of Exodus, all of Leviticus, and into the tenth chapter of Numbers. Throughout this extended centerpiece, Moses acts as God's spokesman to the people and as the people's spokesman back to God. The communication of the law is rehearsed again in retrospect in Deuteronomy, a single day's oration by Moses for the benefit of the new generation that will cross over into the promised land, at the end of Israel's journey. The revelation on the mountain is repeated on the plain (a duplication preserved in the two versions of the Sermon on the Mount in the Gospels of Matthew and Luke). The Book of Deuteronomy stands as a treaty beyond the treaty with its extended presentation of curses and blessings in chapters 27 and 28, one of the six sections of the suzerainty treaty, and in its briefer rehearsal of the other five sections as well. It is a concluding reduplication of the whole generic paradigm of the law.[32]

Within this generic framework of the international treaty or covenant, greatly expanded and freely elaborated upon, the dominant concern of law is God's formation or calling into being of a people. God's people are not simply a set of individuals created in his image but a worshiping community re-created to reflect his distinctive "holiness" in their separation from the rest of the world. The "Holiness Code" of Leviticus, with its reiterated command and invitation "you shall be holy; for I the LORD am holy" (for example, 19:2), is both formally and thematically at the center of the Pentateuch. But as Thomas W. Mann notes, "holiness is not an intrinsic quality belonging to the people; rather, they *become* holy only with respect to Yahweh." This people will be projected into the midst of other peoples in the Promised Land, but they are essentially isolated from such alien cultural influences within the paradigm of the law. In this state of isolation, as Mann observes, "the Israelites enjoy a unique intimacy with Yahweh." "Unlike all other sacral communities, not only the king or the priests have access to the sacred precincts or to ritual instructions, but the people as a whole."[33] As Exodus 19:6 puts it, they are to be a "kingdom of priests."

What is distinctive about biblical law as a paradigm of communication is its record of God being present to his people-in-the-making. Yahweh is before them and among them in any number of auditory and visual manifestations: words addressed to particular individuals ("Abraham," "Moses, Moses"), physical signs addressed to whole groups (the plagues in Egypt, the thunder and lightning on Mount Sinai, the pillar of cloud and the pillar of fire over the Tabernacle or "tent of meeting"). He even appears in person, as it were, to smaller groups—"among the trees" in Genesis 3, as one of "three men" in Genesis 18, upon "a pavement of sapphire stone" in Exodus 24. Even in the verbal rehearsal of earlier events given in Deuteronomy, Moses insists to Israel that "You stand this day all of you before [NIV 'in the presence of'] the LORD your God" (29:10). Moses also insists that the word of God is close at hand, "not in heaven, . . . neither is it beyond the sea. . . . But the word is very near you; it is in your mouth and in your heart" (Deut. 30:12–14).

God meets with his people personally and continuously in law, in a way that he only rarely does in prophecy and almost never does in wisdom. These meetings occur because law presents the dialogue of God and humanity in the form of a covenant in the making. As James Sanders observes, "law in the Bible is phrased in an intimate I-Thou style. . . . It is as though God were personally enunciating royal decrees himself to his personal Israel."[34] Nor is it just that God speaks and men and women listen. God speaks and his people speak back—on the whole, in agreement. The emphasis of law is on the totality of the people's assent, on their ideal, if not actual, response of obedience. "Moses came and told the people all the words of the LORD and all the ordinances; and the people answered with one voice, and said, 'All the words which the LORD has spoken we will do'" (Exod. 24:3).

It is not that the agreement is automatic or uniform or constant on the people's part. There are any number of instances, actual or implied, where individuals or groups are "cut off from Israel." And there are significant moments when God allows his purposes to be shaped, even changed, by human objections to the way he has initially presented them. But "Israel" itself remains intact and integral as far as the law is concerned, even when the whole adult generation of the Exodus, including Moses, has died in the Wilderness before entering into the Promised Land. The precise nature of the offense that disqualifies Moses from entering into Canaan is not clear; it seems to be a ritual offense or "unwitting sin" in Numbers, but in Deuteronomy his death is blamed on the sins of the people. In any case, Moses' solidarity with an ongoing

Israel is assured by his mediation of the Law as a whole—his flesh is made word, so to speak—and the promissory binding of God to his people and his people to God is presented as a fait accompli.

The concern with an obedient, worshiping community in the law is balanced, however, by the centrality of the single figure of Moses, the mediator of the covenant par excellence. Moses represents Yahweh to the Israelites, whose knowledge of him has become remote by the beginning of Exodus. He also represents the Israelites to Yahweh, interceding for them at a number of crucial junctures, appealing to God to "remember" his own words of covenant to Abraham, Isaac, and Jacob in Exodus 32, for example, when God proposes to start over again with a new people, descended from Moses alone. As I suggested earlier, Moses incorporates distinctive features and experiences of the earlier patriarchs of Genesis in his own biography. But he looms as a much larger figure in the law than any of his predecessors in the spiritual formation of God's people. In Deuteronomy, the whole elaborated dialogue between God and Israel, from the giving of the Ten Commandments onward, is condensed and subsumed in Moses' extended monologue. This single utterance of Moses gathers together the numerous utterances of God and of Israel over the forty years preceding, but it does so in order to project them as a single "word which I command you" (4:2) into the unmarked future of Israel's existence in the land of Canaan.

Historical criticism has established beyond any reasonable doubt that Deuteronomy itself was written with hindsight, from the vantage point of Israel's later experience of religious apostasies and political perils, probably in the seventh century B.C.E. The unnamed "place which the LORD your God will choose . . . to put his name and make his habitation there" (12:5) is clearly the city of Jerusalem, which only became the site of the Temple in the early monarchy, and the hortatory style and ethical content of Moses' discourse in Deuteronomy are very close to those of the "Deuteronomic history" that runs from Joshua through 2 Kings in the succeeding canonical division of the Prophets. This historical proximity of sources does not negate the generic distinction between law and prophecy, however, any more than the fact that Shakespeare wrote romances like *Cymbeline, The Winter's Tale,* and *The Tempest* at the end of his career as a dramatist means that his somewhat earlier play *King Lear* should not be regarded as a tragedy. It is true that from the perspective of the historical narratives that make up the first half of the Prophets, as Robert Polzin has argued in his own application of the theories of Bakhtin, there is an implicit dialogism in the bits of narrative in the Book of Deuteronomy that qualifies the monologic authority of the direct discourse of Moses and looks ahead to the larger erosion of religious certainty that is to come.[35] But it is also true that the Hebrew Bible has incorporated Deuteronomy as the climax of the Pentateuch and shaped it according to the treaty form of biblical law. The idea of a "Tetrateuch" advanced by Martin Noth cuts off the final act of the drama of the law, so to speak, while the idea of a "Hexateuch" proposed earlier by Gerhard von Rad, adds to the law's perfected plot an act from a subsequent play in another genre.[36]

Deuteronomy does look ahead from within the paradigm of law to the paradigm of prophecy. It frames a set of thematic concerns common to Samuel, Kings, and Jeremiah, but it does so in the form of a renewal of the covenant, the form that is adumbrated in Genesis and elaborated from Exodus through Numbers. Conversely, the first book of the Prophets, Joshua, consciously adapts the new paradigm of communication, prophecy, to the earlier Mosaic pattern of law. Joshua himself is presented as a second Moses, not merely commissioned by Moses as the leader of Israel to succeed him but also typologically linked to Moses through such actions as his leading of Israel dryshod across the Jordan River into the Promised Land (4:15–18), his circumcision of the younger generation (5:2–7; compare Exod. 4:24–26), and his encounter with an angelic "commander of the LORD's army," who tells him, "Put off your shoes from your feet: for the place you stand is holy" (Josh. 5:15; compare Exod. 3:5). The apparent speed and thoroughness with which the Israelites under Joshua are able to occupy all of Canaan, ending in a Sabbath-like "rest to Israel" given by God (23:1), is a carryover from the totalizing character of the law, an idealized history that will be implicitly corrected by the more problematic, drawn-out narrative of the partial conquest and subsequent defeats experienced by individual tribes in the Book of Judges. There is a final carryover in the ceremony of covenant renewal that Joshua stages in chapter 24, which briefly rehearses the form of the suzerainty treaty so important in the paradigm of the law.

Nevertheless, even in this first book of the Prophets, one can see a significantly different paradigm of communication opening up between God and his people. The concern with forming an integrated community in law is succeeded by a concern in proph-

ecy with reforming a divided constituency. Rahab, a harlot from
Jericho, dwells in Israel "to this day" (6:25) because of her faithfulness to Israel in the opening battle of their holy war. Achan,
from the tribe of Judah, is stoned to death with his family and live-
stock because he violates God's command that all the spoils of
Jericho be utterly destroyed. The ethos of prophecy in the Hebrew
Bible is one of separation; the spiritual community of Israel is
divided again and again by its entry into political history. The
apparent unity of Joshua's campaign gives way to the recurrent
tribal wars of Judges. As Gabriel Josipovici observes, the gruesome
episode at the end of Judges, where a Levite physically dismem-
bers the body of his concubine, symbolizes the disintegration of
the community as well as providing a commentary on the degradation of women.[37] In the Book of Samuel, we see the emergence
of the prophet proper, "twin-born with the monarchy," as Nohrnberg puts it, and the beginning of a long antagonism between
prophet and king as leaders of the nation.[38] After the aborted monarchy of Saul, the redemptive monarchy of David, and the omi-
nously assimilationist monarchy of Solomon, there is a division
of Israel into Northern and Southern kingdoms. First the Northern Kingdom is destroyed with the fall of Samaria in 722, then the
Southern Kingdom collapses with the destruction of Jerusalem in
587. The emblem of prophecy is the drawn sword—in the hand of
the angelic commander who appears to Joshua, in the oracle "the
sword shall never depart from your house" delivered to David by
Nathan (2 Sam. 12:10), and in the "sword for slaughter" described
in terrifying detail in Ezekiel 21, a chapter in which the Hebrew
chereb appears 12 of the almost 150 times it is used in Isaiah,
Jeremiah, and Ezekiel.

   Thus in the paradigm of prophecy, Israel is in perennial crisis.
The point of all God's terrible divisions of the nation is that a
"remnant" of Israel is being preserved and that this redemptive part
is to serve as the basis for Israel's regeneration as a whole. This
remainder is the means God uses to constitute a new and purified
community in the land. God reiterates the promise in Isaiah 35:10
and 51:11: "the ransomed of the LORD shall return, / and come to
Zion with singing." As far as time is concerned, the future itself
is divided between oracles of judgment on the one hand and oracles
of redemption on the other, a pattern essential to prophecy in its
canonical form. But in regard to space both judgment and redemption are seen as taking place within the Promised Land. The liminal space of the Wilderness in law, with Mount Sinai as the locus

of climactic revelation at the beginning, gives way to the historical space of the kingdom Israel, centered in Judah. The city of
Jerusalem and the mountain of Zion are presented as the locus of
the ultimate sovereignty of God over and through his people. Even
the most eschatological or apocalyptic passages in Isaiah and the
other largely oracular prophetic books are centered on "the mountain of the LORD" and the "city of God." A prophecy of Micah is
the most explicit:

> It shall come to pass in the latter days
>   that the mountain of the house of the LORD
> shall be established as the highest of the mountains,
>   and shall be raised above the hills;
> and peoples shall flow to it,
>   and many nations shall come . . .   (4:1–2)

In prophecy, the exile of Israel is never ultimate.

It is a similar case with the prophetic image of the future king,
the Messiah. Biblical prophecy does not suggest that God will
dispense with a distinctive human representative or agent in the
redemptive age to come. Rather it reports that he will recognize a
future king, a descendant of the house of David, as the ultimate
restorer of his people's historical fortunes. This Messiah will combine the power of the kings God's people have known previously
in their history with the justice and compassion demanded by
the prophets who have historically stood over against these kings.
The specifically Davidic Messiah announced in 2 Samuel 7 by the
prophet Nathan and temporarily glimpsed by the writer of 2 Kings
in King Josiah of Judah is modified and generalized in later prophetic books. Isaiah (or Deutero-Isaiah) shows him in the ultimate
form of the Suffering Servant, as well as in the more immediate
form of the Persian ruler Cyrus, to whom the term "his anointed"
is specifically applied (45:1). Ezekiel shows him as a shadowy
"prince" (not a "king") behind the Zadokite priesthood originally
established by David. Haggai and Zechariah show the royal figure
doubled in the high priest Joshua and the governor Zerubbabel.[39]
It is only in the most eschatological prophecies, as in Malachi, the
last book of prophecy in the Hebrew Bible as well as the last book
in the Christian Old Testament, that the specific form of the
Messiah is eclipsed, either by the prophetic "messenger to prepare
the way before me," (also identified by Malachi as a returning
"Elijah the prophet,") or by "the great and terrible day of the LORD"
(3:1, 4:5). Although he is described variously, a single human leader

appointed by God to rule his people is as important in prophecy as the specific land to which the spiritually reconstituted community will be returned.

Most commentary on prophecy in the Hebrew Bible does not pay attention to the prophetic character of the narrative history of the Former Prophets, as they came to be called in later Judaism, and focuses only on the collections of oracles in the Latter or Writing Prophets. But in the paradigm of communication presented in the eight books of the Prophets, which follow the five books of the Law (seven books, plus the composite book of the twelve "minor" prophets), there is a common vision of the way God communicates with his people. The stylistic or presentational mode of the later, oracle-centered books beginning with Isaiah (or Jeremiah in some manuscripts) is certainly different from that of the earlier historical narratives ending with 2 Kings. There is a clearer segregation of narrative from nonnarrative materials in the paradigm of prophecy than in the paradigm of law in the Pentateuch. Even this stylistic distinction, however, is far from absolute. There are short narrative sections in Isaiah, much longer ones in Jeremiah, and Ezekiel is presented almost entirely as narrative history, in spite of its visionary character. And while the earlier narrative histories do give more attention to the figure of the king than to the figure of the prophet, Samuel is a dominant figure in the history of David and Saul, and Elijah and Elisha are prominent in some fourteen chapters of the story of several monarchs in 1 and 2 Kings.

In law, it is clear that God is the initiator and the more powerful party in the covenant he makes with his people. But as we have seen, there is a good deal of attention as well in law given to the people's agreement, even their collaboration, with God in this paradigm of communication. In prophecy, the initiative and authority are more heavily invested in the words of God than in words of the people. The prophetic oracle may be presented in different verbal forms and may be directed at different audiences within and beyond Israel. It even "expects a *reply*, . . . an objection formulated by the prophet, or a prayer," as André Neher observes. Nevertheless, Neher notes, "the true reply to God's *davar* [word] is to repeat that *davar*, to become God's mouthpiece, . . . to put the meaning of the *davar* to a test by introducing it to the world."[40] The prophet who speaks on his own initiative is a false prophet. The paradox of prophecy is that this direct, specific, and unanticipated "word of the Lord" is presented not through the powerful and politically central figure of the king but through the relatively weak, politically marginal figure of the prophet. The view of the prophet as a social outcast popularized in the nineteenth century was overstated, but the reception given to most prophets by their royal audiences in the Bible leaves no doubt about who wielded political power in Israelite society. What the king or any socially powerful person addressed by the prophet's word from God is *supposed* to do is modeled by David in 2 Samuel 12, after Nathan brings him God's judgment on his adultery with Bathsheba and his murder of Uriah. David confesses his sin against God and pleads for mercy. Such repentance is also modeled in the response of Josiah to "the book of the law" discovered in the Temple and read aloud to him as a prophetic word; "when the king heard the words of the book of the law, he rent his clothes" (2 Kings 22:11). The king in his power, in other words, is expected to behave like the prophet in his weakness, like Isaiah with his confession "I am a man of unclean lips, and I dwell in the midst of a people of unclean lips" (6:5) or like Jeremiah in his protest "O LORD, thou has deceived me, / and I was deceived; / thou art stronger than I, / and thou hast prevailed" (20:7). As Walter Brueggeman suggests, following Abraham Heschel, an essential quality of prophecy is its "pathos," ultimately grounded in a pathos that belongs to God himself, God's weakness for his recalcitrant people.[41] The more common response to God's word as delivered by the prophet is the one given to Elijah by Ahab or to Jeremiah by Jehoiakim: the king threatens the prophet with death. For the king to suffer with the suffering of the prophet, which is also the suffering of God, is to align the nation as a whole with God's mercy. For him to use political force against the prophet is to bring the nation under the wrath of God that the prophet has also promised.

The political institution of the monarchy, as presented from 1 Samuel onward, is a spiritually precarious one if left to its own devices. Samuel speaks as prophet when the Israelites demand, "appoint for us a king to govern us like all the nations" (8:5). He reports God's judgment of the proposal—"they have rejected me from being king over them"—even as he also carries out God's ominous accession to the people's demand. From the first, therefore, the communication of prophecy is divided between speaker and audience; indeed, it is radically divi*sive*, as Isaiah learns when he is given his commission to tell the people "Hear and hear, but do not understand; / see and see, but do not perceive" (6:9). Where law dramatizes a single binding agreement between God and his people, prophecy dramatizes a series of polarizing promises. It is not that the utterance of prophecy pits an all-powerful God against an impotent people. It is rather that God's words, delivered by the single figure of the prophet, lead either to the overthrow of the people in their arrogant resistance to God or lead to their restoration as they recognize their weakness and dependence upon him.

Thus in both the narrative and the oracular presentations of prophecy, the movement from "woe" to "weal" and back again is continuous, and it lies beyond human control or prediction. Even the repentance and reform of Josiah in 2 Kings, arguably the greatest instance on record in the Hebrew Bible of a king cooperating with God's corrective word, does not bring the succession of judgments and mercies to an end. Nor does the apparently definitive disaster of the fall of Jerusalem to the Babylonians. Prophecy continues to come to Israel in Babylon during its exile and in Palestine after its return. And even though this dialectic of punishment and redemption is intensely focused on Israel and Judah, it is not limited to this people or this nation alone. "When the Lord has finished all his work on Mount Zion and on Jerusalem he will punish the arrogant boasting of the king of Assyria and his haughty pride," Isaiah announces to the political instrument God uses against his people in the seventh century (10:12). "Assemble yourselves and come, / draw near together, / you survivors of the nations! / . . . Turn to me and be saved, / all the ends of the earth!" his successor-prophet tells the peoples beyond Israel in the sixth (45:20, 22). It is only in the ultimate distance of eschatology, at the historical vanishing point known as the "day of the LORD," that the prophetic division of the kingdom of Israel and the separation of Israel from the rest of the nations will cease.

In the canonical structure of the Hebrew Bible, however, the paradigm of communication presented in prophecy ceases before this projected end is realized. The Prophets are succeeded by the Writings, and prophecy is succeeded by wisdom. This succession is not presented as a historical one first and foremost. The Book of Psalms, the first book of the Writings in most canonical lists, is anchored in the early monarachy of David. Proverbs, the Song of Songs, and Ecclesiastes are linked, directly and indirectly, to Solomon. Job, Ruth, and the first ten chapters of Chronicles are set in even earlier biblical times. And Daniel, primarily a product of the second century B.C.E., is set retroactively in the sixth. Only Esther, Ezra, and Nehemiah refer to the historical period in Israel after prophecy has—canonically speaking—stopped. In this last of its three divisions, therefore, the Hebrew Bible does not move forward in time so much as sideways in genre.

In the paradigm of wisdom, the common ground of the "chronotope" or genre is less evident than in the paradigms of law or prophecy, however. In the individual forms of wisdom, from the single-verse proverbs that predominate in the Book of Proverbs to the comprehensive "biblical historiography" of Chronicles, as Shermayahu Talmon terms this type of narrative, we find specific literary genres more distinctly marked within the canonical paradigm.[42] Instead of the single binding agreement of law or the series of polarizing oppositions of prophecy, biblical wisdom presents an anthology of principles concretely expressed. The Book of Proverbs gathers discrete, highly contrastive proverbs, most of them two half-lines in length, into loose collections with no apparent ordering principle: "the proverbs of Solomon," "the words of the wise," other proverbs of Solomon "which the men of Hezekiah king of Judah copied," "the words of Agur son of Jakeh," and "the words of Lemuel, . . . which his mother taught him" (10:1, 22:17, 25:1, 31:1). "The other books," as the Greek translation of Ecclesiasticus calls the heterogeneous contents of the Writings, gather together different discrete forms of wisdom literature in an explicitly miscellaneous anthology.

In many discussions of the wisdom literature of the Hebrew Bible, only Proverbs, Job, and Ecclesiastes are identified as wisdom proper. But even with these three books, it is obvious that different literary types are involved: practical wisdom in Proverbs versus speculative wisdom, which often assails the practical, in Job and Ecclesiastes; terse poetic parallelism in Proverbs and Job versus loose, gnomic prose in Ecclesiastes; rudimentary dramatic dialogue in Job versus didactic monologue in Proverbs and Ecclesiastes. Rather than claiming that some of the books in the division of the Writings embody wisdom literature pure and simple and others do not, it is more reasonable to note a considerable variety of literary forms that are sapiential in character. These genres present human formulations of the principles that govern the world of nature and human affairs, anthropocentric perceptions of the practical, moral, and philosophical universe. These principles and this universe are assumed to have been instituted by God, but the precise character of God himself is rarely spelled out; it is simply assumed to be enunciated elsewhere. The different wisdom genres represented in the Hebrew Bible include formal debates like the main body of the Book of Job and the poetic lyrics of the Psalms, the Song of Songs, and Lamentations. They also include the didactic poems of the first 9 chapters of Proverbs, the cosmological meditations of Job 28 and Proverbs 8:22–31, and the didactic historiography of Ruth, Daniel 1–6, Esther, Ezra, and Nehemiah. With chapters 7–12 of the Book of Daniel, which belong to the literary genre of apocalyptic, and with the Book of Chronicles, which recapitulates the Pentateuch in the simple form of genealogy and recapitulates the Former Prophets in a revised narrative of the monarachy and its mis-adventures, wisdom elements disappear into the other paradigms of communication. I shall discuss the relationship of the non-canonical apocalyptic literature to canonical prophecy in Chapters 3 and 5. But as far as the paradigms of communication in the Hebrew Bible are concerned, Daniel and Chronicles may be de-scribed as books where the largely sapiential Writings incorporate significant features of prophecy, both canonical prophecy and prophecy from beyond the canon.

This dialogic interplay or interpenetration of paradigms is a phenomenon we have noted already with Deuteronomy and Joshua, where distinctive features of prophecy appear within the context of law and distinctive features of law in prophecy. The overlap-ping of biblical paradigms is not unlike the interpolation of liter-ary genres in Shakespeare's plays, where tragic scenes appear within the comedies (the performance of "Pyramus and Thisbe" in *A Midsummer Night's Dream*, for example) and comic scenes in the tragedies (for example, the several scenes involving the Fool in *King Lear*). The Book of Jonah offers a clear case of biblical wisdom inter-polated within prophecy, to give another biblical example, where a wisdom tale about a disgruntled prophet virtually parodies the prophetic oracles of judgment against Israel's enemies. There are also distinct elements of wisdom in the Joseph story in Genesis, which is a didactic tale of individual virtue in the service of divine providence, as von Rad has pointed out, and thus an instance of wisdom embedded in the Law.[43]

Where the interplay of prophecy and wisdom becomes more difficult to describe as an interpolation or even as a dialogic exchange between paradigms is in Psalms, commonly the first book of the Writings. As noted earlier, Psalms 1 and 2 serve as "canon-conscious" introductions to the Book of Psalms as a whole, itself divided into five books in canon-conscious imitation of the five books of the Law. Psalm 1 is one of a dozen wisdom psalms and Psalm 2 is distinctly prophetic, a royal psalm of a messianic nature. It is well known that other sects within later Judaism, particularly the covenanters of Qumran and the disciples of Jesus of Nazareth, read the Psalms primarily as a prophetic corpus. In his sermon in Acts 2, as reported by Luke, Peter calls David a prophet in connection with another messianic psalm, Psalm 110. It has also been argued that "the Psalms . . . , whatever their origin, came to be read and studied in the context of private meditation or devotion," both in normative Judaism and in Christianity, and thus became a form of wisdom after the fact.[44] In any case, the canonical collection of the Book of Psalms has noticeably diverse types of poems in it. Gunkel identifies hymns of praise, laments (communal and individual), songs of thanksgiving, songs of trust, royal psalms, and salvation history psalms as important specific genres. Robert Alter notes further that genre in the Psalms is often quite flexible, "not a locked frame but a point of departure for poetic innovation."[45]

What all these types of psalm have in common with the more recognizably sapiential types of literature in the Hebrew Bible is what Walther Zimmerli has called the "anthropocentric starting point" of wisdom.[46] They are addressed to God, usually directly and often passionately, but they all express the first-person view of a human individual. It is the "man of God," even if this man is speaking for God's people as a community, who takes the verbal initiative in a psalm. And the single human speaker carries the discourse through to the end, even though his stance and mood may change considerably in the course of the utterance. It is here that the formal diversity of biblical wisdom finds its thematic rationale. The God of Israel may be one Lord, as Deuteronomy asserts, and his people may be of one mind as a worshiping community, as Deuteronomy exhorts. But considered as individuals in the context of the changing generations, which is the way human beings are most often represented in wisdom, God's people are diverse. Wisdom is found in women as well as men. Mothers give advice as effectively as fathers, and the personifications of wisdom, as in Proverbs 8:22–31 and Proverbs 9:1–6, are distinctly feminine if not feminist. Even a single figure like David, with his mood-swings from elation to despair and from fear to trust in the psalms attributed to him, expresses himself in wisdom with a broad palette of emotions.

In this third paradigm of communication, therefore, the balance of divine-human dialogue shifts back from God to the people, away from the single-minded emphasis on the divine initiative of prophecy toward a many-minded concern with the human response.

Instead of historically identified prophets who recite particular oracles and historically identified kings who either receive or reject these words of the Lord, wisdom offers a collective set of teachings, traditional and inherited, often anonymous or generically pseudonymous, that have been passed from one human generation to the next. Law describes the formation or constitution of God's people as a cultic community; prophecy describes their deformation by the influence of other peoples and their transformation by God himself as a kingdom or political state. Wisdom describes the preservation of the people of God on the level of private, domestic personality.

In effect, wisdom is the most secular of the three paradigms of communication in the Hebrew Bible. It is the least explicitly Israelite or Judaic of the biblical modes of utterance. Wisdom focuses on God's ordering of the world in creation rather than on his organizing of a people in history. It speaks of people in the context of civil order, centered on the ordinary household, rather than in the context of political power and conflict. Where prophecy is concerned with the critical differences between Israel and the other nations around her and in her midst, wisdom attends to the common experience of people in all times and places. Indeed, the wisdom literature of the Hebrew Bible has many affinities with the wisdom writings of other ancient Near Eastern cultures like the Egyptian and Mesopotamian. In some cases—as with Proverbs 22:17–24:22 and the Egyptian *Instruction of Amen-em-opet*, for example—biblical wisdom can be shown to have borrowed directly from foreign texts. The prophetic view of such cosmopolitan syncretism is negative. 1 Kings insists that Solomon's wisdom was a direct gift from God, given in response to Solomon's inspired request, and claims that Solomon was "wiser than all other men" from the surrounding nations (4:30–31). But Proverbs, the Song of Songs, and Ecclesiastes associate this patron of biblical wisdom with the pragmatism, sensuality, and skepticism of men and women beyond the boundaries of Israel. Wisdom celebrates and advocates a human responsiveness deeply rooted in general human experience and the order of nature. The quintessential wisdom book, Job, tells the story of a patriarch who has no place in the history or genealogy of Israel; although God finally answers Job, this answer comes quite unexpectedly and comes "out of the whirlwind," cloaked in images of cosmos and creation. Most of the dialogue in Job takes place between the deeply human protagonist and his shallowly human friends on the one hand, and between a natural theologian and the deity he discerns, imperfectly yet correctly in the final analysis, out of his own experience on the other.

It is easy from a modern, literary-critical perspective to exaggerate the humanism of biblical wisdom literature. As historical and theological critics remind us, within the Bible "the wise men began with a faith which was not the product of wisdom."[47] Wisdom stands in ultimate agreement with the paradigms of law and prophecy, even in the case of the Book of Job, as we shall see in Chapter 4, which initially seems to call both law and prophecy into question as adequate forms of communication between God and his people. In terms of the analysis of dialogism provided by Bakhtin, wisdom is the most "centrifugal" of the paradigms of the Hebrew Bible, the most explicit in its recognition of heteroglossia or alternative speaking. Wisdom is overtly didactic in many instances, "selfconsciously educational," in Walter Brueggemann's phrase,[48] and it often idealizes the ultimate order of human morality and divine creativity. But this theoretical respect for authority does not negate wisdom's practical validation of life, human and natural, in its open-ended and energetic diversity.

Indeed, it is only in the paradigm of wisdom that a consideration of the Bible as literature or art is practically sanctioned within the Hebrew canon. The attitude of prophecy toward literary appreciation of the Bible, in contrast, is hostile; it is explicitly condemned by an oracle in the Book of Ezekiel, where God tells his prophet that the people listen to him not as if he were a messenger of God, whose word will come true and should be acted upon by those who hear it, but as if he were an entertainer, whose performance was meant to give pleasure. "And, lo, you are to them like one who sings love songs with a beautiful voice and plays well on an instrument, for they hear what you say, but they will not do it. When this comes—and come it will!—then they will know that a prophet has been among them" (33:32–33). While such an attitude can be found in the Writings—in Psalm 137, for example, where the Babylonian captors of the cultural elite of Jerusalem ask for "one of the songs of Zion" and get a prophetic curse instead— the ironic, reflective stance of Ecclesiastes is more characteristic of wisdom. "I have seen the business that God has given to the sons of men to be busy with. He has made everything beautiful in its time; also he has put eternity into man's mind, yet so that he cannot find out what God has done from the beginning to the end. I know that there is nothing better for them than to be happy and enjoy themselves as long as they live; also that it is God's gift to man that every one should eat and drink and take pleasure in all his toil" (3:10–13). In such a paradoxical vision of life as a pleasurable gift within limits that are disillusioning, even painful, the predominantly religious and ethical discourses of law and prophecy approach a discourse that can be called aesthetic.

Wisdom recognizes, in other words, that God's people are creative agents in the dialogue of humanity and divinity, that they are responsible for giving shape and texture to the words they speak to one another about God and his ways. These utterances are not seen as aesthetic objects to be contemplated for their beautiful proportions but as evidence of aesthetic acts on the part of those who formulate them. Bakhtin himself describes aesthetic activity in a way that captures the idea implicit in biblical wisdom. "Aesthetic activity collects the world scattered in meaning and condenses it into a finished and self-contained image. Aesthetic activity finds an emotional equivalent for what is transient in the world . . . , an emotional equivalent that gives life to this transient being and safeguards it."[49]

It is only in the communicative paradigm of wisdom, I would argue, that the Bible begins to acknowledge its own aesthetic dimensions. Nevertheless, in the closing of the Hebrew canon and the binding of wisdom to the more authoritative discourses of law and prophecy, the Bible refers such activity back to God himself as creator. "The fear of the LORD is the beginning of wisdom" (Prov. 1:7, 9:10; Ps. 111:10) is the recurring formulation that anchors human knowledge and action to the divine order of things. The Bible refuses to develop its aesthetic insight into anything approaching the more developed literary humanism of later Western culture, Jewish and Christian. Literary humanism, seen in figures like Philo and Augustine, supplements the biblical paradigms of communication between God and his people with the self-consciously "poetic" and "philosophical" constructions of Greek and Latin literature, forms that themselves describe a basically anthropocentric rather than theocentric world and an essentially polytheistic rather than monotheistic dialogue between humanity and divinity. What biblical wisdom does produce, out of its rudimentary aesthetic awareness, is the perception of a biblical canon itself—not the contents of a list of sacred or inspired writings but the set of categories and interpretive constructs, the underlying poetics, necessary for "hearing the voice of the same God through historically dissimilar traditions," as Gerald T. Sheppard puts it. Canonization does not fully harmonize these diverse traditions, but it "enhance[s] the presumption of biblical unity by creating explicit interpretive contexts between books or groups of books."[50] It is from the vantage point of wisdom, therefore, that the divisions of the Law, the Prophets and the Writings and the generic constructs of law, prophecy, and wisdom achieve their canon-conscious articulation. In the view of law, one might say, such categories and constructs are merely a transparent window through which the light of revelation passes. In the view of prophecy, they may be thought of as a series of lenses through which the light of God's holiness is focused and concentrated to the point of combustion. In the view of wisdom, however, they are like the pieces in a stained-glass window, filtering the white light of heaven to produce human figures in many colors.

III

This outline of a biblical poetics concludes with an application of the paradigms of communication just described to a particular motif in the Hebrew Bible. It is my purpose to show here the way a particular motif, the image of a "house of God," is treated differently in each of the three paradigms. I am concerned with the way the different treatments of this motif reflect the agendas of concern peculiar to law, to prophecy, and to wisdom. The idea that the God of Israel has a "house" is by no means unequivocally affirmed in the Hebrew Bible. Paul's Hebraic message to the citizens of Athens that "the God who made the world and everything in it, being Lord of heaven and earth, does not live in shrines made by man" (Acts 17:24) has ample precedent in the Jewish Scriptures to which Paul repeatedly refers. But the idea that God meets his people in architecture of his own specification, preeminently though not exclusively, is also affirmed throughout the Hebrew Bible. The dialogues of God and his people often take place in the open: on mountain tops, in the midst of rivers, on the road. But they are frequently (and more normatively) channeled through dwelling places within which God has indicated people are to seek him. The medium is not to be mistaken for the message, the sanctuary for the holiness that it represents. But the "house of the Lord" is a setting within which the communication of God and his people, verbal and otherwise, can be expected regularly to take place.

In law, the house or dwelling of God is exclusively the tabernacle or "tent of meeting." Until Moses is given the elaborate and detailed instructions on Mount Sinai for the construction of this large, portable shrine, there is no thought of God needing or wanting an edifice to dwell in. The patriarchs of Genesis set up altars, but primarily as memorials to particular visitations from God and only in the open, as in the case of the altar Abram builds at Shechem (Gen. 12:7) or the altar that Jacob builds at Bethel (Gen. 35:7), having promised earlier to call the stone he slept on "God's house" (Hebrew, *bet-el*) if God would be with him in his flight from Esau (Gen. 28:22). But with the formal giving of the law comes a formal blueprint for a single structure of divine and human meeting. The portable character of the tabernacle the Israelites are commissioned to build in the Wilderness is significant, reflecting the lack of geographical fixity characteristic of law. As in the burning bush in Exodus 3, which prefigures the tabernacle described later on, "holy ground" is established in a dynamic, temporal manner simply by God's appearing there. Mount Sinai is enshrined in the narrative as the place where God fully revealed himself to all Israel, but it is not a place where God intends his people to seek him thereafter. This a lesson Elijah learns again when he retreats to Mount Sinai, seeking a Mosaic theophany as a prophet in 1 Kings 19. God asks him what he is doing there and sends him back to Damascus. God appears to Israel in the pillar of cloud and fire. The pillar (*ammud* in Hebrew) anticipates a significant feature of the Temple of Solomon to come, but the cloud and fire recall the unrepeatable theophany. In this way, God leads the tabernacle through the Wilderness even as he regularly appears within it.[51]

Historical criticism regards the tabernacle as a utopian fiction of the Priestly writer, an idealized re-creation of the Temple of Solomon probably only composed—certainly only combined with other strands of the Pentateuch—after the Temple was destroyed in the fall of Jerusalem in 586 B.C.E. The generic approach developed in this chapter would describe the relationship differently: the tabernacle in the paradigm of law is subsequently reconstituted in the temple as seen in the paradigm of prophecy. The tabernacle is a house of God tailored to the liminal condition of Israel in Wilderness, in transition between bondage in Egypt and conquest in Canaan. It belongs to an ideal ritual present, not a nostalgic past or a utopian future. The schematic and repetitive elaboration of its cultic details observes only its physical structure and the ceremonial activities within it, not its position in geographical space or historical time. Even the question of ritual time—the cycles according to which the sacrifices are to be performed in the tabernacle—is only specified for certain annual feasts and the Day of Atonement. The more common formula in Leviticus is simply "when any man of you brings an offering to the LORD . . ." (for example, 1:2).

As noted earlier, the main concern of law is with the constitution of a "holy people" among whom the holy God may appear. The institution of the priesthood creates gradations of sanctity within Israel unknown in the Law before the plans for the tabernacle are given. But the genealogical requirements for this office are represented differently in Deuteronomy than they are in Exodus, Leviticus, and Numbers, and both "the Levites" and "the sons of Aaron" are seen mainly as qualified representatives of Israel to God, as a part representing the whole, rather than—like Moses himself—as spokesmen for God to the rest of Israel. At least as their functions are described in Leviticus, in the Holiness Code, their business is to keep Israel ritually clean so that God's presence may be manifest among them in the tabernacle symbolically pitched at the center of their various encampments. God's house is a tent at the center of the tents of the twelve tribes of Israel, and it disappears as such when Israel's nomadic existence comes to its appointed end.

The two main Hebrew words for the tabernacle, *ohel* and *mishkan*, prominent in the Law, appear only infrequently in the Prophets. In the early chapters of Joshua, the ark of the covenant is mentioned a number of times as it crosses the Jordan and accompanies the Israelites in battle, but the tabernacle as a whole is only mentioned at the end of the book, when it is set up, apparently on a permanent basis, at Shiloh. By 1 Samuel, Shiloh has become the site of a temple (*bayit* or *hekal*), to which people like Samuel's father Elkanah travel annually to worship and make sacrifices and within which Samuel himself lives when he ministers before the Lord under the priest Eli. This early temple is corrupt in its priesthood, and it loses the ark, which is first captured by the Philistines in battle, then stored in the house of Abinadab (7:1–2), until David brings it into his new royal capitol of Jerusalem some twenty years later. David wants to build a new temple, a house for God on a magnificent scale. In 2 Samuel 7 he apologetically contrasts his own palace, a "house of cedar," to the mere "tent" that the ark of God dwells in. But he is told through the prophet Nathan that God is not bothered by this disparity. Playing on the double meaning of "house" as "dwelling" and "family," God tells David that he will rather make a house for David, through his descendants. The temple in Jerusalem will have to be built by Solomon.

Thus the representation of the house of God in prophecy shows a characteristic ambivalence toward the imposing and apparently permanent form of the temple. Politically, the temple is too close to the king's palace not to tempt the people to worship the king's power. Religiously, it is too much like the temples of the Philistines and the other Canaanite peoples not to tempt the people of Israel to worship other gods.[52] Before Israel has a king, the judge or charismatic leader Samson pulls the Philistine temple of Dagon down on his and their heads as an act of revenge. When Israel is divided under two kings, the prophet Amos preaches against the temple at Bethel in the Northern Kingdom. And after the Southern Kingdom has had its king taken into exile, Ezekiel has a vision of the Jerusalem temple filled with pagan idolatries; he sees the glory of the Lord ascending from the temple and going off toward Babylon on its spectacular chariot of four-faced cherubim and wheels within wheels.

In prophecy, the fresh word of the Lord may come to the prophet within the precincts of the temple, as it does in the initial call of Samuel and in the call of Isaiah. And the prophet may present a vision of a new and better temple, as Ezekiel does in the last nine chapters at an eschatological distance or as Zechariah and Haggai do in prophetic anticipation of the Second Temple as it was rebuilt after the Exile. But the most prominent attitude toward the temple displayed by the prophets is critical of the false sense of security that it gives the people: that God will protect them in all their political and military affairs. Jeremiah relays an oracle: "Do not trust in these deceptive words: 'This is the temple of the LORD, the temple of the LORD, the temple of the LORD. . . . Has this house, which is called by my name, become a den of robbers in your eyes? . . . Go now to my place that was in Shiloh, where I made my name dwell at first, and see what I did to it for the wickedness of my people Israel" (7:4, 11, 12). Isaiah diminishes the temple by putting it in its cosmic context:

> Thus says the LORD:
> "Heaven is my throne
> and the earth is my footstool;
> what is the house which you would build for me,
> and what is the place of my rest?
>
> (66:1)

Malachi announces that "the Lord whom you seek will suddenly come to his temple," but follows the eschatological promise with a threat. "But who can endure the day of his coming, and who can stand when he appears? For he is like a refiner's fire and like fuller's soap; he will sit as a refiner and purifier of silver" (3:1–3).

The temple in prophecy is thus subjected to the divided, polarizing representation basic to this paradigm of communication. The house of God here is either in a state of corruption or in a state of purification. The centralized temple in Jerusalem may be less subject to idolatry than the "high places," which are merely sacrificial altars and not temples and which may be dedicated to Yahweh rather than to foreign gods.[53] But as far as the prophets are concerned, a temple is continually in need of purification in its effect on Israel's spiritual communion with God. Such a purification comes only through the people taking to heart the prophetic "word of the Lord." This is more far-reaching than the purity that the priestly sacrifices carried out within the temple itself are able to provide. The motto of prophecy may be taken from Samuel's word to Saul: "Has the LORD as great delight in burnt offerings and sacrifices, / as in obeying the voice of the LORD? / Behold, to obey is better than sacrifice, / and to hearken than the fat of rams" (1 Sam. 15:22). The ritual sacrifices of the temple, carried over from the sacrifices of the tabernacle in the Law, are not rejected absolutely in prophecy, but they are shown to be in need of a deeper and wider purification, one in which the temple itself may be completely consumed.

In the paradigm of wisdom and the division of the Writings, the temple continues to be an object of some attention. The First Temple is recalled with celebratory nostalgia in Chronicles, which anchors the house of God built by Solomon to an elaborate planning by David himself and removes the prophetic aspersions cast on this edifice as it is presented in Samuel and Kings. The Second Temple is celebrated more modestly in Ezra and Nehemiah, where the shouts of joy over the laying of the foundations are mixed with weeping among the "old men who had seen the first house" in its larger proportions (Ezra 3:12) and where the satisfaction over the replenished storehouses is mixed with anxiety over the ritual impurities that have been carelessly introduced by the new priests (Neh. 13: 7–9). In any case, as Menachem Haran explains, the Second Temple no longer contained the essential attributes of holiness belonging to the First Temple and the tabernacle—the ark of the covenant and the cherubim above the mercy seat. The Second Temple "marks a stage of transition to a new period which was preparing to give up this institution altogether in practice—even while clinging to it as an eschatological symbol."[54] In wisdom, the literal house of God embodied in the temple is less significant than a series of metaphorical displacements. There is the emotional and spiritual refuge of the "house of the LORD" in Psalms and the emblematic house of Lady Wisdom in Proverbs. There is also the suggestion in Proverbs and in Job that the creation itself is a cosmic dwelling built by God for all his creatures. Finally, there is the palace of the Solomonic king (who is God's representative) in the Song of Songs and Ecclesiastes and the palace of the foreign ruler (which is nevertheless under God's authority) in Daniel and Esther. The single dwelling place of God in history presented variously in law and in prophecy gives way in wisdom to a number of residences throughout the world where God is recognized as the ultimate master.

The "house of the LORD" figures most prominently in the psalms known as songs of trust, psalms of generalized confidence against a background of distress. In Psalm 23, where the speaker describes the table prepared before him in the presence of his enemies and anticipates dwelling in the "house of the Lord" forever (or for as long as he lives), the ceremonial elements of the temple are greatly attenuated. The house of God becomes a place of refuge and residence for God's loyal servant. Psalm 27 uses a series of synonyms in evoking this image of spiritual security: "the house of the LORD," "his temple," "his shelter," "his tent" (27:4–5). In Psalm 52, the speaker compares himself to "a green olive tree / in the house of God," and in Psalm 84 compares "those who dwell in thy house, / ever singing thy praise" to young birds in their nest.

The extension of a particular ritual dwelling of God to a habitation for his servants is developed further in the image of the house of Wisdom in the Book of Proverbs, which culminates a series of scenes of domestic instruction and domestic temptation in the wisdom lyrics of the first nine chapters.

> Wisdom has built her house,
>   she has set up her seven pillars.
> She has slaughtered her beasts, she has mixed her wine,
>   she has also set her table.
> She has sent out her maids to call
>   from the highest places in the town,
> "Come, eat of my bread
>   and drink of the wine I have mixed.
> Leave simpleness, and live,
>   and walk in the way of insight."
>
>   (9:1–6)

Against this life-giving hospitality is the sinister invitation of Wisdom's opposite, "the woman Folly" (NIV), whose guests enter the house only to find themselves "in the depths of Sheol" (9:18). The contrast of two establishments, one leading to life, the other to death, is typical of wisdom literature, as is the sense that while these houses belong to God, he himself is not personally present within them. Fleetingly in Proverbs 8 and in greater detail in Job 38, God is presented not as absent landlord but as architect or master builder of a dwelling place for all his creatures. The "habitable part of his earth" (Prov. 8:31, KJV), has been provided with a "foundation," a "cornerstone," "doors" and "storehouses" (Job 38: 4, 6, 8, 22).

The idea that God is the ultimate owner of the dwellings of those whom he has created is developed in other books of the Writings where wisdom per se is less prominent. Interpretations of the Song of Songs have disagreed over the literal or allegorical nature of the love between a man and a woman that this book celebrates.[55] But whether the mutual longing of the king and his bride is taken as an individual relationship between Solomon and a woman or as a corporate courtship between God and his people Israel, the image of a royal palace hovers in the background, with its "chambers" (1:4), cedar beams (1:17) and "banqueting house" (2:4). The woman speaks in several sections of her own dwelling, "my mother's house" (3:4, 8:2), the king has a sumptuous wooden "palanquin" or carriage (3:9), and many of the imagined rendezvous are presented in pastoral settings—mountains, deserts, woods, and pastures. But in the end the bride represents herself as a palace ("I was a wall, / and my breasts were like towers") and its attached gardens ("my vineyard, my very own, is for myself") (8:10, 12), and the king imagines her as his private garden, "a garden locked, a fountain sealed" (4:12). The royal palace and its ground are evoked more literally at the beginning of Ecclesiastes: "I built houses and planted vineyards for myself; I made myself gardens and parks, and planted in them all kinds of fruit trees," the Solomonic speaker recalls (2:4–5). But as he discovers, in the irony characteristic of this book, such a "house of feasting" is less desirable than a "house of mourning" (7:2), and it is this latter type of dwelling to which he retires in the haunting emblem of the mortal body in decay at the end of life: "in the day when the keepers of the house tremble, and the strong men are bent, and the grinders cease because they are few, and those that look through the window are dimmed, and the doors on the street are shut" (12:3–4). The open, expansive dwelling place under the banner of love in the Song of Songs gives way to the restricted residence of death in Ecclesiastes, man's "long home" (KJV) where "the dust returns to the earth as it was, and the spirit returns to God who gave it" (12:5, 7).

Like the house of Wisdom in Proverbs, these are not houses in which God himself dwells so much as homes he leases to the people he has created. As we have observed earlier, God is not visibly or verbally present in wisdom. Rather he is presumed to be overseeing his creatures and his creation from behind the scenes. This point is underscored in Daniel and in Esther, where a representative of God's people in exile asserts God's authority over a foreign king from within the king's own palace. The Book of Daniel begins with a reference to the "vessels of the house of God" in Jerusalem that are carried off by Nebuchadnezzar to the "house of his god" in Babylon (1:2). Daniel himself is like one of these vessels within Nebuchadnezzar's royal palace, serving in exemplary fashion within Babylon's political administration without compromising his devotion to the God of Israel. He interprets Nebuchadnezzar's dream in which the sheltering tree of his empire is cut down and he is turned into a beast of the field. Nebuchadnezzar has the dream while "at ease in my house and prospering in my palace" (4:4) and Daniel's interpretation comes true as Nebuchadnezzar is "walking on the roof of the royal palace of Babylon" and thinking "Is not this great Babylon, which I have built by my mighty power as a royal residence and for the glory of my majesty?" (4:29–30). When he finally acknowledges the greater dominion of the "King of heaven" (4:37), Nebuchadnezzar is restored to his royal quarters. Other reminders of God as king of kings and owner of their royal houses include the episode of Shadrach, Meshach, and Abednego being preserved in the fiery furnace, the episode of Daniel being preserved in the lion's den, and the writing "on the plaster wall of the king's palace" (5:5), in which Nebuchadnezzar's son Belshazzar is given a warning similar to his father's about honoring God and not believing his own power absolute. Ironically, Belshazzar's response is to promote Daniel to the position of "third ruler in the kingdom" (5:29), whereupon Belshazzar is immediately slain. In the Book of Esther, there is an analogous dramatizion of Jewish influence over a foreign empire in the midst of a royal palace, although in this case, it is the people of God, represented by Esther and Mordecai, rather than God himself, who seem to be in charge of the providential plot and Haman and his Agagite or Amelekite bretheren who are brought low rather than the Persian King Xerxes.[56]

The variety of these tents, temples, royal palaces, and private dwellings in the paradigm of wisdom and the oblique ways in which they figure as "houses of God" reflect the diversity and the metaphorical tendencies of wisdom itself. This figurative diversity of examples contrasts with the single material instance of the tabernacle as the house of God in law and the single institution of the temple divided between its physically real and its spiritually ideal forms in prophecy. Indeed, the different treatments of this motif indicate a difference in the constitution of each of these biblical paradigms. Law is a highly unified—or better, unifying—generic category in the way it presents itself to the reader. In Bakhtin's terms, it is centralizing and monologic, minimizing the dialogic diversity or heteroglossia of the Bible's fundamental organization of its materials. It evokes (from another perspective, it embodies) the kind of harmonizing, theological interpretation that the Torah was to receive in Pharisaic and rabbinic Judaism, in which it is axiomatic that every part of the text agrees with every other part. It also invites the traditional assumption, in Christianity as well as Judaism, that the Pentateuch was written in its entirety by a single author: Moses himself. Wisdom, on the other hand, as we have already suggested, is overtly dialogic. Within the framework of the Hebrew canon, it gives the greatest play to different authors, different intellectual perspectives, different cultural settings, different religious moods.

The heteroglossia of biblical wisdom is certainly restrained in comparison with that of other literary traditions, as we have already noted. The "canon" of Greek literature, with the two Homeric epics at its center and a wide assortment of lyric, dramatic, philosophical, and narrative genres arrayed around them, is considerably more diverse than this third division of the Jewish Scriptures. Nevertheless, Morton Smith has argued that the "belletristic" genres of many of the books of the Writings (gnomic verses, poetic drama, philosophical reflection, romances and erotic poetry) parallel the genres that appear in Greek literature from the sixth through the third centuries B.C.E. in expanding Hellenistic culture of the eastern Mediterranean.[57] And within the canonical system or poetics of the Hebrew Bible, wisdom does sanction a "centrifugal" alternative to the "centripetal" authority of law, in Bakhtin's terminology. It is significant that "deutero-canonical" books that the Christian Old Testament later received into its expanded canon from the Septuagint are predominantly sapiential in nature, not only in the case of the Wisdom of Solomon and Ecclesiasticus among the "Poetical Books," but also in the case of Tobit and Judith among the "Historical Books" and Baruch among the "Prophetic Books." The alternative division of books in the Old Testament (Pentateuch, Historical Books, Poetical Books, and Prophetic Books) is, in fact, a poetics according to wisdom, in which Greek genres that the earlier Israelite and Jewish writers never recognized as such are used to reconstruct the Hebrew canon. The Law is the only Hebrew canonical division that remains unchanged, but in the term "Pentateuch" or "five-volumed," even this division loses its distinctiveness and authority in the translation. Since this other canon only became canonical with the advent of Christianity and the emergence of the New Testament, however, further discussion of these issues will take place in Chapter 3.

3

Spoken to Us by His Son: A Dialogics of the New Testament

I

In Chapter 1 we examined Erich Auerbach's contrast between the forward-looking historical realism of the Gospel of Mark and the traditional comic realism of Petronius's *Satyricon*. In the well-known scene describing Trimalchio's nouveau riche banquet, Auerbach maintains, the lives of ordinary citizens and their common, vulgar speech, are presented as comic, placed within a framework of the classical hierarchy of genres. These lives are treated neither with the seriousness nor with the awareness of revolutionary social forces that are registered for ordinary human existence in the Gospel of Mark. Although these two first-century narratives appear to be close in subject matter, Auerbach argues, they are distinctly different in style.

In one of his rare comments on the biblical writings, however, Bakhtin makes virtually the opposite claim: that the earliest Christian writings and the Greco-Roman novels have important features in common. Both groups represent a radical mixing of traditional generic precedents, a "carnivalization of genres within the realm of the serio-comical," as he puts it. A generic term for this parodic

77

conglomerate of literary forms is Menippean satire, named after Menippus of Gadara whose works are only known through the satiric dialogues of Lucian. Bakhtin stops short of claiming that the New Testament writings belong outright to the genre of Menippean satire, in which the *Satyricon* is usually placed. But he does insist that "ancient Christian narrative literature (including that which was canonized) is . . . permeated by elements of the menippea and carnivalization."[1]

The difference between Auerbach's perception of contrast between the texts of Petronius and Mark and Bakhtin's perception of their comparability proceeds from the different levels of literary form each critic is considering and the different determinants of form that each wishes to emphasize. Auerbach is concerned with style as mimesis, with word-choice and sentence structure as they represent or reproduce a realm of social and psychologial experience beyond language. Bakhtin, on the other hand, is concerned with genre as poesis, with higher-level structures of character, plot, and setting as they shape social and psychological perception within language. Where Auerbach is looking ahead to later European historical realism, Bakhtin is describing the earliest manifestations of the transformational forms that he calls "the novel" and "carnivalistic laughter," forms that find their supreme expression for him in the fiction of Dostoevsky and Rabelais but which also appear throughout literary history in comic genres of literature and in the oppositional culture of folklore.[2] In Bakhtin's historical and populist poetics, the aristocratic or elite genres of literature, systematically coordinated with each other, are continually being challenged—parodically mocked and promiscuously mingled—by common, unofficial genres, complexes of form and theme that, in their exuberant aggregation, confound the idea of a coherent literary system.

Bakhtin is not claiming that the New Testament is a comic novel, rather that it belongs to what he calls "the prehistory of novelistic discourse." There are a great many literary genres that he sees as articulating the fundamental "heteroglossia" that preoccupies him. These genres are produced in societies in which "polyglossia," an awareness of other languages that "frees consciousness from the tyranny of its own language and its own myth of language," predominates.[3] The society of the Roman Empire at the turn of the era was particularly rich in its mixture of languages and literatures, according to Bakhtin, languages and literatures that were conscious of one another's existence and aware of the interpenetration of official and unofficial discourses. An emblem of this sociolinguistic situation, not mentioned by Bakhtin but support-

ing his analysis, may be found in the Gospel of John, where Pilate
has a notice affixed to the cross reading "Jesus of Nazareth, the
King of the Jews" in Hebrew, Greek, and Latin. The Jewish priests
object, wanting the notice to read "This man said, I am King of
the Jews," but Pilate allows his ambiguous "title," ironically meaning more than he knows, from John's point of view, to stand as
written (John 19:19–22).

Much New Testament scholarship in this century has focused
on the relationship between the early Christian writings and the
Hebrew Bible or Old Testament. In this chapter, I shall argue like-
wise, that the deepest and most nuanced dialogues in the New Testament writings take place between the new Christian writings and
the older Jewish Scriptures, especially as these Scriptures were
already being interpreted and extrapolated by contemporary Jewish groups and schools of interpretation. But there is a movement
among recent interpreters of the Gospels, the Book of Acts, and
the Epistles to acknowledge more fully the way these writings also
situate their message "within the Greco-Roman order through the
use of Greco-Roman forms."[4] Vernon Robbins has demonstrated
the ample use the Gospel of Mark makes of rhetorical formulas
and narrative structures typical of the Hellenistic biographical
genre known as the memorabilia. Other critics have shown the
numerous resemblances between the Gospel of Luke and the Book
of Acts and various examples of the ancient novel. And the debt
of Paul's letters to the epistles, legal treatises, and philosophical
writings of Greek and Latin authors is increasingly acknowledged
as more than a matter of superficial form.[5] By the time the New
Testament writings began to appear, in the imperial lingua franca
of *koinē* Greek, the Jewish sect of "the Way" had incorporated a
number of the discourses of Greco-Roman culture into its own
repertoire of utterance.

Bakhtin's perception of the affinity of the early Christian writings with Menippean satire focuses on one common denominator
between the two literatures: the way they bring together spheres
of experience previously considered separate and distinct. Two
thousand years of Christian religious tradition often obscure a
modern reader's perceptions of the way "the gospel of Jesus Christ,
the Son of God" (Mark 1:1) confuses and confounds many of the
cultural categories within which it is proclaimed in the Bible. The
cultural fate of this religious proclamation, blasphemous in its
Jewish context, ludicrous in the Greco-Roman setting, and heterogeneous within its own canonical boundaries, resembles the literary fate that Borges attributes to Cervantes's novel *Don Quixote*,

in which the original opposition between the hero's literary dreams
and the historical reality around him is eventually "smoothed
away" by the passage of time: the dusty plains of La Mancha
become, to twentieth-century readers, as idealized as the romance
landscape of *Amadis of Gaul*.[6] The paradox of a once-upsetting
innovation being stabilized as tradition is more forcefully evoked
by Kafka in his parable of the leopards in the temple: "Leopards
break into the temple and drink to the dregs what is in the sacrificial pitchers; this is repeated over and over again; finally it can
be calculated in advance, and it becomes a part of the ceremony."[7]
Both of these literary paradoxes pale in comparison with the paradox of the novelty-become-norm of the New Testament, the "stum-
bling block to Jews and folly to Gentiles," as Paul describes the
good news of Christ crucified in 1 Corinthians (1:23), becoming,
in the words of the Letter to the Ephesians, "a plan for the fulness
of time, to unite all things" (1:10).

In the terms of Bakhtin's own master polarity, the conflict
between a unifying drive toward central authority and a dispersive
drive toward marginalized diversity, one could say of the New
Testament writings that they offer a peculiar combination of both
extremes, of "authoritative discourse" and "internally persuasive
discourse," as Bakhtin elsewhere calls these opposing forces in
human communication.[8] The New Testament presents us with
extremes of exaltation and degradation, of exclusivity and inclusiveness, of spiritual transcendence and physical embodiment, of
isolated individuality and closely knit community, of appeals to
ancient authority and appeals to contemporary experience, to name
only a few of the opposing categories that it seeks to show con-
verging in and around the person of Jesus of Nazareth, the Christ
of God. In the twenty-seven books of the New Testament canon,
the formulations of this convergence of opposite extremes are various and they are not easily correlated with one another. It is only
in the summarizing creeds and the systematizing theologies that
grow up around the New Testament writings (which, of course,
their authors believe they are reading out of the canon itself), that
these startling transgressions of conceptual boundaries begin to be
harmonized and stabilized within the new tradition of the Christian church. Within the New Testament itself, however, the surprise of the new form of dialogue between God and his people
known as "the gospel" continues to be strongly registered, from
the earthly "amazement" of Jesus's auditors in the Gospel of Mark
to the "great wonders" in the heavens described in the Book of

Revelation. And yet even within the New Testament, these surprising conversions are said to have been "prepared . . . from the foundation of the world" (Matt. 25:34). One of the most surprising things about the new creation, we are told, is that it has already been accomplished in the old one.

This confounding of categories that had hitherto been fundamentally opposed to one another does not only take place in terms of the abstract, general concepts cited above. It occurs in the concrete specifics of daily life recorded in the New Testament as well: for example, in the ordinary event of communal eating or table fellowship as represented in the Gospel of Mark. From the second chapter, where the Pharisees criticize Jesus for eating with "sinners and tax collectors," to the fourteenth chapter, where Jesus eats the Passover meal with his disciples and institutes the new memorial of the Lord's Supper among his followers, Mark repeatedly shows Jesus eating and drinking in transgressive ways. In chapters 6–8, there are six episodes concerned with extraordinary eating that follow one another in close succession. Herod gives a lavish but ultimately brutal banquet, in which the head of John the Baptist ends up on a platter; Jesus compassionately and miraculously feeds five thousand followers; the Pharisees rebuke Jesus' disciples for eating with unclean hands and Jesus replies in a parable that assails the ceremonial nicety of the Pharisees with prophetic denunciation and scatological double entendre ("the things which come out of a man are what defile him"); the Syrophoenician woman engages in parabolic repartee with Jesus about feeding the bread of the children to the dogs, winning from him a healing for her daughter in spite of their not being Jews; Jesus then feeds the four thousand, reenacting the earlier miracle on a slightly smaller scale; and Jesus warns his disciples about the "leaven of the Pharisees and the leaven of Herod," which the disciples mistake for a literal commentary on their lack of bread. The juxtaposition of these episodes, one on the heels of another, provides a continuous overturning, literal and figurative, of the rules of table fellowship in Jewish tradition and the general expectations about hospitality in ancient Near Eastern and Mediterranean culture.

If one considers these chapters in Mark alongside the extended *cena Trimalchionis* chapter in the *Satyricon*, the generic observation of Bakhtin seems more telling than the stylistic analysis of Auerbach. To be sure, the prophetic and charismatic critique of Jewish rituals of table fellowship enunciated and acted out by Jesus in Mark is very different in tone from the comic parody of Roman traditions of hospitality Trimalchio unwittingly provides in his riotous and obscenely excessive feast for freedmen. But an ethos of transgression, of an unholy mixture of classes of people and forms of speech as well as types of food, is common to both these narratives. The sense of the grotesque is heightened in the representation of meals in some of the other New Testament writings—in the sheet full of clean and unclean animals Peter sees in a vision that prepares him for table fellowship with the Gentile Cornelius, when he is told to "kill and eat" indiscriminately (Acts 10:13), or in the discourse on bread Jesus gives in the Gospel of John, when he drives away many would-be followers with the challenge "unless you eat the flesh of the Son of man and drink his blood, you have no life in you" (John 6:53).[9]

Rather than a generic identity of New Testament and Greco-Roman narratives, what I would suggest, refining Bakhtin's formulation, is a proportional analogy between them. The innovative mixing and promiscuous confounding of genres and classes that one finds in the ancient novels, romances, and Menippean satires of the period—from Petronius's *Satyricon* in the middle of the first century c.e. to Apuleius's *Golden Ass* late in the second century— are to the traditional, classical system of separated genres, Greek and Roman, as the New Testament writings are to the canonical order of the Hebrew Bible, with its generic paradigms of law, prophecy, and wisdom. The New Testament does adapt and transform particular formal precedents from contemporary Greek and Roman literature, from historical and biographical narratives and oratorical genres as well as from novels romantic and satiric. And Greek novels do appear with Christian and Jewish subjects (*The Pseudo-Clementine Recognitions, The Acts of Thomas,* and *Joseph and Asenath,* for example). But the two types of literature figure more significantly as parallel transformations of their different traditions, Jewish and Hellenistic, than, as some of Bakhtin's remarks about the period suggest, as a single stream of developing heteroglossia. These new species of writing arise in opposition to the conservative canonization of older traditions, the Judaism of the Pharisees and the rabbis on the one hand and the neoclassicism of official literary culture in imperial Rome on the other. Indeed, the innovations these new types of literature put forward depend on the traditionalism they oppose for their very definition *as* new.[10]

The dialogic relations inscribed in the New Testament writings engage not only the canonical Jewish Scriptures and various forms of Greco-Roman literature, however. They also engage the type of Jewish sectarian writing known as apocalyptic, a radical religious literature both conservative and innovative in its attempt to extend the dialogue of God and his chosen people beyond the canonical boundaries of the Prophets in the Hebrew Bible. Ernst Käsemann's designation of apocalyptic as "the mother of all Christian theology" is only an extreme form of a claim widely accepted among New Testament scholars in one degree or another.[11] Some of the historically earliest New Testament writings, 1 and 2 Thessalonians and the Gospel of Mark, are distinctly apocalyptic in character, but some of the latest—Revelation, Jude, and 2 Peter —are even more overtly shaped by the forms and themes of this sectarian literary genre. As we noted in the last chapter, apocalyptic literature is effectively an extracanonical genre of Jewish (and later of Christian) religious literature; in the Hebrew Bible, at least, it is assimilated into the canonical genres of prophecy and wisdom rather than acknowledged as a genre in its own right. There are chapters of Isaiah and Ezekiel among the major prophets, and whole books like Zechariah and Joel among the minor ones, that interpolate the visionary theatrics—last battles and cosmic conflagrations—of apocalyptic writing into the more chastened and chastening eschatology of classical Hebrew prophecy. And the visionary dreams of Daniel himself in chapters 7–12 are appended to the stories of Daniel as a pious wiseman and interpreter of the dreams and visions of others in chapters 1–6. Within the Hebrew Bible, this distinctive literary tradition never achieves the full and independent articulation it receives outside the canon.

Biblical scholars, not surprisingly, do not agree on the historical provenance of apocalyptic literature. There are those like Paul Hanson who would tie it closely to classical or canonical Israelite prophecy and to certain groups within the Temple priesthood. Others, like von Rad, have linked it with Israelite wisdom literature in its emphasis on the cosmos as a whole and on providential patterns of history. But critics concerned with formal description and analysis of this literature such as John Collins argue that these writings draw from Babylonian, Persian, and Hellenistic literature as well as Israelite traditions and that they constitute a distinctive "genre complex" of their own, independent of the genres of Jewish Scripture.[12] In this formal, generic perspective, apocalyptic has been defined as follows: "a genre of revelatory literature with a narrative framework, in which a revelation is mediated by an otherworldly being to a human recipient, disclosing a transcendent reality which is both temporal, insofar as it envisages eschatological salvation, and spatial insofar as it involves another, supernatural world."[13]

Complicating this analysis is the lack of clear consensus among biblical scholars on when and how the canon of the Hebrew Bible itself was actually closed, as we have already noted in the last chapter. There are those who believe that all three divisions were essentially closed and complete by the second century B.C.E., those who believe that the exact contents of the Writings were only settled at the end of the first century C.E., and a minority who hold that the divisions of the Prophets and the Writings were neither closed nor clearly distinguished from one another within any form of Judaism until well beyond the fourth century.[14]

Nevertheless, if one distinguishes between the theological concept of a canon of revelatory texts and the literary concept of a poetics or system of communicative genres, the historical uncertainty over when and why the Hebrew Bible became fully and definitively canonical need not derail an interpretation of the dialogics of the New Testament writings, their diplomatic relations with types of literature already in existence as they formulate their own distinctive utterance. Some argue, in fact, that it was the proliferation of such alternative or supplementary "scriptures," of Christian writings as well as Jewish apocalypses, that prompted the rabbinical authorities to close the canon of the Hebrew Bible once and for all, whenever this event occurred. A theological canon may contain an implicit poetics, as I have shown in Chapter 2. A literary poetics may also contain an implicit theology or definition of ultimate concerns, as the debate between Plato and Aristotle over the ultimate source and ontological status of poetry reveals. Whether the literary environment within which New Testament writings arose is seen as theologically fixed, as historically fluid, or (more likely) as a mixture of fixed and fluid collections across a number of religious communities, Jewish and Greco-Roman, it is clear that the Christian communication of the "gospel" makes liberal use of the discourse of apocalyptic literature as it re-articulates the discourses of the Law, the Prophets, and the "other books" of the Jewish Scriptures. It is also clear that this extracanonical discourse of apocalyptic was a much more authoritative language for the New Testament writers and their intended audiences than the persuasive and reasonable languages of Greco-Roman literature on which they also drew.

II

The dialogics of the New Testament writings here envisioned is thus more complex than the poetics of the Hebrew Bible described in Chapter 2. The greater complication proceeds in part from the greater amount of written material that has been preserved from the centuries and the communities immediately surrounding the public ministry of Jesus of Nazareth and the spread of that ministry by his followers. We simply know much more about the immediate literary context of the New Testament than we do about the immediate literary context of the Hebrew Bible. But it also has to do with the prior existence of the Hebrew Bible as a (relatively) fixed collection of authoritative texts, sacred writings in relation to which any sect of Judaism was obliged to define itself. At the risk of oversimplifying a complex and still quite incomplete historical record, but in the interests of "hearing the New Testament with biblical ears," the following map of the literary terrain may be offered.

Some sects within the larger community of Judaism explicitly refused to accept the authority of every division of the Hebrew canon. The Samaritans, for example, accepted the Law or Pentateuch as authoritative, but not the Prophets or the Writings. This split occurred, scholars now believe, in the second century B.C.E. rather than earlier. (It was once thought that the party of the Sadducees also only acknowledged the Law as fully authoritative in their controversy with parties like the Pharisees, but this is no longer believed to be the case.) At the other extreme were Hellenistic groups like the Jews of Alexandria, for whom the division of the Writings seems to have included some of the so-called deutero-canonical books like Ecclesiaticus and the Wisdom of Solomon. These groups were not averse, in their apologetics for Jewish culture, to drawing analogies between the Hebrew Bible and Greek philosophy and poetry. Somewhere in between these extremes of canonical restriction and canonical expansion were the writers and readers of apocalyptic literature, who seem to have made a distinction between the public canon of twenty-four books, and another, esoteric set of scriptures that were only to be used by the elite. In the apocalyptic book 2 Esdras, after a special divine dictation has been given to restore the books of the canon that have been destroyed, Ezra is instructed to "make public the twenty-four books that you wrote first and let the worthy and the unworthy read them; but keep the seventy that were written last, in order to give them to the wise among your people." The belief that these seventy secret books are of no less authority than the public ones, at least among the elite, is indicated by God's concluding explanation: "For in them is the spring of understanding, the fountain of wisdom, and the river of knowledge" (2 Esdras 14:45–47).

More important than the actual books that were subtracted from, added to, or appended to the canonical list, however, were the interpretive frameworks that the different Jewish groups used to read the canonical Scriptures. Again, at the risk of oversimplification, one might say that each of these frameworks for reading the Scriptures is primarily concerned with one of the three canonical divisions. The "oral Torah" of what became rabbinic Judaism is focused overwhelmingly on the Law. In this interpretive program, the Prophets and the Writings are considered "tradition," a form of commentary that expounds the "revelation" given in the Five Books; these latter two divisions are not seen as giving additional revelation of their own. In practice, if not in theory, the Prophets and the Writings are treated as the equivalent of "oral Torah," the traditional explanation and application of the Pentateuch supposedly given to Moses on Mount Sinai along with the revelation in the written text.

The interpretive tradition preserved in the Dead Sea Scrolls of Qumran, in contrast, reads the whole canon (with the apparent exception of Esther) in the light of prophetic eschatology. Key texts in the Law and the Writings (especially the Psalms) as well as in the Prophets themselves are interpreted in the light of the rules and expectations of this separatist community. The scriptures are searched for predictions of the present organization and future triumph of this sect, usually considered a branch of the Essene party, a triumph its members believed to be imminent. The interpretive approach of Alexandrian Judaism, on the other hand, especially as expressed in the extensive writings of Philo in the first century C.E., is philosophical and syncretistic in its treatment of the Jewish Scriptures. It treats the Law and the Prophets under the rubric of wisdom, the guiding genre of the Writings. It assimilates the Hebrew Bible through allegorical interpretation to Greek philosophy. Where rabbinic Judaism claims that Torah is the beginning and end of all wisdom, Hellenistic groups see a more comprehensive tradition of wisdom being distinctively but by no means uniquely expressed in Torah.

Most of the authors of the New Testament writings—and Jesus himself in the teaching that lies behind them—were much closer to the Pharisaic precursors of rabbinic Judaism than they were to any other Jewish party or sect. Although New Testament scholars are no longer so confident as they once were of being able to describe the historical Jesus, recent studies suggest that he was in substantial agreement with many of the basic doctrines of the Pharisees, even though he denounced their expanded ceremonial regulations and attacked the unholy attitudes concealed by their religious practice. The Gospel of Matthew reflects a rather positive view of the ethical ideals of the Pharisees, and Paul identifies himself explicitly as a former Pharisee "as to the law" (Phil. 3:5; compare Acts 23:6).

Where Jesus and the Christian community that grew up around him departed radically from all the other sects of Judaism was in their displacement of religious authority away from the Jewish Scriptures and onto a specific historical figure. As Donald Juel puts it, "Christianity began not as a scholarly proposal about the meaning of the Scriptures but as a response to events focusing on a particular person, Jesus of Nazareth."[15] This view is reflected not only by the writers of the Gospels, but also by Paul, who, in the words of Hans von Campenhausen,

> reads the [Jewish] Scripture from the standpoint of Christ, and therefore in a new spirit. This is not simply to say that the biblical statements are now interpreted, with appropriate pains and skill, as referring to Christ and to Paul's own community; Qumran had already done as much. Rather does it mean that now the historical experience of Christians and the new life which flows from this are consciously understood and affirmed as a new and unique starting-point, an independent way-in to the ancient Scriptures.[16]

What this means for a dialogics of the New Testament is that the New Testament presents, in its own right, a new model of communication between God and his people. The paradigms of law, prophecy, and wisdom in the Hebrew Bible are not simply interpreted and extended, as they were in other sects of Judaism. They are supplanted by a new paradigmatic genre, the paradigm of gospel. The term *gospel* was applied to the totality of the Christian message well before and well after it was applied, in a more specific generic sense, to biographical narratives about Jesus. The paradigm of gospel as I shall describe it here presents a form of dialogue in which God speaks anew to "his people," initially to the ethnic Israel he had called into being in the Hebrew Bible but then beyond Israel to the larger humanity of the Gentiles. And in this new form of dialogue God speaks almost exclusively through the unique figure of "a Son" (Heb. 1:1), the historical Jesus of Nazareth, who represents God to this people and this people to God in a type of communication that the Hebrew Bible by itself had simply not prepared its readers to imagine taking place. Jesus agrees with the Pharisees that there will be a resurrection of the dead, but his own resurrection within three days of his death on the cross is something far beyond what was envisioned in their doctrine, as Martha's remark about the "resurrection at the last day" immediately before Jesus raises Lazarus from the dead in the Gospel of John makes clear (11:24).

As the New Testament records his ministry, Jesus often teaches in the formal idiom of wisdom, using parables and proverbial sayings and appealing to common human experience. Nevertheless, he claims a much more intimate and immediate knowledge of God's purposes than any wisdom figure before him in the Hebrew Bible or in Jewish tradition. He also defends the integrity of biblical law and (especially in the Gospel of Matthew) reenacts the experiences of Moses and Israel in the Wilderness in his own activities. But his personal authority in the New Testament far exceeds that of Moses and the Torah, as the Gospel of John and Paul's Letter to the Romans insist. Finally, although Jesus speaks above all as a prophet and is identified first and foremost as the Messiah or Christ, his suffering is more degrading than the pathos of any of the prophets of Israel and his dominion is more transcendent than the power of any form of Messiah they describe in their prophecies. While it is true, as Amos Wilder says, that in Jesus "the discourse of prophet, lawgiver and wise man meet," it is also true, as James Barr puts it, that "the Christian message . . . burst the moulds within which [the Hebraic] heritage had found expression."[17]

The paradigm of communication between God and his people presented in the form of gospel can be characterized at greater length. There is no single title in Jewish or Greco-Roman tradition that is adequate to describe the role that Jesus plays in the text of the New Testament. The one title that has seemed to come closest, the Hebrew 'Messiah' (or its Greek form 'Christ', which as Juel notes is used as "a virtual second name" for Jesus)[18] did not require any suffering, death, or resurrection from the dead in the Jewish Scriptures or Jewish traditions of interpretation, according to recent historical studies. The criminal execution Jesus suffered was not part of the royal authority the Messiah was supposed to exercise on behalf of Israel. "Christian interpretation of the Scriptures arose from the recognition that Jesus was the expected Messiah *and* that he did not fit the picture," Juel argues. Passages from the Hebrew Bible like those from Psalm 22, Psalm 69, or Isaiah 53 that picture a servant or agent of God suffering an unjust punishment were texts that Christians adopted as messianic texts after the fact; they were appealed to by his followers and by Jesus himself in order to account for aspects of Jesus and his career that exceeded the received Jewish image of the Messiah. It is a similar case with less distinctive titles like "Lord," "son of God," "son of man," "savior," and "servant of the Lord." Their application to Jesus in the New Testament expanded and reshaped these terms in Christian understanding as much as they explained his ministry and person according to Jewish preconceptions.

It is not only biblical titles that the life and death of Jesus redefine, but biblical personalities as well. Various figures from the Hebrew Bible are invoked as models of Jesus' ministry. He is a new Moses in the Sermon on the Mount in Matthew (or in the Deuteronomic "sermon on the plain" in Luke), a new Elijah in his raising from the dead of a widow's son and in his miraculous feedings of his followers, a new David in his triumphal entry into Jerusalem. F. F. Bruce argues that particular verbal allusions in the New Testament are intended to evoke the larger contexts of character and action in the Jewish Scriptures.[19] But the Synoptic Gospels also make it clear that these precedents are superseded by this new mediator of God's "word." The scene of transfiguration on the mountain in Matthew 17, Mark 9, and Luke 9 presents a radiant Jesus in the company of a visionary Moses and Elijah, but when the voice from heaven repeats the same testimony (a combination of Ps. 2:7 and Isa. 42:1) that it gave to Jesus after his baptism, it adds the injunction "listen to him," and the figures of Moses and Elijah disappear. Jesus himself signals his supersession of a merely Davidic kingship when he poses his question to the Pharisees about Psalm 110: "If David thus calls him Lord, how is he his son?" (Matt. 22:45). Other New Testament writings—the Gospel of John, Pauline letters like Philippians, Ephesians, and Colossians, and Revelation in particular—identify Jesus with the God of the Hebrew Bible, not merely with the leaders of God's people, though in this case it is a matter not of supersession but of condescension, of Jesus descending from God and ascending back to him. "Though he was in the form of God, [he] did not count equality with God a thing to be grasped, but emptied himself, taking the form of a servant, being born in the likeness of men. . . . Therefore God has highly exalted him" (Phil. 2:6–7, 10). It is true that the specific concepts of Jesus as the "incarnation" of the Godhead and the "second person of the Trinity" appear only in later creeds and theologies and not in the New Testament itself.[20] But Jesus' participation in initiatives that belong to God alone in the Hebrew Bible and the different Jewish interpretative traditions, from the creation of the cosmos to the last judgment of humanity, is amply indicated in a number of places in the New Testament.[21]

Here it may seem that our literary analysis has shifted its ground to theology and has left historical considerations behind. But the kind of literary interpretation that we have been pursuing is one that would deny, or at least postpone, the necessity of limiting the meaning of the text either to historical realities lying behind it (in the mentality of an author or the social setting of an audience) or to theological truths presiding above it (in the nature of God and his relationship to human beings). Paraphrasing Sidney, who was paraphrasing Aristotle, we might say that literary criticism of the Bible is more theological than historical analysis and more historical than theological reflection. In a Bakhtinian conception of the text, moreover, literary criticism is concerned with the formal expression of a variety of voices, voices among and within which unitary and dispersive tendencies struggle for dominance. The text of the New Testament is no less various and composite in its canonical form than the text of the Hebrew Bible. It refers to and proceeds from a much shorter segment of religious history, a number of decades rather than a number of centuries. But the different styles and literary genres that it assimilates in its single canonical paradigm of gospel are no less heterogeneous than those assembled in the paradigms of law, prophecy, and wisdom in the Hebrew Bible before it.

It is not only the different representations of the central person of Jesus, as a human but also a divine being, that burst the molds of the Jewish Scriptures. It is also the different representations of the people of God. The people of God in the Hebrew Bible are a single group of common ancestry, a people initiated into religious community by birth and confirmed as members by later observances, beginning with circumcision. This is true even in the paradigm of wisdom, although the ethnic distinction of this people in wisdom is less explicit. The gospel, on the other hand, describes a heterogeneous group, made up of specially chosen (and specially responsive) individuals from ethnic Israel along with an expanding ethnic diversity of other people with whom God has hitherto had no distinctive verbal communication. Twelve individual disciples represent figuratively the twelve tribes of Israel in the Synoptic Gospels, and seven churches in Asia Minor represent a symbolically sacred number of local congregations in the opening chapters of Revelation. But in the various other groupings of Jesus' followers in the Gospels, larger and smaller than the twelve, and in the miscellaneous collection of churches and individuals that Paul addresses in his letters, the eclectic, open-ended nature of the new people of God is obvious.

In this newly reconstituted holy people, confidence in the importance of one's natural birth is an obstacle to accepting the new birth that is required, and in the apocalyptic perspective that opens up continually throughout the generic paradigm of gospel, natural death (the first death of Revelation 20) does not cut individuals off from the community of the faithful. From the parable of the sheep and the goats at the end of the Gospel of Matthew to the lake of fire and the heavenly city at the end of Revelation, previews of heaven and hell distinguish the people of God above and beyond history from the people who belong, finally, to God's angelic enemies. Two of Paul's letters, 1 Thessalonians and 1 Corinthians, make special reference to the fate of individual believers beyond the grave. There are ideas and images of personal afterlife in some places in the Hebrew Bible (though only Daniel 12:2 seems unequivocal about the heavenly reward of faithful individuals per se) and the Sadducees seem to have been the only Jewish sect to deny that there would be some kind of resurrection of the dead. But the pervasive correlation between the earthly and heavenly assemblies of God's people is unique to the New Testament in the canonical Scriptures.

There is finally in the paradigmatic gospel an intimate identification of the people of God with the person of Jesus, the Christ. The individual followers singled out for particular mention in the Gospels are identified collectively as "the disciples" and "the twelve" in the Synoptics and are drawn into more intimate communion by "the Spirit" in John, a communion expressed by a number of different figures of speech (cup of water and spring of water, sheep and shepherd, vine and branches) and in a more abstract language of incorporation and oneness (for example, "I in them and

thou in me, that they may become perfectly one" [John 17:23]).
This communion between Jesus and his followers through the
agency of the "Holy Spirit" is effected more literally on the Day
of Pentecost in Acts, chapter 2, where the disciples become active
ministers and founders of new congregations after they are "filled"
with this Spirit. And it is given greater metaphorical detail in the
image of the church as the "body of Christ" composed of different
"members" in chapter 12 of 1 Corinthians, where anatomical diversity is as important as organic unity. It is characteristic of the
way the church and the Lord are seen as models for one another
in the paradigm of gospel that the passage about Jesus being "in
the form of God" but emptying himself, cited above, is set in the
middle of Paul's exhortation to the Philippian church to "have this
mind among yourselves" and not to act competitively with one
another.

Once the distinctive character of the communicative paradigm
of gospel is recognized, however, its dialogic relationship in the
New Testament with the paradigms of the Hebrew Bible, rearranged within the Christian Bible as the Old Testament, must also
be acknowledged and may be described in greater detail. It is particularly important for a literary criticism of the New Testament
writings to distinguish the Hebrew Bible of Judaism, with its three
divisions and three generic paradigms, from the Old Testament of
Christianity, with its four categories of books—Pentateuch, Historical, Poetical, and Prophetic Books—and its single hermeneutic
construct of "salvation history." As I shall go on to show, the
canonical process of reordering the books in the Hebrew Bible and
of adding other Jewish books excluded by the rabbis was only completed for the Christian Old Testament centuries after the contents
of New Testament were canonically fixed. And the Christian perception of the Old Testament as a single "salvation history," a
series of mighty acts of God leading up to and prefiguring the coming of Christ, only became dominant in the later typologies developed by the Church Fathers in their efforts to harmonize the two
Testaments in a systematic fashion. The writers of the New Testament itself, however, think of the Hebrew Bible in its traditional
divisions of Law, Prophets, and Writings. They engage the Jewish
canon in literary dialogue by means of the generic frameworks of
law, prophecy, and wisdom, not simply by citing specific precedents—incidents, characters, or phrases—selected at random. Here
we must begin to distinguish among the different New Testament
documents instead of considering them together.

The first book of the canonical New Testament, the Gospel "according to Matthew," is the most comprehensive in its dialogic engagement with the Hebrew Bible, giving attention to the paradigms of law and wisdom as well as to prophecy, the genre closest to the scriptural imagination of the Christian sect. In Matthew 23:34 Jesus tells the Pharisees that he is sending them "prophets and wisemen and scribes," whom they will reject and persecute; the three roles correspond to the three paradigmatic genres of the Hebrew Bible and suggest that Matthew himself envisions a threefold Christian Scripture modeled on the Jewish one. (Luke mentions only "prophets and apostles" in his version of this saying [11:49].) The wisdom elements are particularly pronounced in Matthew's birth story, where the angelic annunciation occurs to Joseph in a dream, rather than to Mary awake as in the Gospel of Luke, and where the first witness to Christ comes from Gentile "wise men" alerted by a cosmic sign, the star in the East. Further dreams instruct the wise men not to return to Herod. Dreams also instruct Joseph to take the child to Egypt for protection, recalling the Joseph of Genesis, a sapiential figure within the Law, as well as the Israel of Exodus specified in the reference to Hosea 11:1, "Out of Egypt have I called my son."

Matthew gives particular emphasis to Jesus' role as a teacher, a characteristic wisdom role in the Hebrew Bible, and Jesus' teachings in Matthew refer to the natural world more copiously than in the other Gospels. The lessons drawn from the birds of the air, the lilies of the field, the weeds among other crops, the pearl of great price, and the good and bad fish are all unique to his narrative. Both Matthew and Luke show Jesus drawing on two wisdom psalms as he delivers the Beatitudes, Psalm 34 and Psalm 37, and both mention his reference to himself as "greater than Solomon," the biblical patron of wisdom (Matt. 12:42, Luke 11:31). But in the course of their Gospels Matthew refers to "wisdom" itself twice as often as Luke does.[22]

On the other hand, Matthew takes much more care to present Jesus in the context of biblical law than the other Gospel writers do. The notion of a five-part structure in Matthew modeled explicitly on the Five Books of Moses, proposed by B. W. Bacon, may not be widely accepted today, but it is generally recognized, as Brevard Childs observes, that "no problem is more central to Matthew's Gospel than his presentation of Christ's relation to the law."[23] It is in Matthew that the Beatitudes lead into a "Sermon on the Mount," a setting that recalls Moses on Mount Sinai, and it is Matthew who juxtaposes the oral recitation and outward observance of Torah ("You have heard that it was said, 'You shall not commit adultery'") with the new authority of Messianic speech and the internalization of righteousness ("But I say to you that everyone who looks at a woman lustfully has already committed adultery with her in his heart") (5:27–28). It is also in Matthew that the written text of the Law is most hyperbolically defended—"till heaven and earth pass away, not an iota, not a dot, will pass from the law until all is accomplished" (5:18). This idea of a sacred written word, a concept derived from the elevated status of Torah in Pharisaical Judaism, is reflected by Jesus when he resists the temptations of the devil in the wilderness with quotations from Deuteronomy prefaced by the phrase "It is written." It may also be reflected by Matthew himself when he notes that incidents in Jesus' early life take place to fulfill what was "written by the prophet" (for example, 2:5). Even when the formula is "spoken by the prophet," a specific textual quotation from Scripture is provided.

This is not to say that the Gospel of Matthew is less deeply informed by the discourse of prophecy than the rest of the New Testament writings, the discourse of the Hebrew Bible that is most extensively engaged by the proclamation of the gospel. But it is to note how idioms and incidents from the other forms of dialogue between God and people in the Hebrew Bible are more prominent in Matthew than in the other Gospels, how the idea of Jesus fulfilling the Law but also speaking the language of wisdom is most explicit and most affirming of the validity of these earlier discourses in its dialogic engagement with the Jewish Scriptures as a whole. It is only in Matthew that Jesus tells his disciples that "every *scribe* who has been trained for the kingdom of heaven is like a householder who brings out of his treasure what is new *and what is old*" (Matt. 13:52, emphasis added). Paul's Letter to the Galatians and Letter to the Romans engage the Law more explicitly, perhaps, but also in a much more critical, transumptive fashion; the ethical stipulations emphasized by rabbinic Judaism are in Paul's view replaced by the story of salvation.[24] And while in 1 Corinthians Paul devotes much attention to wisdom, he does so in a way that replaces the traditional idea of a general human capacity for understanding with a "secret and hidden wisdom of God" (1 Cor. 2:7).

The Gospel of Mark, in contrast, gives ample dialogic expression to the extrabiblical discourse of apocalyptic, and it uses the discourses of biblical law, biblical prophecy, and biblical wisdom much more sparingly than the other Gospels. The enigmatic character of Mark is both cause and symptom of the way it holds the idioms of the Hebrew Bible at an ironic distance in its presentation of "the gospel of Jesus Christ," most famously in Jesus' insistence that he not be identified as the Messiah when people—and demons—spontaneously testify that he is. Where Matthew uses the terms of the "old covenant" to articulate the "new" one in a largely positive manner, Mark dramatizes the way the old terms fall short of the new revelation. It is perhaps for this reason that Matthew was placed first in the canonical order of the Gospels (occurring in this position in all the early Gospel lists) and for this reason that the historical priority of Mark, upon whom Matthew and Luke seem to draw so extensively, went so long unnoticed. The Messianic secret makes more canonical sense as the second proclamation of the gospel than as the first one.

With Luke succeeding Mark in the canonical order of the New Testament, the older forms of dialogue in the Hebrew Bible are again extensively engaged. But they are engaged in a more generically literary fashion than in the Gospel of Matthew and with a greater emphasis on prophecy than on law or wisdom literature. Luke's story of the birth of Jesus is modeled on the story of the birth of Samuel, the first full-fledged prophet in the canonical division of the Prophets. It is not merely that Mary's Magnificat resembles closely Hannah's prayer of rejoicing after Samuel's birth. There are more complex reworkings of the plot of 1 Samuel 1–2. The barrenness of Elizabeth, the skeptical priesthood of Zechariah, the annunciation of John's birth in the Temple, the dedication of Jesus in the Temple after his birth all recall features of Samuel's birth and calling. The complications are due in large part to the doubling of the story in Luke, to his overlapping the account of the birth of Jesus with the account of the birth of John the Baptist. But this very narrative device (which occurs elsewhere in Luke's Gospel—in the doubled civil trial of Jesus before Pilate and Herod, for example) is one of the striking features of 1 Samuel itself, which is famous for its numerous (and less clearly coordinated) "doublets." For example, there are two prophetic messages telling Eli of the fall of his house in 1 Samuel 2–3, the first delivered by an anonymous "man of God," the second by Samuel himself.[25] Furthermore, like both 1 and 2 Samuel, Luke and Acts are concerned throughout with the problem of succession and continuity within the inspired leadership of God's people, most notably the succession and continuity in Acts of the ministries of Peter and Paul.

Where Matthew evokes prophecy mainly through the quotation of oracles from the so-called Latter or Writing Prophets, written texts that are "fulfilled" in specific detail in the life and ministry of Jesus, therefore, Luke re-creates the literary ambiance of the Former Prophets in which God is shown—and also assumed to be—working continuously in history. Luke borrows from conventions of Greco-Roman historiography in his Gospel and in Acts. But he also creates a stylistic replica of the historical narratives that figure so prominently in the generic paradigm of prophecy in the Hebrew Bible. In this linear, progressive model of God's dealings with his people, specific typological resemblances between individual persons and particular acts are not emphasized. What is stressed is a more generic concept of precedent. Thus Luke reports that after his resurrection, "beginning with Moses and all the prophets," Jesus "interpreted to them in all the scriptures the things concerning himself" (Luke 24:27), a Scripture lesson that is tantalizing in its lack of specificity. Luke himself directs attention to more general patterns of interaction between divine initiative and human response. The story he tells is not limited to the personal ministry of Jesus described in his Gospel but continues with the growth of the early Christian community in Acts. If the Gospel of Luke re-creates the narrative mode of 1 and 2 Samuel, with its focus on a few charismatic individuals, the Book of Acts recalls 1 and 2 Kings in the way it pursues the development of larger and more widely scattered groups of the faithful.

The Gospel of John treats the Hebrew Bible in a manner notably different from any of the Synoptic Gospels. The law is no longer seen as a viable model for gospel, as it was in Matthew. "The law was given through Moses" but "grace and truth came through Jesus Christ" (John 1:17). A new dispensation replaces the old. A positive typology of events like the feeding of the five thousand fulfilling the giving of the manna to Israel in the Wilderness, a typology strongly indicated in Mark, becomes here a point of controversy between Jesus and "the Jews." These Johannine opponents resist Jesus' miracle with the claim that Moses gave them bread from heaven; Jesus counters that *he* is the bread of life come down from heaven. This is one of many occasions in John when Jesus delivers the Jewish reading of the Scriptures from the bondage of literalism into the liberty of figurative speech. Physical places and events, like the well of Jacob where Jesus meets the Samaritan woman in chapter 4, become metaphorical vehicles for the communication of spiritual realities, as in the "spring of water well-ing up to eternal life" that Jesus offers the woman on that occasion (4:14).

John's metaphorical transformation of the Hebrew Bible also eschews the discourse of prophecy that is so prominent, in different forms, in Matthew, Mark, and Luke. There are very few Old Testament "testimonies" to Jesus given in the Fourth Gospel, and in the first chapter of this gospel, John the Baptist denies that he is Elijah, an identification that Jesus makes for John the Baptist in Mark 9 and Matthew 17 and one that he claims for his own ministry beyond Israel in Luke 4. Nevertheless, John does engage the Hebrew Bible in a pervasive fashion through the discourse of wisdom. The type of wisdom John invokes is not the practical, ethical wisdom invoked by Matthew, a classic Old Testament form of wisdom that is also picked up in the Letter of James, but the speculative or "theological" wisdom contained in certain passages of Proverbs and Job and developed at greater length in Hellenistic wisdom books outside the Hebrew Bible canon like the Wisdom of Solomon. This "sapientializing process" in John, as it has been called by Childs, is most evident in the prologue to the Gospel, which puts the birth of Jesus in a cosmic perspective that evokes the poetic speech delivered by a female Wisdom in Proverbs 8.[26] But it is also evident in the numerous discourses of Jesus, much more extended and much more philosophical in John than in the Synoptic Gospels. In these speeches, Jesus presents to a literal-minded audience a spiritual vision of the heavenly truth that has now come down to the earth. The riddling quality of the numerous doubly signifying phrases such as "born anew" (born from above) (3:3), "wind" (spirit) (3:8), "lifted up" (exalted) (3:14) and "living water" (running water) (4:10) begins in John's ambiguous designation of Jesus as *ho logos* and culminates in Jesus' own play on the name of God, "I am that I am," in his *ego eimi* sayings. Samuel Beckett's ironic paraphrase "In the beginning was the pun" captures an important element of John's wisdom christology, as it has been termed.[27]

The discourse of theological wisdom in John has its counterparts in Pauline letters like Ephesians and Colossians, which emphasize the preexistence of Christ and Christ's role in the predestination of believers and the creation of the universe. In these letters (which most scholars attribute to a Pauline school rather than to Paul himself), the paradoxical "secret and hidden wisdom of God" (1 Cor. 2:7) contained in the scandal of the crucifixion gives way to a more foundational "Christ, in whom are hid all the treasures of wisdom and knowledge" (Col. 2:2–3), a cosmic figure who holds the whole universe together. Speculative wisdom, in its most Hellenistic-Alexandrian form, finds further expression in the anonymous Letter to the Hebrews. Here we see the most explicit instance of essential elements of law—the office of the priesthood, for example—being reinterpreted according to a hermeneutic based on wisdom. The law provides mere "copies of the heavenly things" (9:23); it offers "but a shadow of the good things to come instead of the true form of these realities" (10:1). The true form, of course, is provided once and for all, in history but for eternity, by the sacrifice of Jesus Christ. Here the discourse of wisdom from the Hebrew Bible approaches the discourse of Platonic philosophy, as it already had in a Jewish context in the writings of Philo and as it was to do later in a Christian context with Origen and Augustine.[28] But to imply that this is the dominant discourse of the New Testament as a whole, as Gabriel Josipovici does in his essay on Hebrews in *The Literary Guide to the Bible*—to say, as he does, that in contrast to the "fruitful dialogue" within the Hebrew Bible the New Testament is "single-minded" in its abstract spirituality— is to listen too intently to a single inflection of one of several major languages of Scripture in which these writings speak.[29]

III

Thus the dialogue of the New Testament with the Hebrew Bible is carried on to a considerable extent in response to the generic paradigms that this older testament created to frame the dialogue between God and his people Israel over the many centuries of their joint venture of revealing his nature to a larger world. The new paradigm of gospel cannot be adequately understood in terms of law, prophecy, and wisdom alone. But it cannot be adequately understood apart from these biblical genres or discursive constructs either. There is obviously a great deal more that could be said about the different ways that these generic paradigms are inflected. And there are other types and levels of intertextuality between the testaments (Harold Bloom suggests calling them the "Original Testament" and the "Belated Testament"), than those that can be subsumed within these three generic categories and the interpretive traditions they generated.[30] But a dialogics of the New Testament according to Bakhtin must also consider the dialogue within, the way in which the New Testament canon itself is organized in different generic patterns of similarity and difference.

The internal echoes or dialogic answerings within the New Testament, like the repeating patterns within the Hebrew Bible, occur on many levels and in many different forms. They occur first of all within a single Gospel or letter, where one passage or pericope seems pointedly shaped or accented in response to others in close proximity to it. We have already noted the sequence of episodes involving communal meals or table fellowship in chapters 6–8 of the Gospel of Mark, where the changes are rung on the breaking of bread, literal and figurative. The fact that the simple though miraculous hospitality extended by Jesus in feeding the five thousand follows a grandiose banquet given by Herod in the course of which John the Baptist is executed is clearly not an accidental juxtaposition by Mark as author. The significance of the juxtaposition cannot be reduced to a single or simple formula, but the *Sitz im Lesen* is surely as important as the different historical situations from which the two events are taken. There is a similar sequence of meals recorded in Luke 14–16, involving different incidents with different implications. First we are told of Jesus going to eat at the house of a prominent Pharisee. Then Jesus offers several "parables" concerning meals, the first directed to the guests in the form of straightforward advice about not rushing to occupy the place of honor at a wedding feast, the second directed to the host, advising him to invite guests who cannot reciprocate so that he will be repaid "at the resurrection of the just," when a messianic banquet is expected to take place. A guest exclaims at the good fortune of the man "who will eat bread in the kingdom of God," whereupon Jesus tells a version of a parable proper, the parable of the great banquet. What is distinctive about Luke's association of these thematically similar passages is the way he locates them in a conversation that takes place in a single setting. The meal at which Jesus is present provides a realistic occasion for the several sayings about meals that he goes on to offer. The scene shifts at 14:25, when we are told of crowds accompanying Jesus, presumably on the road. But a realistic motivation for additional meal parables that follow—the Prodigal Son, the Unrighteous Steward, and the Rich Man and Lazarus—is provided by a comment of some Pharisees and scribes: "This man receives sinners and eats with them." Jesus tells these parables as answers to such criticism: mine is the kind of hospitality extended by God himself.

Such associational clustering of sayings and acts occur in all the Gospels. There is the gathering of parables concerning seeds and harvests in Matthew 13, following the inaugural parable of the sower, which is itself a parable *about* parables. But the dialogic interplay is often more complex than it appears at first sight. The parable of the sower stresses the different types of reception that the "word of the kingdom" receives, at least in the interpretation that Jesus provides the puzzled disciples. But the parable of the weeds that follows it emphasizes the need for the servants of the Son of Man to leave such distinctions to the discernment of angels at the apocalyptic harvest. The parable of the Mustard Seed comes at the topos of spiritual seeds from yet another angle; here the stress falls on the disproportion of the size of the seed to the size of the plant it produces. Given the oral nature of Jewish teaching at the time, as Birger Gerhardssen argues, it is quite possible that Jesus told the same parable in different ways on different occasions, even that he strung different parables together to suit the situation.[31] But in a literary criticism of the written text, one is obliged to notice how additional dimensions of meaning are generated by the way one saying appears to pick up and reemploy the metaphorical vehicle of another. There is a similar, slightly different dialogue among the seed stories in Mark 4, where the parable of the sower is followed by the parable of the growing seed, in which the ground is all the same and the sower has no idea how the seed sprouts and grows, then by the parable of the apparently insignificant mustard seed.

Dialogic relations, established by verbal and conceptual resemblances within a particular New Testament book, can also be found in the letters of Paul. Such apparently fortuitous linkages sometimes have profound thematic—hence theological—implications. There is, for example, in 1 Thessalonians an implicit comparison of the "coming" or return of Christ with Paul's own desired return to the church at Thessalonica. Paul does not use the same word (*parousia*) for his own coming that he does for Christ's in this passage. But the juxtaposition of his own eagerness to come back to Thessalonica (1 Thess. 2:17–18) with the mention of "our Lord Jesus at his coming" (1 Thess. 2:19), followed by his reference to Timothy coming to and from this church in Paul's service (3:1–10), establishes suggestive parallels between the messianic and the apostolic roles in a letter that is quite concerned throughout its five chapters with both kinds of second coming.[32]

A more substantial series of analogical parallels that speak across logical distinctions can be found in the various evocations of the "body" (*soma*) and the "flesh" (*sarx*) in Romans. In the first half of this most extended and treatiselike of Paul's letters, the emphasis falls on the radical separation of the physical dimensions of human existence from the spiritual: of behavioral "works" from attitudinal "faith," of the body that is subject to death in the world from the spirit that can live forever in Christ, of the "carnal" self, "sold under sin" (7:14), from "the Spirit of life in Christ Jesus" that sets the self "free from the law of sin and death" (8:2). In the second half of the letter, in chapters 9 through 16, the emphasis shifts to reintegration: the ultimate regrafting of Israel back into the people of God in which "all Israel will be saved" (11:26); the presentation of "your bodies as a living sacrifice, holy and acceptable to God, which is your spiritual worship" (12:1); and the integration of the many callings or offices in the church as "many members" of the "one body in Christ" (12:4,5). The positive images of corporeal and corporate existence in the second half of this treatise constitute a reprise, illogical but highly significiant, of the negative bodies in the first half. In effect, the "body of death" in the abstract theological formulations of the first eight chapters is resurrected—raised to new, concrete but figurative life—in the more specific, ethical instructions of the last eight chapters, a transformation of imagery often undervalued in discussions that focus on Paul's apparent asceticism or dualistic thinking in the first half of this letter alone.

In considering the internal dialogues of the New Testament writings, we have concentrated so far on relations within particular books, on recurring motifs within a narrative Gospel (or within a single-authored sequence like Luke–Acts) and within a particular Pauline letter. But there are also revoicings between passages in different books and by different writers. Some of these have been studied at great length in New Testament scholarship—the relations between similar episodes in the different Synoptic Gospels, for example, or between similar theological formulations and rhetorical formulas in the different letters of Paul. In most cases, these studies are given a genetic slant. Critics examine how Matthew and Luke elaborate upon a particular passage in Mark (or Q), sometimes with the additional consideration of noncanonical Gospels like Thomas. Or they look at the way Romans develops and revises a theme in Galatians. But in the generic approach we have been pursuing, under the aegis of Bakhtin, other kinds of dialogue appear as well, sometimes in less predictable contexts. The lines of compositional genealogy are not always clear in these cases—it is harder to prove that one episode is the textual progenitor of another—but the dialogic alterity is more significant within the larger semantic sphere of the canon. A brief discussion of two such instances of New Testament cross-talk will indicate what is at stake.

Mark and Matthew both report the incident in which Jesus pronounces a curse on a barren fig tree. The incident occurs immediately before or immediately after he drives the money-changers out of the temple—in Mark, the cleansing of the temple is characteristically sandwiched between Jesus' curse and the disciples' observation of the tree's withering—and it is a sign of the impending judgment against an Israel that will not accept God's Messiah. The incident as such, during the Passion Week, is omitted in Luke. Nevertheless, Luke reports Jesus telling a parable about a fig tree earlier in his Gospel that has some interesting family resemblances with the literal, prophetic enactment in Mark and Matthew.

> And he told this parable: "A man had a fig tree planted in his vineyard; and he came seeking fruit on it and found none. And he said to the vine-dresser, 'Lo, these three years I have come seeking fruit on this fig tree, and I find none. Cut it down; why should it use up the ground?' And he answered him, 'Let it alone, sir, this year also, till I dig about it and put on manure. And if it bears fruit next year, well and good; but if not, you can cut it down'" (13:6–9).

In a dialogic reading, this parable in Luke can be seen as a displacement and mitigation of the miracle or eschatological sign performed by Jesus at the end of his ministry in Mark and Matthew. Jesus gives the prophetic threat in Luke in speech rather than in deed; he delivers it in front of "the multitudes" (12:54) before he has come to Jerusalem rather than to the disciples in private after he arrives there. Furthermore, within the parable there is a voice that asks for mercy as well as one that demands judgment. That the fig tree is planted in the man's "vineyard" connects Luke's parable with the famous Song of the Vineyard in Isaiah 5, where another unproductive fruit-bearing plant is consigned to destruction. The Isaian passage is the basis for still another New Testament parable, the parable of the *tenants* of the vineyard told by Jesus in Jerusalem in all three Synoptic Gospels, in which the emphasis is again on the severity of judgment. (In Luke's version, Jesus says explicitly that "the owner of the vineyard . . . will come and destroy those tenants" who have rejected his servants and his heir [20:15–16].) But in the parable of the fig tree, given in Luke alone, the extra year and extra attention requested by the owner's servant (a "vine-dresser" rather than a fig-tree specialist) interpolate a space of salvation-history before the eschatological end, a time of redemptive ministry that will find its full expression, for Luke alone among the Gospel writers, in the Book of Acts. This time of redemptive ministry extends to Jews as well as Gentiles, it should be noted, just as the fig tree is given more time to produce fruit.

My second example of dialogic cross-talk involves a parable in Luke and a miracle in John. In Luke 16 Jesus tells the parable of Lazarus and an anonymous rich man; in John 11 Jesus raises Lazarus of Bethany, the brother of Mary and Martha, from the dead. In a historical analysis, one would hesitate to assume any connection between the two episodes. Lazarus was a common enough name, a Greek version of a Hebrew name meaning 'he whom God helps', and in the words of a recent reference work, "no relationship between the two individuals has been demonstrated."[33] But in a literary criticism, where the odd assumption of a historical reference to "*two* individuals" may be ignored, one may notice some peculiar similarities between the two stories, in spite of their obvious differences.

In Luke's parable, the story begins with a simple contrast between the misery of the poor and the complacency of the rich. Lazarus is a miserable beggar in this life but is comforted in the bosom of Abraham in the life to come. The rich man, denied a proper name, has it all in this life but is made to pay later. But the emphasis shifts from the afterlife moral to the question of instruction while people are still alive on earth. When the rich man learns that "a great chasm has been fixed" between those in the bosom of Abraham and those in Hades, he asks that Lazarus be sent back to warn his five brothers, still living, to mend their ways. Abraham tells him that his brothers already have "Moses and the prophets," the Hebrew Scriptures. The rich man replies that they nevertheless need more instruction, that "if some one goes to them from the dead, they will repent." But he is told that "if they do not hear Moses and the prophets, neither will they be convinced if some one should rise from the dead."

In John 11, of course, someone does rise from the dead, and within the context of the four canonical Gospels of the New Testament, this second Lazarus does seem to be speaking back to the first one. John's Lazarus does not testify to Moses and the Prophets, as Luke's Lazarus does, but to Jesus himself as a manifestation of "the glory of God" (11:40). The resurrection of Lazarus leads directly, in John's narrative, to the decision among the Jewish leaders to have Jesus put to death, when Caiaphas makes his ironically prophetic statement "it is expedient for you that one man should die for the people, and that the whole nation should not perish" (11:50). But it also prefigures, midway through John's narrative, the resurrection of Jesus (first witnessed by another Mary) that takes place at the end.

The probable genetic relationship between these two "resurrections" of a man named Lazarus is not easy to determine. Given the general view that the Gospel of John is later than that of Luke, one might assume that John's Lazarus is a christological and soteriological counterexample to the more generalized prophetic-ethical lesson offered by the Lazarus of Luke. In Luke, Lazarus points to the importance of providing for the needs of the poor, a lesson taught throughout the Hebrew Bible. In John, Lazarus points to salvation through faith in someone who is, uniquely, "the resurrection and the life" (11:25). Historical and theological readers may be uncomfortable with the implication that John invented his Lazarus for the occasion. But there is no need to deny Lazarus of Bethany a historical existence in this reading of his resurrection as an answer to the refusal of resurrection for Lazarus in Luke's parable. It is clear that John has subjected his historical materials to a theological transformation throughout, that he has shaped his account of virtually every natural event to make a distinctively supernatural point. It is also possible, given the almost certain existence of separate sources and traditions on which John draws for his later Gospel, that Luke was responding to an earlier version of the Johannine Lazarus of Bethany in his parabolic figure. In this hypothesis, it is striking that Luke's Lazarus is the only character in the parables of the Synoptic Gospels who is given a proper name. In this alternative analysis of the dialogue of scriptures, Luke would be bringing John's heavenly lesson down to earth, redirecting the vertical vision of the individual believer out to the wider, horizontal community of the faithful and the needy. In either account of the textual relationship, however, the isolated *Sitze im Leben* are connected by a common *Sitz im Lesen*. The reader is made aware of hearing the good news in different voices.

IV

In the view of many scholars, the canonization of the different Christian writings into a New Testament is a purely extrinsic matter, an imposition of a "catholic" orthodoxy after the fact on a much more extensive and heterogeneous collection of written documents and oral traditions. The Gnostic scriptures unearthed at Nag Hammadi in 1945 have strengthened modern interest in the New Testament apocrypha, the considerable array of early Christian writings that describe the ministry of Jesus and his disciples in ways sometimes quite similar and sometimes quite divergent from the representation of these ministries in the canonical writings. This concern with the "other Bible," as it has been called in a recent edition of these writings, is perfectly legitimate from a literary as well as a historical perspective, as is the more traditional concern with the New Testament writings prior to their canonized form and apart from their canonical context.[34] But in the literary criticism according to Bakhtin that we have been pursuing here, the literary dimensions of the canon itself are far from irrelevant. Like the Hebrew Bible before it, the New Testament was eventually arranged as a canon according to rudimentary notions of genre. Furthermore, there are "canon-conscious" utterances within the New Testament itself, passages that point to larger patterns of integration and coherence in the emerging collection of documents.

The latter phenomenon, which might also be thought of as meta-scriptural reflection on the formal character and coherence of the Christian writings, occurs in all parts of the New Testament canon, in texts or passages usually considered "late." The supplementary endings to the Gospel of Mark, beyond the statement "for they were afraid" at 16:8, which is now widely regarded as the original conclusion, serve to harmonize this stark, enigmatic Gospel with the other, more discursive ones.[35] The editorial opening of the Gospel of Luke alludes in a harmonizing manner to other versions of "the things which have been accomplished among us," explaining its own intention to produce "an orderly account" of these materials (1:1–3). One of the most important earlier versions that Luke assimilates to his broader historical account, of course, is the Gospel of Mark. The Gospel of John ends with a similar reference to "many other things which Jesus did," which if they were all written down, would make for more books than the world itself could contain (21:25). In this case, the author seems to be justifying his own selectivity, perhaps even his failure to mention numerous incidents recorded in the Synoptic Gospels.

There are canon-conscious gestures in the letters of the New Testament as well. The Pastoral Epistles reshape the historical Paul into a figure of canonical authority speaking to his apostolic successors in the church.[36] The Letter to the Hebrews, a letter strikingly different in style and method from Paul's, has a Pauline closing in its last three verses, a passage that reinforced its claim to apostolic standing in the early church. 2 Peter formulates a doctrine of scriptural inspiration, comments on the apostolic authority of 1 Peter, and notes the complexity of Paul's teaching in the canonical collection of "all his letters" (3:16). Even in the Book of Revelation, which often seems sublimely unconcerned with the rest of the New Testament writings, the letters to the seven churches in the first three chapters anchor the apocalyptic vision of this last book of the canon to the epistolary collection, Pauline and catholic, that precedes it.

What we see in this last example is not simply a belief about the unity or relatedness of the New Testament writings considered as a whole but an awareness of certain genres of Christian writing. Like the canonical paradigms of the Hebrew Bible that we considered in Chapter 2, these Christian genres seem to have been partly inherited and partly created in the process of canonization. The narrative "gospel" and the apostolic "book of acts" seem to be largely Christian creations, new types of narrative for dealing with the distinctive events of this new religous sect, although some scholars argue that even these types of writing can be seen as transformations of existing Greco-Roman genres. The apostolic letter and the apocalypse, on the other hand, are literary forms that Christianity took over with few formal changes. There are numerous examples of Greco-Roman epistles and Jewish apocalypses before the New Testament writings were produced. Like the Hebrew Bible before it, the New Testament only became a theological canon by organizing its contents, possible and actual, into a rudimentary poetics or system of literary genres.

This process of generic differentiation is less comprehensive and less profound in the New Testament than in the Hebrew Bible. As the previous discussion in this chapter has indicated, the three paradigms of communication between God and his people in the Hebrew Bible are succeeded by what is best seen as a single paradigm in the New Testament. The New Testament conceives of itself as presenting a single "gospel" in the words of different witnesses—the gospel according to Matthew, Mark, Luke, and John; the gospel as revealed to Paul, to Peter, or to James. But in the better-documented canon-formation of the New Testament, one can observe a growing perception among second-century Christians that the single paradigm by which God had recently spoken anew to his people in the person of Jesus, his Christ, could itself be broken down into different types of testimony as well as into the reports of different apostolic personalities.

Thus in the second century Justin Martyr begins to apply the term "gospel" to the biographical narratives of the ministry of Jesus, even though he considers the usage novel enough to supplement it with the more common term *apomnemoneumata* or "memorabilia." Vernon Robbins, who notes this double usage, suggests that it was the unwillingness of Marcion to recognize any other narrative gospels beyond the single, reduced version of the Gospel of Luke that he included in his preliminary canon of the New Testament that hastened the application of the term among orthodox Christians to a particular type of writing.[37] On the other hand, Marcion made a distinction between "gospel" (*euangelion*) and "apostle" (*apostolikon*), the latter a category describing the ten letters of Paul that Marcion recognized as authentic. Although the Church Fathers declared Marcion's highly restricted New Testament to be heretical, they did so by insisting that there were more gospels and more apostolic letters that belonged in each of these two classes of writings. Furthermore, they soon found themselves excluding other gospels and other letters beyond the ones that they considered canonical. The Muratorian canon list from the end of the second century inveighs against letters to the Laodiceans and to the Alexandrians, "forged in Paul's name for the hersey of Marcion." A few centuries later the Gelassian decree declares nine additional "gospels" to be apocryphal.[38]

The Christian canonizers added two more genres to the poetics of the New Testament when they included the Acts of the Apostles and the Revelation of John. The Muratorian Canon List observes that "the acts of all the apostles are written in one book," unlike the Gospels, which appear in four books.[39] It notes, however, the omission of Peter's crucifixion and Paul's journey to Spain from the Book of Acts, apostolic episodes apparently in wide circulation in the church. And already in the second century, apocryphal books of acts had begun to appear; the Acts of Peter and the Acts of Paul are mentioned by Tertullian at about the same time as the Muratorian Canon List was written. The canonical claims of additional apocalypses or books of revelations, beyond the Revelation of John, are weighed by the Muratorian Canon List itself. It mentions the Revelation of Peter as a disputed book, accepted by some but not by others, and the Shepherd of Hermas as an apocryphal one.

Thus by the end of the second century, the period at which the canonization of the New Testament is commonly held to have been completed, we can observe a basic poetics or genre system of the Christian gospel in its canonical form. There are memoirs of the words and deeds of Jesus himself in four Gospels; there are memoirs of the actions and speeches of the apostles in a single Book of Acts; there are written instructions of the apostles to particular churches, to individuals, and to Christians in general in letters of Paul and of four or five other apostles; and there is an apocalypse or book of prophecy in the Revelation of John. The major genres are presented in this roughly chronological order (the acts of the apostles presumably taking place before their letters and the apocalypse obviously looking ahead), even though the letters of Paul are now known to have been written before any of the other canonized documents and even though the Book of Acts is clearly a second part of the narrative begun in the Gospel of Luke.

This sequence of New Testament genres, in turn, seems to have influenced the ultimate canonical form assumed by the Christian Old Testament. As we have seen, most sects of Judaism during the first century, including early Christianity, knew a Hebrew Bible composed of the Law, the Prophets, and the Writings. Those more familiar with the Greek Septuagint version probably accepted as part of this Bible additional books beyond the twenty-four Hebrew books (sometimes counted as twenty-two by combining Ruth with Judges and Lamentations with Jeremiah), and there was most likely no consensus on the exact order of the books beyond the Five Books of the Law. There may not even have been a completely fixed canon, in the later Jewish and Christian sense of the word, until the very end of this century or later. Nevertheless, there was widespread agreement that the Hebrew Bible was composed of three parts.

By the beginning of the fourth century, however, the Christian Old Testament, now preserved in Greek and Latin translation, had lost or abandoned the tripartite scheme of the Jewish Scriptures. It is difficult to tell exactly when the Christian ordering of the Old Testament became definitive. Canon lists were more concerned with fixing the books of the New Testament than the books of the Old, and until the advent of printing, one-volume or single-codex Bibles were much less common than smaller codices of a few books copied and bound together. Nevertheless, a consensus was eventually reached in the Western Church distributing the books of the Old Testament into four different sections: the Pentateuch, the historical books, the poetical books, and the prophetic books. The books of the Law remained the same in order and number in the Pentateuch. The last two divisions of the Hebrew Bible, the Prophets and the Writings, were considerably rearranged and supplemented. The Old Testament established three new generic categories by separating the narrative books of the "Former Prophets" (Joshua through Kings) from the oracle collections of the "Latter Prophets" (Isaiah through the Twelve), by placing five books from the Writings (Job, Psalms, Proverbs, Ecclesiastes, and the Song of Songs) between the historical and the prophetic books, and by reassigning the remaining five books of the Writings to one or the other of these new Christian categories. Ruth, Chronicles, Ezra-Nehemiah and Esther became historical books; Lamentations and Daniel became prophetic. In addition, the historical books were supplemented from the Septuagint with Tobit, Judith, and First and Second Maccabees, the poetical books with Ecclesiasticus and the Wisdom of Solomon, and the prophetic books with Baruch.

A traditional explanation for this new arrangement has been that the early church simply took over an "Alexandrian canon," an ordering and list of books produced by the Greek-speaking Jews of Alexandria who were responsible for the translation of the Hebrew Scriptures beginning with the Pentateuch in the third century B.C.E. The existence of such an alternative Jewish canon has been thrown into considerable doubt in recent decades, however, and it seems increasingly likely that the structuring of the Christian Old Testament as a canonical whole occurred quite independently of Jewish precedent.[40] The text of the Greek Septuagint can only be traced back through the massive editorial efforts of Origen in his Hexapla and thus can only be grasped in a thoroughly Christianized form. Jerome, who translated his Latin Old Testament from the Hebrew with the help of Jewish informants, became aware after Origen of the divergence of the Christian Old Testament and the Hebrew Bible of rabbinic Judaism. He seems to have been the last major Christian scholar to be aware of the threefold division of the Hebrew Bible among the Jews. But Jerome's insistence on the *"Hebraica veritas,"* as he called it, was overridden by the conviction of Church Fathers like Augustine that the Septuagint was itself an inspired text (based on the legend of Aristeas about the miraculous translation of the Pentateuch by seventy Jewish scribes) and should take precedence over the rabbinic Jewish canon.

What a study of the early Christian lists of Old Testament books reveals is a "bewildering diversity," as the *Cambridge His-*

tory of the Bible puts it, in the ways these books were ordered
beyond the five books of the Pentateuch.[41] Of twenty-two surviving lists, all but one place the so-called historical books second,
supplementing Joshua through 2 Kings with history-like books
from the Writings such as Ruth and Chronicles. But in nine of these
lists one or more of the historical books appear elsewhere in canon.
Only fifteen of the twenty-two lists place the poetical books in
third position, and of these only nine group Job, Psalms, Proverbs,
Ecclesiastes, and the Songs of Songs (in various orders) together.
Only fourteen lists, less than two-thirds of the twenty-two, place
the prophetic books—the Latter Prophets plus Daniel—in fourth
position, and in six of these fourteen, one or more books from other
parts of the canon come after the last prophetic book. Five lists,
in fact, end with some set of the poetical books as the last major
section of the Christian Old Testament.

This relative fluidity in the ordering of the Old Testament,
compounded by the inclusion of a varying number of books from
the Jewish books in Greek versions not included in the rabbinical
canon, confirms the perception that the Christian Bible was essentially bipartite in the early centuries of the church.[42] The most
important distinction, literarily as well as theologically, was
between the two Testaments (Latin *testamentum* as a translation
of Greek *diatheke*) or two "instruments," as Tertullian preferred
to call them. From the Christian perspective, all the "scriptures
of the Lord" testify to Christ. The Old Testament testifies propheti-
cally, through the salvation-history of Israel before the birth of Jesus
of Nazareth. The New Testament testifies historically, through the
apostolic witnesses to the Messiah in his human form and in his
resurrection power and presence.[43] In this sense, all the books of
the Old Testament are "prophetical books." Nevertheless, by the
time of Augustine's treatise *On Christian Doctrine*, a distinction
is made between historical and prophetic books within the Old
Testament itself. The books from Genesis through Chronicles,
Augustine says, "are made up of history and are arranged
according to the sequence of time and the order of things," but
other books—he cites Job, Tobit, Esther, Judith, 1 and 2 Maccabees,
and Ezra-Nehemiah—are also historical, even though they "are
arranged in a different order" and are not "connected among themselves." The category of "the Prophets," on the other hand, is
extended to cover Psalms, Proverbs, the Song of Songs, Ecclesiastes,
Ecclesiasticus, and the Wisdom of Solomon as well as "those books
called Prophets in a strict sense," the twelve minor and four

major prophets, who now include Daniel.[44] Finally, in what was probably the gradual ascendency of one manuscript tradition of the Latin Vulgate over others, a single order of Old Testament books became canonical in the Christian Bible. This order involved not simply a sequence of specific titles but a series of four canonical classes: the Pentateuch or books of Moses, the historical books concerned with Israel, the poetical books of psalms and wisdom literature, and the prophetic books composed mainly of recorded oracles and visions. This order persisted even when the Reformation removed the additional books of the Greek Septuagint and returned the Protestant Old Testament to the narrower canon of the Hebrew Bible.

Although there is no historical evidence that any particular church official or council made a conscious decision to this effect, it appears from a literary-critical perspective that it was the four-part canon of the Christian New Testament that provided the basis for the eventual four-part arrangement of the Christian Old Testament. The sequence of four New Testament genres seems to have "*created* its precursor," in Borges's phrase, in the sequence of four Old Testament genres. The first type of literature in each testament recounts the original giving of divine instruction, through Moses in the Old, through Jesus in the New. The second type recounts the historical development of the religious community, extensively in the case of the nation of Israel, more concisely in the case of the Christian church in the Book of Acts. The third type of literature provides the religious community with theological reflection and moral instruction on its ideal order. As John F. A. Sawyer notes, the poetical books of the Old Testament, including the Psalms in their Christian use, are concerned not with the historical past but with the practical present,[45] and the New Testament Epistles, Pauline and otherwise, are similarly oriented as far as later readers are concerned. The fourth type of literature, represented by five major books (Isaiah, Jeremiah, Ezekiel, Daniel, and the Minor Prophets) in the Old Testament and by a single book, Revelation, in the New, provides a prophetic vision of the community's future.

This is not to say that the literary impact of the New Testament upon the Old Testament occurred only, or even most importantly, on this large-scale generic level. The search for witnesses to Jesus Christ and morals for Christian living in what had been— and continued to be—the Jewish Scriptures involved a great variety of interpretive strategies, both before and after the canonization of the New Testament. The simple, fourfold parallel of genres between the Testaments proved to be much less significant than the complex, fourfold allegory developed by the Church Fathers from Origen onward. It is also not to deny that the exposition of the Old Testament by Christian writers made liberal use of Greco-Roman literary categories as well as New Testament genres. James Kugel has described at length the ingenious ways in which early Christian apologists likened the Old Testament writings to Homeric epic, Greek drama, and Latin lyric poetry.[46] But it is to argue that the canon of the Christian Bible as a whole has a literary logic of its own and to claim further that this logic emerged from the extended dialogue between the New Testament writings and the Hebrew Bible. This dialogue began in the first century of the Common Era and continued for several centuries thereafter. By the fifth century, with the death of Jerome, the Church Father most aware of the difference between the Hebrew Bible and the Greek versions of the Jewish Scriptures, the ongoing interaction of the Christian Scriptures with the Hebrew Bible per se virtually ceased. But an extensive record of the conversation was laid down for later ages to rediscover when it was taken up again, not only during the Reformation but in the historical criticism of the Bible that followed.

This conversation between the Bibles, Hebrew and Christian, is still being attended to in new and different ways in literary criticism of the Bible today, a criticism that would succeed, or at least supplement, the primarily historical reconstructions of the text presented by biblical scholarship in the last two centuries. In this particular study, I have described it as a dialogics, a dynamic complex of dialogic relations, in which the Christian Scriptures are neither independent of the Jewish Scriptures that precede them nor dependent on these writings in any simple or single-minded way. The dialogics of the New Testament has its internal as well as its external dimensions, and it results in the incorporation of the Hebrew Bible of Judaism, in a somewhat different form and with a somewhat different content, within the Bible of catholic Christianity. The basic premise of such a dialogue was of course denied by rabbinic Judaism, which separated and elevated the five books of the Law above all the other Jewish Scriptures and surrounded the Law itself with the "fence" or "hedge" of commentary that became the Talmud. On the other side of the widening sectarian divide, the premise was challenged by Gnostic Christianity, which considered the Hebrew Bible as the revelation of an inferior or even antithetical deity and tried to banish the Jewish Scriptures from Christian use. But in the Letter to the Hebrews, which stands as an answer to both these types of objection, the premise is baldly stated: "In many and various ways God spoke of old to our fathers by the prophets; but in these last days he has spoken to us by a Son, whom he appointed the heir of all things, through whom also he created the world" (1:1–2). In Bakhtin's terms, the author of this letter is claiming that the heteroglossia of the Old Testament is superseded by a monologic discourse of the New Testament. But as our analysis conducted under the aegis of Bakhtin has shown, there are also many and various ways in which God speaks to his people within the New Testament—many and various ways in which this Son enters into the conversation of those fathers.

4

Who Is This That Darkens Counsel? Cross-Talk in the Book of Job

I

In any discussion of the Bible as literature, the Book of Job is apt to figure prominently. Although rabbinic commentators were not much interested in the literary qualities of this (or any other) biblical book, the Church Fathers, developing approaches of Hellenistic Jews like Philo and Josephus, were appreciative of its artistic dimensions. Jerome believed that the bulk of the book was composed in Hebrew poetic meters analogous to Greek meters, and Theodore of Mopsuestia introduced the idea, still occasionally proposed today, that Job was modeled on Greek drama.[1] In the Renaissance, with the renewed appreciation of biblical and classical models and the deliberate merging of biblical and classical traditions with one another, it became commonplace to include the Book of Job among the great works of Western literature: as epic, as drama, or as lyric poetry. Job was not the only book of the Bible whose poetic qualities were highly esteemed. Sidney mentions "David in his Psalms; Solomon in his Song of Songs, in his Ecclesiastes, and Proverbs; Moses and Deborah in their Hymns; and the writer of Job."[2] But with the increasing value accorded to the literature of the "sublime" in the eighteenth century and the corresponding devaluation of didactic or religiously tendentious art, Job was widely regarded as the greatest contribution of the Hebrew people to the treasury of world literature. "A noble Book; all men's Book!" Thomas Carlyle proclaimed of the Book of Job. "There is nothing written, I think, in the Bible or out of it, of equal literary merit." Carlyle's friend J. A. Froude went even further; he thought of Job as "towering up alone, far above all the poetry of the world."[3]

The question of the specific kind of literature Job represents, however, has produced less of a consensus than the question of its general merit. Even today, critics attempt to classify the book within traditional classical genres like epic or drama or lyric, acknowledging that these generic categories must be redefined to fit Job or that they only apply to parts of the book, not the whole. Critics of the previous generation were often convinced that Job was a tragedy, as in Richard Sewell's eloquent analysis of the book as "a classic example of the dynamics of tragedy." But it has been argued more recently, with no less conviction, that Job is a critique of the concept of tragedy in human affairs. Comedy has also been proposed as the most appropriate generic model.[4] Although Job can be more easily detached from the canon of Scripture than any of the other books of the Bible, Hebrew or Christian, its place within the canon or within a poetics of literature has been uncertain. Many commentators have contented themselves with the claim that it is sui generis, a literary specimen in a class by itself, or with the observation that it stands at the head of a long line of later literary imitations, from the Testament of Job in the second or first century B.C.E., through *King Lear, Paradise Regained,* and Goethe's *Faust* in the Renaissance and the Romantic era to the dramatic adaptations and travesties of Robert Frost, Archibald MacLeish, and Neil Simon in the twentieth century.[5]

A more ingenious and more suggestive solution to the problem of the literary genre of Job is offered by Richard Moulton in his *Literary Study of the Bible,* published in 1896. Moulton begins his consideration of the "literary morphology" of the Old and New Testaments with an analysis of the Book of Job, in which he discovers six major types of "universal literature," three genres of prose and three of poetry, within this one biblical book. Job is not contained by any one of these genres (history, philosophy, rhetoric, epic, drama, and lyric) but incorporates them all within its aesthetic boundaries. All of the major "interests" of literature are brought into play in this one book of the Bible.[6] In Bakhtin's terms, this would make Job a special case of heteroglossia, an encyclopedic or Menippean aggregation of genres that are themselves more single-voiced or limited in scope. This is, in fact, a traditional way of coming to terms with problematic literary genres like the novel —to say, as A. W. Schlegel did long before Bakhtin, that the novel was the genre that contained every other genre within itself. But from a Bakhtinian perspective, the weakness of Moulton's claim for Job (apart from the fact that he goes on in a later chapter to classify it more modestly as an epic that has been invaded by the dramatic impulse) is its anachronistic nature. It too clearly reads back into an ancient Hebrew text of uncertain date and provenance an arbitrarily limited set of classical genres and disciplines first recognized as such in Greece in the fifth century B.C.E. The idea that Job is polygeneric or many-voiced is plausible enough. As historical critics have observed for the last two hundred years, the received text of the biblical book seems to be composed of distinctly different literary parts, not only in the laconic prose narrative of the opening and closing chapters and the expansive poetic speeches in between, but also in the several different styles and genres of poetry represented in chapters 3–41. But the character of these parts and the way in which they are orchestrated in the book as a whole can be better appreciated by situating Job in its biblical—and pre-biblical—literary context.

Once again, we shall be considering the canonical setting of Job rather than its situation in a history beyond the Bible. Indeed, the historical origin of the Book of Job is even less certain than the origin of the other books of the Hebrew Bible. Scholarly opinion on its date ranges from the tenth to the fourth centuries B.C.E. and commentators are divided on the question of whether some parts should be dated substantially earlier than others. This is not surprising, considering that Job contains no reference to the historical experience of Israel, which figures so prominently in the other books of the Hebrew Bible. With one editorially suspect exception, God is never identified by his covenant-name of "Yahweh" in the speeches of Job and his friends, which compose the bulk of the book.[7] It is only in the prose of the prologue and epilogue and the stage directions introducing God's speeches "out of the whirlwind" in chapters 38–41 that he is identified by the name of the God who revealed himself to Israel. And among the various people and places in Job, only Elihu, the son of Barachel, has a name that is properly Hebrew. The name "Job" has an ancient Western Semitic character, the names of his friends are associated with the Edomites and Moabites, and "Uz" is generally identified with either Edom or Hauran, both beyond the borders of

Israel at its greatest extent. What all these historical (or history-like) details add up to is that Job is the only book in the Hebrew Bible that deals specifically and exclusively with people and places that have no direct bearing on the history of Israel. In biblical terms, Job presents itself as a Gentile book, apparently set in a time before the nation of Israel had taken shape as the people of Yahweh or before Israel had become widely known as a political force in the ancient Near East.

The precise debt of Job to ancient Near Eastern literature is uncertain. The surviving texts of Egyptian and Mesopotamian laments and debates that resemble Job in their basic plots and rhetoric are too scattered and (apparently) too much older than the biblical text for scholars to claim that any one of them had a direct influence on Job or to claim that Job makes direct allusion to any particular ancient Near Eastern work. The so-called Babylonian Job, an Akkadian lament also known from its opening line as "I Will Praise the Lord of Wisdom," presents the complaints of a sufferer, but there is no argument between friends, and the sufferer ends by giving thanks to the god, Marduk, without making any claims for his own innocence or righteousness. The "Babylonian Theodicy" does take the form of a dialogue between the sufferer and a more pious friend, but the friend ends up being convinced by the sufferer that the gods have done a bad job in creating humanity. The Egyptian "Dispute Between a Man and His Soul" is a internal dialogue in which a man persuades his soul that suicide is preferable to a mortal life of suffering.[8] While it is possible that the author of the Book of Job knew some or all of these texts, texts only known today through the discoveries of modern archeology, it is more likely that the relationship is a self-consciously generic one. Shakespeare used Roman and Italian settings in many of his plays to create a symbolic geography, a culturally displaced ambiance in which subjects of interest to late sixteenth- and early seventeenth-century English society could be explored within conventions or stereotypes about another country. The opening words of Job—"There was a man in the land of Uz"—seem designed to evoke a similar set of geographically generic expectations: this is a pagan tale from ancient times, when individuals suffered individually and complained to their gods loud and long. In commenting on the lament "I Will Praise the Lord of Wisdom," W. G. Lambert notes, "Much of the material, even complete couplets, and the themes are traditional. The Babylonians had long been accustomed to mention or expatiate on their troubles both in letters addressed to their gods and in literary prayers."[9]

There is no question that Job, written in Hebrew and filled with echoes of other books of the Bible, is addressed by an Israelite author to an Israelite audience. The idea that it was an Arabic book translated into Hebrew, voiced by Thomas Carlyle among others, has been long discredited. Rather it is a Hebrew book in ancient Near Eastern dress, probably drawing on a legendary figure from outside Israel (see, for example, the mention of the generic righteous figures of "Noah, Daniel [or Dan'el] and Job" in Ezekiel 14:14 and 20) in order to speak to the more overtly Israelite literary tradition—a literary tradition already well on the way to becoming canonical, if the majority opinion that associates Job with sixth-century exile in Babylon is allowed. As we have already noted in Chapter 2, the wisdom literature that dominates the canonical division of the Writings in the Hebrew Bible is international in flavor and cosmopolitan in character, less exclusively concerned with ethnic and national Israel than the law of the Five Books and the prophecy of the Prophets. But in addition to the unself-conscious appropriation of Egyptian and Babylonian wisdom material in books like Proverbs—where direct borrowings have been detected in the biblical writings—there is also the more pointed use of "pagan" characters and settings in books like Daniel and Ruth. Part of the lesson of Daniel is that the captivity in Babylon is best seen not as a historical punishment for the nation of Israel but as a persistent condition of righteous individuals in an oppressive world order. It is surprising that the oppressor Nebuchadnezzar, after his own period of punishment as a beast of the field, is reinstated as a human being and blesses God, "the Most High," for his mercy. This theme of divine mercy extended to pagans who repent is presented even more pointedly in Jonah, which has been described as a sapiential parody of classic Israelite prophecy. Jonah must learn to extend his hope for God's redemption beyond the kingdom of Israel to the evil empire of Assyria. In the Book of Ruth, the lesson seems to be directed against the concept of the ethnic purity of Israel as promoted by Ezra after the return from Babylon. Ruth is a woman from pagan Moab who adopts the faith of her mother-in-law Naomi, redeems Naomi's inheritance in Israel, and becomes the ancestress of David, Israel's greatest king. This wisdom tradition, critical of religious exclusivity, is continued by Jesus in the Gospel of Luke in his parable of the Good Samaritan, the compassionate man from the despised neighborhood.

The ethnic symbolism of Job is less clear-cut than the ethnic symbolism of these other books but no less important from a dialogic perspective. From its position within the canon of the Hebrew

Bible, Job speaks as a half-outsider. Historically considered—that is, from the point of view of the Bible's own historiography—Job is one of the antediluvians, the heroes of the primeval period in Genesis 1–10, before the idea of a specific chosen people was presented by Yahweh to Abraham. (In the view of James Sanders, the Book of Job reflects a "sixth-century B.C. renaissance of interest in the Bronze Age, the age of the patriarchs.")[10] Or at least Job continues this antediluvian tradition onward, with no personal awareness of the covenants that God has made with Israel. The righteousness of Job, like the righteousness of Noah, is achieved without the benefit of special revelations, as far as we are told. Job knows to make burnt offerings on behalf of his children in the prologue, and he is instructed to intercede in prayer for his friends in the epilogue. But these are acts of natural religion or universal piety familiar to the generations before Abraham in Genesis. They do not descend from the Law given to Moses and Israel on Mount Sinai, nor do they lead up to it, as the sequence of dialogic encounters between God and the major human figures in the Book of Genesis clearly do. Job enters into communication with the God of Abraham, Isaac, and Jacob without the benefit of their example. His story inserts itself, as it were, between the primeval and the patriarchal dialogues of Genesis that we considered in Chapter 1.

The fact that Job can speak "what is right" (42:7) of God and receive corrective instruction from him face to face apart from the dialogic apparatus of law and prophecy is unsettling enough. But the fact that he does so in the generic mode of a Babylonian lament is a distinct challenge to the requirements of the Law and the Prophets. Where most of the wisdom literature in the Writings either takes the paradigms of revelation in law and prophecy for granted or suggests that the people of God should be a little less presumptuous in their appropriation of the Scriptures, the Book of Job appears to call the paradigms themselves into question as privileged descriptions of the way in which God has communicated with humanity. In the final analysis, Job doubts neither God's authority nor his own integrity. What the record of his struggle to bring these two extremes of his faith together implies is that the Law and the Prophets are not so authoritative and absolute in mediating the communication between God and his people as some of the claims presented within them would lead a pious Jewish reader to believe.

It is accepted by many historical critics that in its canonical context, the Book of Job constitutes a critique of the Deuteronomic history, books that place strong emphasis on retributive justice as it describes God's dealings with Israel. This "terrestrial eschatology," as it has been called, is most apparent in the Book of Deuteronomy itself, in the lists of curses for disobedience and blessings for obedience to the Law, and in 1 and 2 Kings, in the close correlation of the spiritual condition of the reigning monarch and the political fortunes of the nation. But J. Gerald Janzen argues that such a contrast between the Deuteronomist and Job "provides much too narrow and static a basis for analysis," that Job offers a much wider "critique, deepening and the seeds of a transformation" of the whole religious history of Israel.[11] From the Bakhtinian perspective of the present study, it is not too much to claim that Job offers a critique of the Hebrew Bible as a whole. It calls into question the authority of this Bible's generic paradigms of law, prophecy, and wisdom, at least wisdom in its more traditional, practical form. This critique is not a simple rejection, a parody, or an alternative scheme of revelation. Nor does it represent the biblical paradigms accurately, in all their flexibility and variety, especially the paradigm of wisdom, which after all managed to include Job itself within its canonical embrace. It is rather a literarily fictive critique of a historically realistic literature, a literature in the process of becoming scripture by fixing and restricting its play of possibilities in its presentation of the dialogue of God and his people. In Bakhtin's terms, Job is a self-consciously dialogical reflection on a literature that was becoming, or that its author thought was in danger of being perceived as, reductively monologic.

II

It is obvious that the Book of Job calls into question "the counsel from the wise," as Jeremiah 18:18 calls this type of biblical utterance. The gross misapplication of proverbial truth by Job's three friends or "comforters" has itself become proverbial. Eliphaz's opening remarks, after Job has cursed the day of his birth in chapter 3, suggest that Job himself has been one of the wise counsellors and now must accept a dose of his own medicine:

> Behold, you have instructed many,
> > and you have strengthened weak hands.
> Your words have upheld him who was stumbling,
> > and you have made firm the feeble knees.
> But now it has come to you, and you are impatient.
>
> (4:3–5)

Eliphaz continues with proverbs that have a familiar biblical ring. "Is not your fear of God your confidence" (4:6) recalls the proverb of proverbs "The fear of the LORD is the beginning of wisdom" (Prov. 9:10), and "Think now, who that was innocent ever perished" (4:7) recalls the orthodox wisdom of Psalm 37:25: "I have been young, and now I am old; / yet I have not seen the righteous forsaken / or his children begging bread." Job himself, of course, has just found out how unreliable this particular piece of wisdom can be.

It is not merely the content of wisdom but the form in which it is characteristically expressed that the speeches of the three friends evoke. Their advice and observations are cast in the mold of the practical and prudential sayings concentrated in the Book of Proverbs but scattered throughout the Hebrew Bible as well: the pithy parallelisms ("But a stupid man will get understanding, / when a wild ass's colt is born a man" [11:12]), the general types ("the fool," "the wicked," "the righteous"), the examples and images from the natural world (plowing and reaping, papyrus and reeds, the lion, the spider). Job, of course, replies with proverbs of his own, but he mocks the sapiential stance and style of the friends as well. "No doubt you are the people, and wisdom will die with you," he says (12:2). "Your maxims are proverbs of ashes, / your defences are defences of clay" (13:12). Again, it is not just the content of what his friends tell him that antagonizes Job. It is the form, the speech genre, in which they deliver their misguided consolation. One of the weaknesses of collections or anthologies of proverbial sayings is that they ignore the crucial issue of the context in which one proverb rather than another is appropriate, a weakness that Shakespeare satirizes in the character of Polonius and Cervantes comically exploits in Sancho Panza, both of whom have an overabundant supply of proverbs on the tips of their tongues. Job objects to the volume of wisdom, much of it contradictory, that his three friends offer him. By the third round of speeches, he is able to anticipate their different lines of attack. In chapter 25 he cuts Bildad off after six verses and completes his speech for him. And in the last ten verses of chapter 27, "after waiting in vain for the Zophar to speak, . . . Job then offers what Zophar might have said had he spoken, in a second display of expert mimicry."[12]

Job's parody of wisdom literature goes beyond specific responses to the style of his friends. There is the well-known parody of a hymn of praise in chapter 7, where Job mocks the exclamation of Psalm 8, "What is man that thou art mindful of him, / and the son of man that thou dost care for him?" with "What is man, that

thou dost make so much of him, / . . . and test him every moment?" (7:17–18). Other ironic hymns, praising God's brutal power
rather than his creative majesty, appear in chapter 9:4–12 and chapter 12:13–25. This is not to say that Job himself has the last word
about the validity of biblical wisdom, that his mockery of the
"counsel from the wise" represents the attitude of the Book of Job
as a whole to this anthropocentric form of religious discourse,
however. In chapter 28, a "hymn to wisdom" is assigned to Job in
the received text; unless one wants to treat it as a beautiful but
irrelevant interpolation, one is forced to notice a surprising modu-
lation in Job's attitude. Before he rests his case in his aggressive
summation for the defense in chapters 29–31, Job seems to allow
his mind to play over the created world in a hypothetical quest.
Men mine precious metals and stones in the depths of the earth,
he observes,

> But where shall wisdom be found?
> And where is the place of understanding?
> Man does not know the way to it,
>   and it is not found in the land of the living.
>
> (12–13)

On one level, this discourse can be read as a final critique of the
advice of the friends, who have no doubt of their own possession
of this precious commodity and dispense it freely to Job. But on
another level, Job is led to acknowledge that a higher form of wisdom does exist:

> God understands the way to it,
>   and he knows its place.
> . . . .
>   he established it, and searched it out.
> And he said to man,
> "Behold, the fear of the Lord, that is wisdom;
>   and to depart from evil is understanding."
>
> (23, 27–28)

If we grant Job the depth and flexibility of character necessary to
utter this radically different speech in chapter 28, we may see him
beginning to relinquish his confident denunciations of wisdom as
embodied in his three friends and moving toward the frame of mind
necessary for him to be able to respond to the speeches of God out
of the whirlwind.

If Job calls the traditional forms of wisdom into question in the course of his speeches, he does so on the basis of forms from the Law and the Prophets. In a literal sense, of course, on the level of the dramatic action, Job himself has never heard of the Law and the Prophets; he has no portion or inheritance with Israel. Nevertheless, the *author* of the Book of Job is fully aware of these authoritative parts of the Hebrew Scriptures, however far along the road to canonization they had traveled when he wrote his own dissident contribution. The model for the vast majority of Job's complaints against God is the model of the covenant, as set forth initially in the five books of the Law and as prosecuted subsequently in the eight books (the Twelve counting as one) of the Prophets. Again, this allusion has been perceived by other commentators. Janzen notes an allusion to the Book of Exodus "which calls into question not only the Deuteronomic theology but the covenantal relation itself as inaugurated at Sinai."[13] Also recalling Mount Sinai and the giving of the law on stone tablets is Job's exclamation in chapter 19, "Oh that my words were written! / Oh that they were inscribed in a book! / Oh that with an iron pen and lead / they were graven in the rock for ever" (23–24). Greenberg observes the way Job's self-defense in chapter 31 is modeled on the curse-sanctions of Leviticus 26 and Deuteronomy 28 and goes on to suggest that "all of Job's speeches assume the character of a 'covenant lawsuit' in reverse: man accusing God, instead of God accusing man [Israel] as in the books of the Prophets."[14] The messianic form of prophecy is evoked in four different places in Job's speeches. References to an "umpire between us, / who might lay his hand upon us both" (9:33), to a time when God would "cover over my iniquity" (14:17), and to "my witness . . . in heaven" (16:19) culminate in the famous affirmation of 19:25: "For I know that my Redeemer lives, / and at last he will stand upon earth." The capital "R" of the RSV is a reminder of the way Christianity (though, interestingly, not the New Testament itself) has read this last passage with christological hindsight. But in the more immediate canonical context of the Hebrew Bible, it appears as Job's untutored intuition of the messianic hope held out in various prophetic oracles and visions from Nathan's word to David in 2 Samuel through the concluding oracle in Malachi.

Although the messianic prophecies of the Hebrew Bible were magnified in later sects of Judaism and became the cornerstone of the Christian understanding of Jesus, their status in the Book of Job is dubious. As with Job's confidence that he has a convenant

with God, his "imaginative outreach" to a divine redeemer, as
Janzen calls it,[15] is best understood, from a literary perspective, as
a questioning and a critique by the author of the book of this distinctly prophetic motif. Within the book that presents Job's case,
the response he receives from God is not at all messianic. The
recurrent figure he invokes is his own invention, and it is one that
is implicitly rejected. Indeed, in the intervening figure of Elihu, who
jumps into the discussion unannounced, there seems to be a specific attempt to discredit the institution of prophecy. If the three
friends are misguided wise men, Elihu is a self-appointed prophet,
and as such he exposes the would-be prophet in Job himself. As
Gordis observes, "Elihu" stands out as the only genuinely Israelite
name in the book, and it is a version of "Elijah," the name of the
archetypal Israelite prophet.[16] Other commentators have taken this
insight further, noting that Elihu is the only human speaker who
claims to be speaking under divine inspiration rather than from
traditional knowledge.[17] It is true that he rehearses some of the
sapiential arguments and rhetoric of the friends, in spite of his
announced intention of saying something new. But it is also the
case that he introduces some different ideas into the discussion:
that pride is a sin and that suffering may be redemptive as well as
punitive. But again, while these ideas are often validated in biblical prophecy, in the Book of Job they seem to be put, like Job himself, in their place. God does not even dignify Elihu's defense of
his ways with a critical comment, as he does the speeches of the
three friends. While God's own speeches from the whirlwind do
expand on particular images that Elihu introduces, as Robert
Alter points out—most notably the images of the storm in chapter 37[18]—the dramatically more powerful poetry of chapters 38–
41 deflates Elihu's own claim to inspiration. The thoroughly biblical ideas that man must approach God through the covenant of
law or through the summons to judgment and blessing of prophecy are in the long run no more affirmed by the Book of Job than
the thoroughly biblical idea that God rewards the righteous and
punishes the wicked.

III

What, then, does the Book of Job affirm about the communication
between God and man? If it calls the canonical paradigms of the
Hebrew Bible into question, is there anything that it offers in their
place? It will come as no surprise, in a literary-critical study

under the aegis of Bakhtin, if I advance the argument that what the Book of Job offers is a heightened awareness of the concept of dialogue itself, a concept, as I have been arguing, that underlies almost everything that has found its way into the Bible over the centuries of its canonical formation. To put it in other terms, the Book of Job is a reflexive text, testing, in an alien or alienated literary mode, the adequacy of the Scriptures that Israel claims to have received from God. Just as God invites the testing of its hero with his question to Satan (or the satan), "Have you considered my servant Job?" the author of Job invites God's people to test the integrity of God's historical "word" to them. In the final analysis, I will argue, the integrity of this word is affirmed, along with the integrity of the servant, but not without a vigorous and unsettling interrogation of both.

Dialogue is of course prominent in the Book of Job in the formal sense of an extended verbal interchange between speakers. Chapters 3–41:6 are often referred to by commentators as "the Dialogue," as distinguished from the narrative "prologue" and "epilogue," and with the exception of the Song of Songs and certain antiphonal speeches in the oracular prophets, Job is peculiar in the literature of the Hebrew Bible for its presentation of unmediated speech back and forth between characters.[19] But this formal expression of dialogue is not by itself a particularly important manifestation of the concept, according to Bakhtin. "Dialogic relationships are a much broader phenomenon than mere rejoinders in a dialogue, laid out compositionally in the text; they are an almost universal phenomenon, permeating all human speech and all relationships and manifestations of human life."[20] It is in Bakhtin's broader, more philosophic sense that the Book of Job is especially dialogic, a dialogue raised to the second power.

In its critique of the established biblical genres of divine-human communication, Job reduces the complexities of law, prophecy, and wisdom to a generalized discourse of justice. As we have seen in Chapter 2, there are important differences between the concept of covenant that structures the paradigm of law and the concept of spiritual reform that polarizes prophecy, not to mention the difference between these and the concept of established moral order that informs wisdom in its practical mode. Nevertheless, the author of Job lumps them all together as a single discourse concerned with justice, a language of vindication that is spoken by virtually every speaker in the book—by Job as well as his friends, by God as well as Satan. It is interesting that the first hint of such talk comes from Job himself when he offers sacrifices on behalf of his sons (his daughters are apparently not liable) after their feasts: "It may be that my sons have sinned, and cursed God in their hearts" (1:5). The sins of the sons, in Job's primeval thinking, may be paid for by the sacrifices of their father. But the discussion of justice also breaks out in heaven. God's question to Satan (the adversary is one of his own "sons" in this text) about whether he has considered his servant Job virtually invites Satan's accusation that Job's integrity and piety are merely situational, that Job will "curse thee to thy face" if God's benefits are taken away (1:11). Curses are important in the discourse of justice—so important that the Hebrew text uses the euphemistic "bless" (*barak*) to express them—but they have a strong legal connotation of bringing a formal charge against (and requiring a formal defense of) someone in a judicial proceeding. Thus in chapter 3, Job launches into a curse upon the day of his birth, a curse that would remove his day of personal beginning from the annals of history inaugurated in Genesis. Where God said "Let there be light" and blessed the creatures made in his image, Job commands the day of his birth to turn into darkness and the night of his conception to be stricken from the calendar. Job's three friends are fluent in this language of justice as they enter into the proceedings. "Think now," says Eliphaz, "who that was innocent ever perished? / Or where were the upright ever cut off?" (4:7). "Does God pervert justice?" Bildad demands, "Or does the Almighty pervert the right?" (8:3). Even Elihu, who rises at the end of the three elders' speeches as a character witness for God, speaks of the relationship between God and man in these terms: "far be it from God that he should do wickedness, / and from the Almighty that he would do wrong. / For according to the work of a man he will requite him, / and according to his ways he will make it befall him" (34:10–11). In this view, God is not above his own code of justice. Job himself is still more practiced in legal terminology, alternately mocking the friends' abstract arguments from precedent and framing his own defense from the concrete evidence of his life. He rests his case in chapter 31 with a long series of conditional self-imprecatory oaths: if I have ever committed any of the following offenses, may I be visited with the following punishments.

God comments wryly on Job's preoccupation with law in chapter 40: "Will you condemn me that you may be justified?" (40:8). Nevertheless, God sets up his own judicial proceeding in the epilogue when he brings charges against the friends for their poor attempt at defending him. "You have not spoken of me what is right, as my servant Job has" (42:7), he tells them, and announces that he will spare them his wrath only as Job intercedes in prayer on their behalf. Many commentators have puzzled over how to explain that Job has "spoken what is right" about God. But even more are offended at the restitution that God goes on to give Job after his trial is over. It seems as though God is vindicating the traditional legal theory of the friends—that the righteous are always rewarded—after all, although Job's first set of ten children must be left off the balance sheet in this settlement. Unless one is prepared to believe that God raises Job's original sons and daughters from the dead, as a recent analysis argues was the case in the original legend behind the book and is still implied in the epilogue,[21] or unless one assumes that the epilogue is part of the inherited folk tale that the author of the poetic dialogue felt constrained to preserve in its original, theologically primitive state, as most historical critics do, one is forced to conclude that this discourse of justice is contradictory and incoherent.

If one assumes, however, that the received text is responsibly assembled, that a single author or ultimate redactor is answerable for the different voices that the Book of Job convenes within its boundaries, one may consider that this peculiar conclusion is intentional. The discourse of justice is prominent, even dominant, in the Book of Job, but it is not the discourse in which the book speaks most persuasively. From the very beginning, there has been another way of talking about the relationship of God and man, a discourse of providence. The discourse of providence sets up a meaningful cross-talk with the discourse of justice and offers a way out of the impasse that the various judicial proceedings have reached.

The first hint of this alternative mode of relationship comes in the parallelism of the first description of Job as a man "blameless and upright, one who feared God, and turned away from evil" (1:1). The Hebrew words rendered as "upright" (*yashar*) and "turned away from" (*sur*) are frequently used in connection with Israel's convenant.[22] But *tam*, in spite of its rendering as "blameless" in most English translations, has the sense of "integral," "whole" or "complete"; it describes the intrinsic ethical consistency of an individual (or the physical perfection of an animal to be sacrificed) rather than performance according to an extrinsic standard. "Fearing" God (*yare*) describes an attitude or predisposition, not an action like turning away from evil. In the normal expectations evoked by biblical parallelism, such differences of emphasis are secondary, not matters on which to build a theology. But the difference between Job's created character and his covenantal behavior turns out to be crucial as the story of his suffering and his protest unfolds.

Where the discourse of justice rests on the concept of a covenant or treaty with specific requirements, the discourse of providence rests on the idea of general creation. Creation in the Hebrew Bible is not something accomplished by God in the beginning that runs on its own thereafter but something that is initiated and then actively sustained by God through time in the existence of individual creatures. The discourse of providence speaks not of a transcendent standard of righteousness to which both God and his people subscribe. It speaks of an immanent relationship of power and weakness, of protector and protected, of maker and made. We hear Job voicing it in his first response to disaster in the prologue, "Naked I came from my mother's womb, and naked shall I return; the LORD gave, and the LORD has taken away; blessed be the name of the LORD" (1:21). These words are spoken in shock rather than in full comprehension, but the language of dependence and nurture carries over into Job's first expression of anger and grief in chapter 3: "Why did I not die at birth, / come forth from the womb and expire? / Why did the knees receive me? / Or why the breasts, that I should suck?" (3:11–12). Job articulates the relationship of protection even as he regrets ever having experienced it.

The appeal to the nurturing wholeness of a created order appears again in the speeches of Eliphaz, Bildad, and Zophar from time to time, particularly in the genuine words of comfort they try to offer Job at the end of each of their speeches in the first round. "You shall know also that your descendants shall be many, / and your offspring as the grass of the earth. / You shall come to your grave in ripe old age, / as a shock of grain comes up to the threshing floor in its season," Eliphaz concludes in his first address to Job (5:25–26). Understandably, Job cannot accept this consolation. "O that my vexation were weighed, / and all my calamity laid in the balances," he retorts in the language of justice (6:2). The creational language of providence recedes from the discourse of the friends in the second and third rounds of the speeches. The utterances of both sides in the debate become more law-conscious and vindictive. But it surfaces again, mysteriously, in Job's expansive "hymn to wisdom" in chapter 28. And it enters into the speeches of Elihu in chapters 32–37. "Behold, I am toward God as you are,"

Elihu assures Job; "I too was formed from a piece of clay. / Behold, no fear of me need terrify you; / my pressure will not be heavy upon you" (33:6–7). Elihu cannot sustain this discourse. He does come down hard and legalistically on Job as his speech unfolds. But he also keeps recurring to "God my Maker, who gives songs in the night" (35:10) and the "wondrous works" of the natural world (37:16).

Where the discourse of providence and its "creation theology" come to the fore, of course, is in the extended speeches from "the LORD," here identified as Yahweh, that come forth from the whirlwind. The theophany is not something that Job seems to have anticipated as he rested his case in chapter 31 and it does not seem to be something that Elihu expected when he described the thunder and lightning, wind and rain in chapters 36 and 37. The Hebrew word translated as "whirlwind," *seara,* is the same as the one used to describe Elijah's disappearance in 2 Kings 2. But instead of being the means by which the prophet makes his visual disappearance it is here the means by which God manifests his verbal presence. Only in the books of the Law, nowhere else in the Prophets and the Writings, does God speak, directly and uninterrupted, at such length. And nowhere else in the Hebrew Bible is God's concern for the natural world described in such variety and detail. Everything that God says to Job, or asks of Job, is couched in elements of the created and sustained universe: "the foundation of the earth" (38:4), the stars, the sea, the dawn, the rain, the snow, and then the cavalcade of animals. Allusions to lions, goats, deer, donkeys, ostriches, and horses culminate in the extended descriptions of the more exotic "Behemoth" and "Leviathan."

For many readers this celebratory itemizing of the fullness of heaven and earth has seemed magnificent in its own right but largely irrelevant to Job and his suffering. Northrop Frye suggests that God "triumphantly displays a number of trump cards that seem to belong to a different game."[23] René Girard is more indignant; "it is difficult to take this farce seriously," he writes of chapters 38–41. "This sort of showman who passes for God has nothing in common with the Defender to whom Job appeals."[24] Nevertheless, Robert Alter has demonstrated in a brilliant close reading that these speeches from the whirlwind are closely linked in their images of light and dark, birth and death, and the weather with earlier speeches by Job, by his three friends and by Elihu. "The entire speech from the storm is not only an effectively structured poem in itself but is finely calculated as a climactic development of images, ideas, and themes that appear in different and sometimes antithetical contexts earlier in the poetic argument," he writes. This is especially the case, Alter shows, in the way God's speeches at the end emerge as a "brilliantly pointed reversal" of Job's curse on the day of his birth at the beginning of his poetic lament.[25]

Alter still follows the majority view of the speeches, however, when he claims that what God evokes in his speeches is "a creation that barely reflects the presence of man."[26] While this is objectively and literally true—there is no mention of humans among the creatures that are conjured up—it ignores the all-important dialogic situation in which the speeches are delivered. God is not speaking *about* men in general; he is speaking *to* a man named Job. God has "answered" Job out of the whirlwind, as 38:1 puts it. He has not missed the point of Job's cry for justice so much as he has placed this point in a wider context.

What is striking about the hundred-plus verses of God's direct speech is the way they represent the creation and its creator in peculiarly human terms. "Where were you when I laid the foundation of the earth? . . . Who determined its measurements . . . ? On what were its bases sunk, / or who laid its cornerstone . . . ?" (38: 4–6). The images of building here are presented not as literal or objective descriptions of how God actually constructed the universe in the beginning. They do not challenge the ordered cosmogony described in Genesis 1:1–2:4, for example. Rather they appear as particularized metaphors, framed in the hypothetical mode of rhetorical questions, designed to impress on Job himself the limits, but also the basis, of his own human powers. God makes Job see that it would take a great householder to set the world on its foundations and keep it in order. He makes Job see that it would take a powerful patriarch to domesticate and provide for all the individual elements and animals within the universe, given the force with which these things are able to assert their independence. But these are the primary terms in which Job has been presented throughout the book—as an exemplary householder and patriarchal provider for those under his care. God's creation discourse, with its peculiarly domestic metaphors, appears as a dialogic response especially tailored to Job himself. Where Genesis 1 describes the human species, male and female, made in the image of God, Job 38–41 describes God the maker and sustainer of the creatures he had made in the image of a particular human being.

The domestic dimensions of Job are first established in the prologue. His seven sons and three daughters are adults, with their own houses, but he remains ritually responsible for their well-being with his sacrifices on their behalf. It seems pointed and poignant that the death of his children comes from a "great wind" over which he has no control, although the Hebrew word here, *ruah*, is different from the *seara* or "whirlwind" of 38:1 and 40:6. Job is further defined by his ownership of animals, not only the common sheep and oxen but the more unusual camels and she-asses. And he is particularly restrained as a husband as well. In the face of his wife's bitter counsel, which unwittingly echoes Satan's prediction, to "curse God, and die," he replies with tactful circumlocution: "You speak as one of the foolish women would speak. Shall we receive good at the hands of God, and shall we not receive evil?" (2:9–10).

These images of Job as provider and protector are not limited to the prologue. They are confirmed by references to Job's former state by the friends and they are reinforced, in a wider social setting, by Job himself as he sums up his defense in chapters 29–31. "When I went out to the gate of the city, / when I prepared my seat in the square, / the young men saw me and withdrew, / and the aged rose and stood" (29:7–8). "I was a father to the poor, / and I searched out the cause of him I did not know" (29:16). It is in the light of the special characteristics of Job himself that many of the images of domestication and nurture in God's creation speeches taken on personal signficance. "Where is the way to the dwelling of light, / . . . that you may discern the paths to its home?" (38:19–20), God asks. "From whose womb did the ice come forth?" (38:29). "Who provides for the raven its prey, / when its young ones cry to God, and wander about for lack of food?" (38:41). Such images speak not to the general problems of justice Job and the friends have raised in their dialogues but to the specific human need for nurture beyond what the safeguards of law can provide. Even the terrible Behemoth is evoked mainly in terms of God's domestic provision for him:

> For the mountains yield food for him
> > where all the wild beasts play.
> Under the lotus plants he lies,
> > in the covert of the reeds and in the marsh.
> For his shade the lotus trees cover him;
> > the willows of the brook surround him.
> Behold, if the river is turbulent he is not frightened;
> > he is confident though Jordan rushes against his
> > mouth.
> > > > > (40:20–23)

In the parabolic indirection typical of wisdom literature, God is telling Job that—like Job himself in his days of prosperity—he provides for the needs of those under his care. In this sense, Job is made to understand that he is like his maker.

Of course this motif of domestic solicitude is only one side of the creation discourse of these concluding chapters. On the other side is the fierceness and pride of the natural world, both animal and inorganic. God points to the "proud waves," the hail "reserved for the time of trouble," the horse who "exults in his strength" and "laughs at fear" (38:11, 23; 39:21, 22). These images of creaturely assertiveness are also directly responsive to the particular personality of Job, the man who has been challenging God so vociferously in the course of responding to his friends.

The sketches of powerful independence within the creation culminate in the extended portrait of Leviathan. What God dwells on in this evocation is not only the power of the beast but also the integrity with which his individual parts are bound together, his "limbs," his "goodly frame," his back "made of rows of shields / shut up closely as with a seal" (41:12–15). The emphasis is more on Leviathan's defensive strength than on his offensive energy. The portrait ends with God's approving assertion: "He beholds everything that is high; / he is king over all the sons of pride" (41:34).

In these lower, animal orders of the creation, Job is invited, rather tactfully, to see two things. First, he is invited to see that in spite of his resemblance to God as protector and preserver of his creation, he is a good deal closer to the subject animals than to the sovereign God in the scale of being. His sphere of influence as a patriarch, even at the height of his prosperity, is only a microcosm within a much larger animal world. Second, he is shown how God can accept him in his integrity and self-assertiveness, just as God accepts—even points proudly to—Leviathan and Behemoth. "Behold Behemoth," God says, "which I made as I made you" (40:15). This statement echoes suggestively God's question to Satan, the adversary angel, at the beginning of the story, "Have you considered my servant Job?" (1:8, 2:3). "Have you considered my servant Leviathan?" God seems to be asking Job, in response to Job's adversarial accusations of his management of the universe. It is worth noting that Job has already aligned himself with wild animals in his own speeches, calling on those "who are skilled to rouse up Leviathan" (3:8), telling Zophar to "ask the beasts" whether or not God has done these things to him (12:7) and claiming "I am a brother of jackals, / and a companion of ostriches"

(30:29). God agrees that Job belongs to the animal kingdom and invites him to see that his response to suffering is natural but hardly unique.

Of course in holding up to Job this mirror of nature, God is allowing him to adopt a more appropriate and intelligent attitude toward his creator—which Job promptly does. Job stops conducting himself as one of the animal "sons of pride" that Leviathan is king over and withdraws his own prescriptions for justice. "I have uttered what I did not understand, / things too wonderful for me, which I did not know" (42:3). It is significant that immediately before repudiating in general his own earlier words of accusation, he rehearses in particular (with slight variations) the opening questions in God's two answers to him. "Who is this that hides counsel without knowledge," Job repeats, and "Hear, and I will speak; / I will question you, and you declare to me" (42:3–4; compare 38: 2–3 and 40:7). As Janzen observes, this revoicing by Job of God's rhetorical questions is a confessional response in the literal sense of the word, a concise speaking-in-agreement that is completely different from the extended speaking-in-dissent that precedes it. Although historical critics sometimes regard these lines as "misplaced variants" of the earlier ones they echo, there is no literary reason to suspect the integrity of the text.[27]

Thus in this indirect dialogue, conducted in the discourse of providence, Job is assured of his place within the vast but by no means impersonal or static order of the creation. The would-be adversary of God allows himself to be reinstated in the all-inclusive vitality of the universe, if only because he is shown the family resemblances between himself and the creator as well as between himself and the creation. The process of reinstatement is continued, although in a distinctly different literary style, in the eleven verses of the epilogue. Reverting to the language of justice, God tells Eliphaz that his wrath is kindled against him and the two other friends, but his accusation that they have not spoken "what is right" (Hebrew *kun*) of him is better understood as 'what is true' or 'what is the case' than 'what is righteous' or 'what is permitted by the law'. Furthermore, God's claim that Job *has* spoken "what is right" about him, although it conceivably refers only to Job's recent statements of repentance, seems to separate even further the idea of the whole truth about God from the idea of his ruling passion for righteousness. The friends are humiliated or humbled by having to go to Job with their burnt offerings and have him pray for them, but they are not punished for their offenses.

Like Job himself, they are led back into the sphere of God's provision. It has bothered many readers that there is no mention of the
other would-be advocates or would-be adversaries presented earlier
in the book in this tying up of loose ends. Job's wife disappears
from the story, and although one may assume her reinstatement
is implied in the mention of ten new children, in the time of the
patriarchs one cannot be sure. Eliphaz is neither rebuked with the
three friends nor honored with Job, a fact that has been used as
evidence that his speeches are an interpolation and not a dramatic
intrusion into the ongoing discussion. And finally, there is complete silence about Satan, the adversary, who in the prologue
seemed to set the whole story in motion with his accusation
against Job. It would seem to be a more logical ending for God to
tell Satan that he had not spoken what is right about Job than for
God to tell Eliphaz and the other two friends that they have not
spoken what is right about him.

A clue to what these omissions mean is supplied by the later
Testament of Job, which moralizes the story in a crude fashion.
Here Job becomes the direct antagonist of Satan—he has destroyed
a pagan temple dedicated to this enemy of the one true God—and
Elihu becomes a follower of Satan, denounced as "evil Elious" by a
repentant Eliphaz.[28] This is clearly antithetical to the vision of God
as creator and sustainer of his whole unruly creation presented in
chapters 38–41. In 38:7, Satan, one of the "sons of God" in the prologue, seems to be implicitly included in "all the sons of God [who]
shouted for joy" at the moment the universe was established on
its foundations.[29] Leviathan, king over all the sons of pride but
nevertheless a creature God himself takes pride in, provides a more
prominent model for the universal gathering-in of all those agents
who try to set themselves over and against.[30] In other words, the
inclusiveness of the creator-creature relationship, benevolent and
universalistic, triumphs over the exclusiveness of the relationship
between a righteous God and righteous—or unrighteous—human
beings, a relationship marked by rigorism. Therefore we can only
conclude, against the Testament of Job, that God's embrace of his
primary adversary Job implies his embrace of all the other, lesser
adversaries in the story—those who think they are on God's side
as well as those who think they are against him.

There is one more surprising reversal in the epilogue: "the LORD
restored the fortunes of Job." God does this, the narrative speci-
fies, "when he had prayed for his friends" (42:10), but the suggestion that Job has had done to him what he has just done to others
is not sufficient to mitigate the scandal to the ideal of justice that

this restoration poses. We have already noted the conclusion of many historical critics: that this was the traditional ending to the ancient folktale about the righteous Job that the later poet inherited and did not feel free to change. But as Janzen notes, this is an odd conservatism to ascribe to the author of the iconoclastic speeches of Job in the dialogue. Greenberg's characterization seems more to the point: "In its reversal, the conclusion is of a piece with the rest of the book, so consistently subverting expectations and traditional values."[31]

Indeed, what this final turn of the screw in the epilogue suggests is that God is an author and finisher of human plots who is so free that he can follow the traditional rules as well as break them. He is not finally bound by his people's expectations concerning his behavior, even when these expectations are based on a careful reading of the record of his actions on their behalf. But neither is he bound *not* to satisfy these expectations. The discourse of justice, which for the author of the Book of Job represents the essence of the Hebrew Scriptures as a whole, is ironically reinstated in a place of honor in the story of this righteous and pious man, but its authority is no longer absolute. God's covenant with the chosen people at the center must be read against his providential relationship with other people—individuals rather than ethnic groups—at the margins of biblical awareness.

The Book of Job thus offers a creationist corrective to the historical redemption offered to Israel in the Law and the Prophets. Job's testing is not simply the test of a man, but a test of the creation as a whole. Against the suspicions raised by Satan, Job proves that the "good" that God saw in his workmanship in Genesis is not just a paradise lost at the beginning of things. Nor is it simply a paradise to be regained at the eschatological end of history, in a new heaven and new earth. Rather the goodness abides in the integrity and independence of all the creatures who exist, under God's authority and provision, in the time of the present. Humanity, male and female, is only one species among many, Job discovers, but in its capacity for language—for listening as well as speaking forth—it can find its proper place or range between heaven and earth.

IV

It remains to be pointed out that this "minority report filed against the dominant religious orthodoxy," as Bruce Vawter calls Job, is not so isolated a voice within the biblical canon as this dialogic interpretation of its literary critique of scripture might imply.[32] There are scriptural critiques of scripture in the Hebrew Bible as well, reconstructions of traditional forms of communication between God and people that parallel the humanizing initiatives of the Book of Job while insisting on the continuing covenantal authority of God and covenantal responsiblity of Israel. A close parallel to the revisionism of Job can be seen in Second Isaiah (chapters 40–55), which some historical critics believe either influenced the Book of Job or was influenced by it. The enigmatic figure of the Suffering Servant in the four separate songs devoted to his redemptive presence in Israel resembles Job in several respects, particularly in the indications that this servant is a unique individual rather than just a personification of the nation as a whole. There is also the emphasis in these chapters of Isaiah on the power of God as creator of the universe. "It is he who sits above the circle of the earth, / and its inhabitants are like grasshoppers; / who stretches out the heavens like a curtain, / and spreads them like a tent to dwell in" (40:22). The picture of the creation here puts more emphasis on God's transcendence of it than the picture presented in Job 38–41, and in the related attacks on the makers of idols Second Isaiah makes less of a place for human creativity within the creation than the Book of Job does. But the appeal to God's authority over nature "from the foundations of the earth" (Isa. 40:21) works in a similar way to supplement the traditional appeal to his authority over history.

There are also many songs of suffering and many celebrations of God as creator and provider in the Psalms. There is the suffering of the victim in Psalm 22, ascribed to David, in which wild animals, metaphorical but vividly presented nevertheless, are ranged against the human figure and in which the speaker arrives at a vision of his restoration in advance. And there is the mixture of humility at man's insignificance and pride at man's exalted place within the creation in Psalm 8, the psalm that Job bitterly parodies in his distress. The idea of humanity having authority or "dominion" over the lower orders of the creation, proclaimed at the creation in Genesis and reaffirmed after the Flood, is discovered anew by the psalmist (also identified as David); there is even mention of "whatever passes along the paths of the sea" as being under his verbal authority through the name of God (Ps. 8:8). In Psalm 77, the lament by the sufferer and the praise for the creator come together. God asserts his power over the natural world in a storm that conflates the dividing of the waters of the Red Sea in the Exodus with the bringing of dry land out of the waters in the Creation and again after the Flood. The psalmist's composite memory of these events brings him from the virtually blasphemous depths of his complaint ("the power of the Most High is no longer what it was," he ventures, in the Jerusalem Bible's rendering of verse 10) to a proper covenantal conclusion: "Thou didst lead thy people like a flock / by the hand of Moses and Aaron" (77:20). In Psalm 139, to offer a final example, there is a "striking rapprochement with the Book of Job," according to one critic, in the meditation by the creature on his creator and on the creator's meditation on him.[33] Nevertheless, the intimacy between the psalmist and the God who has created him, a relationship not without its anxieties, gives way at the end to a violent denunciation of God's enemies: "O that thou wouldst slay the wicked, O God, / and that men of blood would depart from me" (139:19).

What these parallels show is that the cross-talk of the Book of Job with earlier, substantial portions of the Hebrew Bible is not unique. Rather it is a special case of a heightening of recessive elements and dampening of dominant ones that occurs in a number of the historically later books of the Hebrew Bible. It is also worth remembering that the Book of Job can hardly be said to have had the last word on these matters. For all its antagonism to forms of religious discourse in the canon, Job was itself given a place of prominence in the third division of the canon, the Writings, and exercised a considerable influence on the way in which Jewish wisdom literature was understood. It most likely paved the way for another "strange book of the Bible," as it has been called, Ecclesiastes, to be included in the Scriptures.[34]

Furthermore, Job began to attract its own revisions. It has been suggested that Ecclesiastes itself is an "answer to Job," rejecting man's attempt to understand the ways of God in the first place.[35] The Testament of Job, from the second or first century B.C.E., recasts the story in the form of apocalyptic literature; Job is told in advance that he will be assaulted by Satan and has a clear vision during his time of suffering of a "throne . . . in a supra-terrestrial realm" awaiting him after his death.[36] Rabbinic midrash and haggadic legend read Job's story back into the story of Israel in the Law, claiming in one tradition that Job was a counselor to Pharaoh at the time of the Exodus and that God allowed him to be attacked by Satan in place of Moses to provide a diversion while Israel escaped.[37] In the literature of the New Testament, the Book of Job is curiously uncited for the most part. Paul quotes approvingly from one of Eliphaz's speeches in 1 Corinthians 3:19 and from the speech of God from the whirlwind in Romans 11:35; James mentions "the patience of Job" in his epistle (perhaps thinking of the Testament of Job rather than the canonical book). But in the writings of Church Fathers like Jerome and Theodore of Mopsuestia, Christians began to appreciate its poetic style and dramatic form, as we have seen, and in the thirty-five books of his *Morals on Job*, Gregory the Great used this dissident biblical book as the basis of the allegorical exegesis of Scripture that was to dominate Christian reading of the Bible throughout the Middle Ages. Job was an important text in the Reformation as well. Calvin preached 159 different sermons on Job, and the lessons that he drew from this Old Testament book helped to shape his *Institutes of the Christian Religion.*

The moral of this brief religious reception history of the Book of Job, in which the half-outsider to the canon becomes a pillar of orthodoxy, may be taken from Bakhtin. In "Toward a Methodology for the Human Sciences" Bakhtin writes,

> there is neither a first nor a last word and there are no limits to the dialogic context (it extends into the boundless past and the boundless future). Even *past* meanings, that is, those born in the dialogue of past centuries, can never be stable (finalized, ended once and for all)—they will always change (be renewed) in the process of subsequent, future development of the dialogue. At any moment in the development of the dialogue there are immense, boundless masses of forgotten contextual meanings, but at certain moments of the dialogue's subsequent development along the way they are recalled and invigorated in renewed form (in a new context).[38]

In its earliest canonical context, as I have tried to reconstruct it in this chapter, the Book of Job speaks into an emerging scripture from a self-consciously literary position. But the relationship between literature and scripture is never fixed and final, canons notwithstanding, and the dialogic cross-talk of Job has continued to transgress disciplinary boundaries in both directions. The Bible may belong to literature, Job suggests in one of its voices, but in another voice it proclaims that literature also belongs to the Bible.

5

Coming Down out of Heaven from God: The Orchestration of an Ending in the Book of Revelation

The Book of Revelation, although part of the canonical New Testament, has been received with reservations by the established Christian church. Suspicions of its extremist character were aroused in catholic Christianity in the late second century by the way it was embraced and imitated by Montanus and his followers, a sect that was declared heretical. It was classified in the fourth century by the Roman church historian Eusebius as both a "recognized" and a "spurious" book in the New Testament canon, and it was either omitted or explicitly rejected in still later canon lists of the Eastern Church. During the Reformation, Luther was reluctant to accord it full canonical status, complaining that "Christ is neither taught nor known in it,"[1] and Calvin pointedly omitted it from his otherwise complete set of commentaries on the books of the New Testament. In the centuries that followed, Revelation continued to attract great minds, such as Sir Isaac Newton's, and it still continues to attract large readerships for books that claim to open its mysteries. *The Late Great Planet Earth*, a popularizing application of its eschatological scenario to recent world events, has been a best-seller in the United States for the last two decades.[2] But it has been often regarded by much of established Christian-

ity as "a happy hunting ground for all sorts of bizarre and dangerous interpretations."[3] Where the staunchly skeptical Book of Job
was drawn into the center of the Christian canon of scriptures, the
deeply confessional Book of Revelation has remained on the pe-
riphery.

This is not to say that Revelation has been widely regarded as
a conspicuously literary text, either. Again unlike the case with
Job, few commentators have thought that it was the intention of
its author to write an imaginative or artistic work, even if the
record of his visions did inspire literary and artistic masterpieces
over the centuries: Dante's *Divine Comedy*, Michelangelo's "Last
Judgment," Handel's "Messiah," and Blake's *Jerusalem*, to name
only the most prominent examples. In *Apocalypse*, the visionary
commentary on the Book of Revelation finished the year he died,
D. H. Lawrence expressed a low opinion of the artistic intentions
of its author. "What we realise when we have read the precious
book a few times is that John the Divine had, on the face of it,
a grandiose scheme for wiping out and annihilating everybody
who wasn't of the elect, the chosen people, in short, and of climb-
ing up himself right on to the throne of God."[4] It was only in
Lawrence's reconstruction that the work of imaginative genius
buried in Revelation, a vision of man gloriously reunited with the
cosmos, was to be uncovered. Even in the one literary critic who
might seem to be an exception to this rule, Northrop Frye, in whose
poetics the genre of apocalypse occupies a place of literary honor,
the critic's attention turns away from the specific, objective form
of the Book of Revelation, which Frye calls a "panoramic apocalypse," to what he calls a "second or participating apocalypse," a
generalizing elaboration that "ideally, begins in the reader's mind
as soon as he has finished reading." Frye describes this reader's
response as "a vision that passes through the legalized vision of
ordeals and trials and judgments and comes out into a second life.
In this second life the creator-creature, divine-human antithetical
tension has ceased to exist, and the sense of the transcendent person and the split of subject and object no longer limit our vision."[5]

What Frye and Lawrence testify to in their imaginative leaps
beyond formalism is what William Beardslee, one of the more
astute biblical critics of Revelation's literary dimensions, calls the
"profound thirst for total presence" in apocalyptic writing. "'All'
is one of the great governing apocalyptic words," he observes.[6] This
concern with totality is readily observed in chapter 5, in John's
vision of the worship of "the Lamb who was slain," where innu-

merable angels—"myriads of myriads and thousands of thousands" —all speak with one voice and "every creature in heaven and on earth and under the earth and in the sea" repeat an almost identical doxology (5:11–13). In the terms of Bakhtin's descriptive categories, Revelation is a prime example of unifying discourse and the centralizing force in language. If the Book of Job accentuates the dialogic character of the biblical writings, as I have argued in Chapter 4, the Book of Revelation puts heavy emphasis on their contrasting, monologic tendency, their presentation of an "authoritative word" from God that seems to override all the "internally persuasive discourses" of men and women.

I

The contrast between Revelation and Job, though not a comparison commonly made, is nevertheless an instructive one. If Job is the most overtly "literary" of the books of the Bible, Revelation is the most explicitly "scriptural." Job is a story of a man living before (or at least apart from) the special revelation or written word God gave to his chosen people. The book is a self-consciously oral performance, even in the folk-tale quality of the prologue and epilogue. Revelation is acutely conscious of being a written document; in it the visionary author is repeatedly told to "write" what he has seen and heard and additional "books" and "scrolls" figure prominently in a number of the visions. Revelation insists on the sanctity of its exact wording, pronouncing a curse on anyone who tampers with its contents. It is true that other books in the Bible refer in an authoritative manner to "what is written," but unlike Deuteronomy or Matthew, for example, which point to earlier divine commandments or sacred texts, the Revelation of John insists on the sacred character of its own textuality. Those who read it aloud and those who listen to it being read are quite literally "blessed" (1:3). This textuality is based on the contemporary form of the papyrus scroll rather than of the later vellum codex, and it presumes an oral proclamation of the document rather than the later habit of private, silent reading. But the ethos of a fixed verbal communication valid for all listeners is strikingly different from the ethos of spontaneous and personalized interchange in the Book of Job.

The difference in ethos between Revelation and Job is evident in other aspects of these two biblical books as well. They both deal with situations of adversity, but Job's is the adversity of a single

individual while the suffering of the "saints" in Revelation is communal through and through. Where the Book of Job affirms the
integrity of the person apart from the holiness of the nation, the
Book of Revelation insists that consolation and redemption are an
essentially corporate affair. God appears to large groups of his servants, "a great multitude which no man could number" (7:9), not
just to a paragon among them. The first thing John is told to do is
write to the seven churches of Asia. Nor does God listen in Revelation, as he does in Job, to the angelic adversary, "the accuser of
our brethren," as Satan is called in the later book. Once the
"authority of [God's] Christ" has come, John learns, the angel who
"accuses [the saints] night and day before our God" is "thrown
down" from heaven (12:10). Finally, there is a curious, linguistic
connection between the figures of Behemoth and Leviathan, affec-
tionately embraced by God in the Book of Job, and the "beast" and
the "dragon" whom God emphatically rejects in the Book of Revelation, casting them into the lake of fire. As Austin Farrer notes,
the Greek words used for these figures in Revelation, *therion* and
drakon, are the same words used by the Septuagint to render the
Hebrew *behemot* and *livyathan* in Job.[7] The inclusive and immanent providence of God over the creatures he made in the beginning is replaced by an exclusive and transcendent redemption that
produces "a new heaven and a new earth" at the end of human
history.

These differences between Revelation and Job are immediately
explicable in terms of their respective genres. The Greek word
apokalupsis, the term by which the Book of Revelation identifies
itself in its opening, was later used as the label for a special kind
of revelatory literature, first Jewish and later Christian as well,
which had existed for several centuries before the Common Era.
As we noted in Chapters 2 and 3, the type of literature eventually
known as apocalyptic was incorporated into the Hebrew Bible and
the Christian New Testament, but Revelation is the only book in
either canon in which the forms and themes of this primarily
extracanonical genre are dominant. There are apocalyptic visions
scattered throughout the Latter Prophets; the last six chapters of
Daniel are a classic example of the genre; and there are apocalyptic predictions in the narrative Gospels (Matthew 24–25, Mark 13,
Luke 21) and in the New Testament epistles (1 Corinthians 15,
1 Thessalonians 5, 2 Thessalonians 2, 2 Peter 3). The Letter of Jude
even refers directly to apocalyptic writings, the Book of Enoch and
the Assumption of Moses, that did not become part of the canon.
Nevertheless, within the canonical writings it is only the Book of

Revelation that can be called a "full-blown apocalypse" according to the pattern of the Jewish visionary literature that was popular for centuries before and centuries after the formation of the New Testament.[8]

Theological commentaries on Revelation have often denied or minimized this generic identification, confusing the question of literary source with the questions of rhetorical purpose and canonical authority. As we have seen throughout this study, a literary criticism of the biblical writings cannot afford to ignore the question of genre, but it should not regard generic forms as fixed and unchangeable; nor should it consider a genre's characteristic themes as foreordained. There are Christian as well as Jewish apocalypses— the Apocalypse of Peter, the Shepherd of Hermas, and the Apocalypse of Paul, for example—and among the Jewish examples there are philosophical, Hellenistic versions, such as the Sybilline Oracles, as well as prophetic, sectarian ones like the Enoch writings. There are even forms of revelatory literature, journeys to heaven and tours of hell, that have nothing to do with the biblical tradition: Plato's myth of Er in *The Republic* and Virgil's account of his hero's descent to the underworld in the *Aeneid* are well-known instances that were adopted as "precursors" by later Christian apocalypses.[9]

As we saw in the last chapter, the Book of Job uses the ancient Near Eastern genre of the sufferer's complaint to signal its questioning of the traditional religious literature of Israel. An apparently "foreign" literary form is deployed in the service of an ultimately "native" biblical conclusion. In the case of the Book of Revelation, I would argue, the effect is virtually the opposite. An overtly "Jewish" or "Semitic" literary form is used to bind more tightly the emerging Christian literature to the authority and precedent of the Hebrew Scriptures. If one insists too literally on the formal features of the apocalyptic genre as doctrinal ends in themselves, one can easily lose sight, as Luther did, of the Christian content of the communication. But if one interprets the form of the book as a deliberate and systematic attempt to ground the Christian gospel in the scenes and images of "the Law and the Prophets"—especially as these scenes and images were characteristically interpreted in Jewish sectarian literature—one can see that the Book of Revelation provides a distinctive, intertestamental finale as it brings the Christian canon to a close.

The thesis that Revelation is a self-conscious Judaizing of New Testament literature is borne out by well-known peculiarities of the text. First there is the matter of the style. As early as 250,

Dionysus of Alexandria observed that the use of Greek was consistently barbarous and ungrammatical, strikingly different from
the pure and elegant style of the Gospel of John and thus unlikely
to have been written by the same author. While the irregular syntax and vocabulary have often been taken as a sign of linguistic
incompetence on the part of the author of Revelation, they are
systematic and insistent enough to be described by recent commentators as "a peculiar, contemporarily Semitizing Greek" written as
"a kind of protest against the higher forms of Hellenistic culture"
or as "imposing Hebrew or Aramaic language patterns on Greek
in such a way as to produce . . . a hieratic speech, a language
appropriate to the renewal of prophecy."[10] Second, there is the evidence of the peculiar and extensive allusiveness to the Hebrew
Bible. There are no direct quotations from the Hebrew Bible (in its
Hebrew or its Greek form) in Revelation, such as one finds everywhere in the other New Testament writings. Yet there is an overwhelming amount of allusion to the Hebrew canon: 348 distinct
references to 250 separate passages of the Old Testament by one
count, with 278 or 69% of the 404 verses of Revelation referring
to the canonical Jewish scriptures by another. Allusions to Isaiah,
Daniel, Psalms, and Ezekiel are most common, with more than
forty allusions to each of these books. But there are a significant
number of references to Genesis, Exodus, Jeremiah, and Zechariah
as well, and of the twenty-four books as reckoned by Jewish tradition, only Job and Ecclesiastes escape John's allusive attention altogether.[11]

The mere number of references does not indicate the way Revelation invokes and reconstructs the Hebrew Bible, but from a
Bakhtinian perspective, the fact that this New Testament book
consistently paraphrases the Old Testament rather than citing
scripture "as it is written" is significant. In his essay "Discourse
in the Novel" Bakhtin refers to two basic types of learning in
school, "reciting by heart" and "retelling in one's own words." In
this second type of verbal transmission, he argues, "the tendency
to assimilate others' discourse takes on an even deeper and more
basic significance in an individual's ideological becoming, in the
most fundamental sense. Another's discourse performs here no
longer as information, directions, rules, models, and so forth—but
strives rather to determine the very bases of our behavior; it performs here as *authoritative discourse*, and an *internally persuasive
discourse*."[12] Ideally, this type of utterance brings together the two
embattled tendencies, centripetal and centrifugal, that Bakhtin

finds pitted against one another in all verbal communication. Thus the recurrent, allusive paraphrasing of Jewish Scripture in Revelation is not the kind of monologic Judaizing objected to by Paul, in which, he argued, the Christian gospel was being subordinated to the Jewish law, the new paradigm of biblical communication being nullified by an old one. Rather it is the kind of appropriation of the authority of the old discourse for the proclamation of the new utterance practiced by Paul himself, where the words of the law are not simply canceled but are shown to be referring beyond themselves to Christ. Indeed, it is the kind of appropriation of "the law of Moses and the prophets and the psalms," as Luke 24:44 puts it, that Jesus himself claimed for his ministry, a prophetic "fulfillment," that incorporates the traditional, public authority of scripture with the spontaneous persuasiveness of new and intimate speech.

In the light of this analysis, we must revise our initial, comparative perception that the Book of Revelation is a monologic book, an assertion of authoritative words at the expense of internally persuasive discourse. Compared to the Book of Job, the assertion of verbal authority is certainly pronounced, but within the context of New Testament literary forms, Revelation may be more accurately described as a dialogic appropriation of an earlier collection of writings that it treats as a monologic authority. This last book of the Christian Bible, as it became, is not unconnected to the writings of the New Testament. As we have noted briefly above and as we shall see at greater length in the last section of this chapter, there are a number of parallels between Revelation and other books of the New Testament, some of them deliberately signaled by the text of Revelation itself. Nevertheless, it is the Hebrew Bible that Revelation calls upon, not any of the New Testament writings, as the scriptural precedent for its own proclamation.

A scene especially rich in Old Testament appropriations is the vision of worship in heaven in chapter 4. John is invited through an open door by a voice like a trumpet; he sees God seated on a throne surrounded by four living creatures and twenty-four elders who proclaim God's holiness and worthiness. Although the only furniture or architecture described is the throne of God and the thrones of the elders around it, the scene evokes many of the different images of the "house of God" in the Hebrew Bible that we observed in Chapter 2, the royal dwellings where God meets with his people. The earliest allusion is to Exodus 24:9–11, where Moses and seventy "elders of Israel" behold God and eat and drink in his presence, out of doors, on Mount Sinai. The "sea of glass, like crystal" of Revelation 4:6 recalls the "pavement of sapphire stone, like the very heaven for clearness" although the image of a solid sea evokes as well the Red Sea crossing of Israel earlier in Exodus, described in the Song of Moses as "the deeps congealed in the heart of the sea" (Exod. 15:8). The image also recalls the "firmament" in Genesis 1 that separates the waters of earth from the waters of heaven. The "twenty-four elders" of Revelation may come from the seventy elders of Exodus 24, but they have a more precise functional and numerical precedent in the twenty-four priests and twenty-four dozens of musicians enlisted for service in the Jerusalem Temple in 1 Chronicles 24–25. In 2 Chronicles 7, these are part of the congregation who "bowed down with their faces to the earth on the pavement, and worshiped and gave thanks to the LORD (7:3), just as the twenty-four elders in Revelation "fall down before him who is seated on the throne and worship him who lives for ever and ever" (4:10). The lightning and thunder that come forth from the throne in Revelation 4 have numerous precedents in the Hebrew Bible, from the theophanies on Mount Sinai in Exodus to visions of God among the prophets and in a number of the psalms. The throne of God itself and the thrones of the elders surrounding it recast the vision of Daniel 7:9, where "thrones were placed / and one that was ancient of days took his seat; . . . / his throne was fiery flames," although the act of judgment that ensues in this passage in Daniel is deferred in the Book of Revelation to the following chapter and the appearance of the slain Lamb. There is also an allusion to the earlier temple vision in Isaiah of "the Lord sitting upon a throne, high and lifted up" (Isa. 6:1), and there is an even closer resemblance of the vision in Revelation to the throne of God described by Ezekiel. This throne is placed above "a firmament, shining like crystal," and the divine figure seated on it has a nimbus "like the bow that is in the cloud on the day of rain" around him (Ezek. 1:22, 28), a precedent for the "rainbow that looked like an emerald" in Revelation 4:3. The "living creatures" in Revelation draw most explicitly on the visionary cherubim of Ezekiel 1 as well. The four faces on each of Ezekiel's creatures are reduced to a single countenance—one is like a lion, another like an ox, the third like a man, and the last like an eagle—and in their heavenly station they lack the accompanying wheels that Ezekiel sees on earth. But they retain the multiplicity of eyes from Ezekiel's vision. Isaiah's vision makes its presence felt in other details of the "living creatures," however. Their six wings and their three-fold chorus "Holy, holy, holy, is the Lord God Almighty" evoke specifically the call-vision of Isaiah 6: "I saw the Lord sitting upon a throne, high and lifted up; and his train filled the temple. Above him stood the seraphim; each had six wings: with two he covered his face, and with two he covered his feet, and with two he flew. And one called to another and said: 'Holy, holy, holy is the LORD of hosts; / the whole earth is full of his glory'" (Isa. 6:1–3).

This collage or palimpsest of Old Testament images of God and his worshipers, human and angelic, condenses a series of episodes from the history of God's appearances to his people into a single image of this relationship beyond historical time and space. In the Old Testament scenes, God and his attendants come down to meet with the leaders of God's people—on Mount Sinai, in the Temple in Jerusalem, in visions beside the river Chebar or in dreams dreamt in Babylon. In chapter 4 of Revelation, a leader of this people is taken up to heaven from the island of Patmos, but as the successive visions unfold, heaven and earth move progressively closer together. In the final vision of the New Jerusalem, "coming down out of heaven from God," the spatial and temporal boundaries between the dwelling of God and the dwelling of his human worshipers are erased. The new images that John sees "in the Spirit" (a phrase repeated in 1:10, 4:2, 17:3, and 21:10) are composed of elements from ancient scriptures. A further and important implication is that John's role as the latest human messenger from God can be traced back through the prophets of Israel to Moses himself.

This hypertypology, as it might be called, occurs throughout Revelation, and across chapters as well as within particular scenes. The scene of the sealing of the 144,000 in chapter 7, where angels seal the servants of God from each tribe of Israel on their foreheads to save them from the destruction unleashed by the four winds, recurs in demonic parody in chapter 13 where the "name of the beast or the number of its name" is marked on the forehead or the right hand of those who serve this false deity in order to escape from poverty and famine. The motif of sealing or marking is last mentioned in chapter 20, where among those who sit on thrones in the Millennium are "the souls of those who had been beheaded for their testimony to Jesus and for the word of God, and who had not worshiped the beast or its image and had not received its mark on their foreheads or their hands" (20:4).[13] The loss of the martyr's head for refusing the demonic mark takes the place of the earlier divine seal on the forehead of the saint.

In the course of these repetitions and reversals of the peculiar motif, a number of Old Testament precedents are evoked and gathered together. The initial and obvious recapitulation is of the scene or vision in Ezekiel 9, where an angel with an inkhorn is instructed to "Go through the city, through Jerusalem, and put a mark on the foreheads of the men who sigh and groan over all the abominations that are committed in it" (9:4). Those who are so marked will be spared when the rest of the inhabitants of the city are slaughtered by other angels with "destroying weapons" in their hands. But the image of salvational marking also reaches back to the Passover story in Exodus 14, where the blood of the lambs placed on the lintel and the doorposts spares the Israelites from the angel of death who kills the firstborn of the Egyptians. This association is reinforced by the identification of Christ in Revelation as "the Lamb who was slain." Prior to the Passover, the sacrificial marking reaches back to the rite of circumcision, particularly as it is reenacted in the mysterious assault by God on the uncircumcised Moses in Exodus 4, as Moses is on his way back into Egypt.[14] And this mark on the flesh, first required of Abraham as a sign of God's covenant with his offspring in Genesis 17, looks back further to the mark of Cain given by God as protection in his exile. This negative mark, a sign of Cain's rejection as well as a reminder of the sevenfold vengeance that God has promised to take on his murderer, is especially relevant to the mark of the beast in chapter 13 of Revelation. Although Abel is not mentioned directly in Revelation, "the blood of Abel" (Luke 11:51) is synonymous with martyred righteousness in the New Testament, the "way of Cain" (Jude 11) with martyring evil.

It is not that these associations of widely separate episodes are necessarily important, or even suggested, within the Hebrew Bible itself, or even that they were perceived by other New Testament writers as they searched the Jewish Scriptures for patterns and precedents. Rather it is that the Book of Revelation itself works as a powerful agent of typological consolidation, telescoping the authority of Israel's distant past into its own proclamation of the church's immediate future. The basic technique of prophetic exegesis, of treating details of the largely historical narrative of the Hebrew Bible as predictions of recent events and impending disasters in the life of a sectarian community, is common to Jewish apocalyptic texts and to Christian formulations of the gospel. But the depth, the scope, and the indirectness of the appropriation of Old Testament particulars is unique to the Book of Revelation.

II

Also peculiar to Revelation among Jewish apocalypses and among New Testament books is its internal complexity. "The Apocalypse of John is more structurally complex than any other Jewish or Christian apocalypse," David Aune observes, "and has yet to be satisfactorily analyzed." As Austin Farrer puts it, the Book of Revelation "has a great deal of framework."[15] Farrer's own analysis of this structure, first in *A Rebirth of Images* and then in a commentary, *The Revelation of St. John the Divine*, is the most elaborate and systematized account of the book's inner form in recent times. *A Rebirth of Images* finds Revelation organized in six sets of sevens, according to liturgical patterns of the week and the year. *The Revelation of St. John the Divine* argues for a basic structure of three parts plus an introduction and a scheme of three and a half days, the "time, two times, and half a time" of Daniel 12:7. Most other commentators have felt that the symmetries, sequences, and numerologies of the patterns Farrer has perceived are forced, even though they have adapted elements of these patterns for their own elucidation of the way the different visions of the book are organized. What I would argue, following the suggestion of Leonard L. Thompson that the "recurring numbers of equivalent value contribute toward the unity of Revelation,"[16] is that the various sevens, fours, threes, and twelves that appear so insistently in the book are symptoms of a will to system that is never fulfilled by any single numerical set. Farrer himself observes, in a skeptical moment of reflection, how Revelation exists "in perpetual tension between the claims of the part and the claims of the whole: each section being almost allowed, but never quite allowed, to become an apocalypse whole in itself."[17] There is no single framework within which all the visions granted to John can be accommodated, I would argue, but the ideal of such a single framework, of such a centralizing, monologic design, is one that the book pursues with considerable energy and conviction. The closest we come to such a framework, or "architectonics," in Bakhtin's terms, is in the vision of the New Jerusalem elaborated upon in the last two chapters, a vision of human worshipers in the shape of a symmetrical city, with twelves and fours and threes abounding. But this gigantic, gemlike, cubic structure remains an icon within the text rather than a discernible pattern informing the book as a whole. It is a symbolic form aspired to rather than a formal coherence successfully embodied.

The formal unity of Revelation, in other words, reflects the thematic concern of the book with the unity of the people of God. It is a unity that lies beyond the horizon of human vision, even the inspired, God-given vision of the prophet. It is a unity grounded in the church's faith in its "one Lord," as proclaimed in Deuteronomy 6:4 and Ephesians 4:5, but even this divine person is doubled in the two figures who are worshiped together, "the Lord God the Almighty and the Lamb" (21:22). There is one throne, revealed first in heaven and then in the new heaven and new earth, but the throne is occupied, from chapter 5 onward, by "God *and* the Lamb." All the voices and visions of Revelation originate in and look toward a divine presence, but this presence is guaranteed in the end only by a promise—"he who testifies to these things says, 'Surely I am coming soon'"—and an agreement and appeal: "Amen. Come, Lord Jesus" (22:20).

The tension between assertions of ultimate unity and acknowledgment of persisting diversity in Revelation are best described from a Bakhtinian perspective not as the failure of a monologic ambition, however, nor as the triumph of dialogic sanity in the face of such ambition, but as an affirmation of agreement. As Morson and Emerson observe, "Bakhtin cautions that it is a crude understanding of dialogue to picture it as 'disagreement.' . . . Agreement is as dialogic as disagreement. Agreement has countless varieties, infinite shadings and gradations, and enormously complex interactions." They continue: "to agree with a discourse is already to have tested it, deprived it of unconditional allegiance, and integrated it into one's own framework. One has retold it in one's own words, and, whether those words seem acceptable or unacceptable, they are still partially one's own."[18] The Book of Revelation dramatizes agreement, as we have already seen, through its peculiar use of Old Testament allusions retold in its own language. It also dramatizes such "creative uses of authoritative discourse," as Morson and Emerson call them,[19] in its recurrent scenes of worship.

The preeminent scene of worship—actually a double scene, focused first on God as creator and then on the Lamb as redeemer—occurs in chapters 4 and 5. Direct description of the divine figures themselves is sparing. What is given more extended attention is the composition of the worshipers: four living creatures, twenty-four elders, the "saints" whose prayers are presented as incense (5:8), countless angels, and finally "every creature in heaven and on earth and under the earth and in the sea." (5:13). Each of these groups joins in a doxology or canticle; five of these are either sung or said, from the opening *trisagion* "Holy, holy, holy" to the final ascription of "blessing and honor and glory and might for ever and ever."

This account of worship in heaven, to which John has access through the "open door" of his vision, is the most elaborate act of worship in the book but it is not the first one presented in Revelation. The initial act occurs in the first chapter when John is "in the Spirit on the Lord's day," the normal time and common mode of worship in the early church.[20] He hears a prophetic call to "write what you see in a book and send it to the seven churches" (1:11), turns and sees a vision of Christ ("one like a son of man") composed of elements from Exodus, Zechariah, and Daniel, and falls at Christ's feet "as though dead" (1:17). The two most common biblical words for worship, the Hebrew *shachah* and the Greek *proskuneo*, both have the root meaning 'to fall prostrate'. John's prostration is rendered by a similar word, *pipto*, used also when the twenty-four elders "fall down" before God in worship several times in chapters 4 and 5 and used again ironically in chapters 19 and 22, when John mistakenly throws himself at the feet of an angel and is told that worship of anything less than God is forbidden.

There are seven such scenes of worship in the course of Revelation, developed at varying length and with different emphasis. The first is John's spontaneous and inarticulate response to his commissioning vision (1:10–1:20), the second the universal chorus of praise in heaven in chapters 4 and 5. A third description of worship occurs between the opening of the sixth and seventh seals, beginning in 7:9 with the "great multitude . . . from every nation" who sing "Salvation belongs to our God who sits upon the throne, and to the Lamb!" and ending in 8:4 with "the smoke of the incense" rising "from the hand of the angel before God." Details from previous worship scenes recur (for example, the incense-prayers), but the movement in this scene is from the lower orders of the creation up instead of from the higher orders downward.

The fourth scene of worship is more extended and episodic; like the second scene, it covers two complete chapters, 10 and 11. The initial episode is the presentation by an angel to John of a "little scroll," which he is told to eat. As Adela Yarbro Collins notes, this is not only a recapitulation of an incident in the third chapter of Ezekiel but also a reprise of John's first vision, in which he is told to write in a book (or scroll, *biblion*), and a reprise of the opening of the scroll (also *biblion*) with the seven seals by the Lamb.[21] In chapter 11 John is instructed to measure the temple (like the angel in Ezekiel 40) and "those who worship there." The preeminent worshipers seem to be the "two witnesses" who are killed, resurrected after three and a half days, and ascend to heaven in a cloud. Worshipers in heaven then proclaim that "the kingdom of the world has become the kingdom of our Lord and of his Christ" (11:15), and the chapter ends with the opening of God's temple in heaven and a revelation of "the ark of his covenant" within the temple.

There are three remaining worship scenes in Revelation. They come in the form of shorter interludes. In chapter 14:1–7, John sees the 144,000 singing a new song in heaven before the throne and an angel flying "in midheaven" calling people from every nation on earth to join in. In chapter 15:2–8, the ones who have conquered the beast and refused his false marking stand before the sea of glass with "harps of God in their hands" and "sing the song of Moses, the servant of God, and the song of the Lamb." The primary allusion is to the song sung by Moses and the Israelites after they cross the Red Sea, but several other Old Testament songs of victory and praise are woven in as well, including Psalm 145. In chapter 19:1–10, John hears the most extended hymn of praise, its "Halleujahs" echoing the opening exclamations of the last five psalms in the Psalter. When he falls at the feet of the angel, John is told to "worship God" instead (19:10).

Seven scenes or episodes of worship thus punctuate the Book of Revelation, scenes that bring those in heaven and those still on earth increasingly close together. In between these scenes, however, come the sequences of judgments, more memorable for many readers in their images of punishment and destruction, in which those in heaven and others on earth are cut off from one another. The most memorable of these are the judgments of the seven seals, with their four horsemen, but as commentators have noted from early on, the catastrophes unleashed by the opening of the seals—conquest, war, famine, death, and cosmic collapse being discernible among them—seem to be recapitulated by the "plagues" subsequently announced by the seven trumpets and the closely corresponding plagues poured out from the seven vials or bowls still later.[22] Some interpreters have gone as far as to argue that there is no progression at all from one of these sevenfold judgments to another—that they should be taken as different perspectives on the same eschatological sequence.[23] But in a literary-critical view, especially in a dialogic interpretation, there is no reason to deny that there are significant differences along with the significant repetitions. What a dialogic reading can show in addition is that these recapitulating judgments extend beyond the three sequences of seven in the book and that they are all closely connected to the scenes of worship that precede them as well. *One* of the ways the Book of Revelation is organized—to avoid exaggerated claims about *"the* structure" of the book that its monologic tendencies have evoked from too many of its interpreters—is that it moves back and forth between scenes of worship and sequences of judgment, between harmonious agreements among those who confess the one true God on the one hand and violent conflict between those who are loyal to this God and those who are in rebellion against him on the other.

In the intensifying eschatological perspective of the Book of Revelation, there is finally no middle position between agreement with the community of God's worshipers and disagreement in solidarity with those who reject his authority. This ultimate separation occurs not between a preexistent heaven and hell, where earth is an ultimate nullity in the middle. It takes place between an emerging "new heaven and new earth," a resurrected cosmos, and a henceforth everlasting "lake of fire," a transformed and permanent chaos or "deep" that has replaced the no longer existing "sea" (21:1) of the first heaven and earth. More important from a literary perspective, the process of separation begins not with the cosmic judgments of chapter 6, but with the prophetic messages to the seven churches in chapters 2 and 3. Here, in historical time and space, we find worship and judgment in intimate proximity with one another.

Many commentators regard the letters to the seven churches of Asia as prefatory material that is essentially alien to the apocalyptic body of Revelation. But it is clear from the start that these epistolary sections are closely bound to the content of the opening scene of vision and worship. The opening of each letter identifies the sender by details from the description of the messianic figure in the first chapter; "the words of him who has the sharp, two-edged sword" in 2:12, for example, refer back to the sharp, two-edged sword issuing from Christ's mouth in 1:16. And the close of several (though not all) of the letters promises something from the concluding visions of Revelation to those who are faithful in each congregation—the "tree of life" from 22:2 to "him who conquers" in 2:7, the "rod of iron" from 19:15 to the conqueror in 2:27. What the body of each letter offers to each congregation, in fact, is a particular judgment. Most of these judgments mix praise with blame, and all of them offer encouragement to the faithful to renew their commitment to the Lord. But in the context of the septenary judgments that follow, those in this preliminary sequence (also seven in number) are notable in their restraint. Even in the denunciation of renegade believers—the "Nicolaitans," "the woman Jezebel," the "synagogue of Satan"—the punishments with which they are threatened (sickness, having to bow down before the faithful) are mild in comparison with those that come later.

It is also important to recognize that these judgments are delivered in the context of worship itself. Apostolic letters were normally read aloud in the public worship service in the early Christian churches, administering correction as well as encouragement, as Paul's letters so often do, and it is clear that John has a circular letter in mind as he combines all seven letters in the same book. Furthermore, it is evident from various New Testament writings that the exercise of prophetic "gifts" was common in early Christian worship services. Overindulgence of the various charismata in a congregation might create confusion, as Paul makes clear in his attempts to restore to order the worship of the Corinthian church. But Paul advises in chapter 14 of 1 Corinthians, at the end of his instructions, that believers "earnestly desire to prophesy" in public gatherings. In *New Testament Apocalyptic*, Paul Minear discusses the second and third chapters of Revelation in the midst of a collection of passages describing the normal order of worship of Christian worship, in which words of correction from God and acts of repentance on the part of his followers were as expected as songs of thanksgiving and hymns of praise.[24]

Thus the opening chapters of Revelation show a sequence of judgments, verbal but vivid, closely bound to a scene of worship. Worship is people's response to a God who has been faithful to them; judgments are God's response to people who have been unfaithful to him. The initial correlation of these two dialogic acts, as we might call them, continues in the alternating scenes of worship and judgment that follow. It is in the midst of worship in heaven that the Lamb appears and opens the seven seals that unleash the judgments; it is from the altar and censer in heaven that the fire is thrown down on the earth to initiate the judgments of the seven trumpets. And it is after God's temple in heaven is opened to his worshipers that the great red dragon is thrown down from heaven and the dragon and the beasts exercise their power on earth. Although no simple, causal connection is ever established, each celebration of the holiness of God by his faithful followers leads to a further revelation of the unholiness of his unrelenting enemies.

Not all the judgment sequences come in sevens. The fall of Babylon, celebrated in an extended reworking of an oracle in Jeremiah 51, is appended to the plagues of the seven bowls in the sixth set of judgments. (Like the plagues of the trumpet-judgments presented earlier, the bowl-plagues recapitulate the ten plagues of the Exodus.) The last series of judgments in Revelation begins with the "last battle" fought by the messianic rider on the white horse and ends with the famous "last judgment," when the dead who are not written in the book of life are thrown into the lake of fire along with Death and Hades. (Hades is presumably the shadowy, unmoralized underworld of the first heaven and the first earth described in the Hebrew Bible and classical literature.) In between there are the judgments during the Millennium rendered by "those to whom judgment was committed" (20:4) (including the beheaded martyrs but probably not limited to them, as argued above), another last battle against "Gog and Magog," and another trip to the abyss, now a lake of fire, for Satan and his assistants. Any attempt to reduce these last two sequences of judgment to numerical rule or typological order seems doomed to failure, although the number of judgment sequences overall, like the overall number of worship scenes, does come to a probably symbolic seven.

The episode that brings this interplay of worship and judgment to a conclusion is the vision of the New Jerusalem, "coming down out of heaven from God" (21:2). At first glance, this celestial city seems to represent simply one last scene of worship, of worship triumphing over judgment now that all the elements that resisted the acknowledgment of God's authority as creator and redeemer have been banished forever to the lake of fire. It also seems to be a triumph of architectural order, with the city's "great high wall, with twelve gates," its equal measurements in length, breadth and height, and its jeweled foundations and construction of "pure gold, clear as glass." Like the vision of the eschatological temple in the last nine chapters of Ezekiel on which it is modeled and like the cubic "holy of holies" of the tabernacle and the temple that lies behind Ezekiel's blueprint, the New Jerusalem seems to be a structure without inhabitants, a house of God too holy for the people of God to enter, except on special occasions and through special representatives. But the impression of petrified purity and symmetry conveyed by the description of the city from 21:10 to 21:21 is dialogically complicated by the descriptions that precede and follow it. In fact, the vision is given twice in chapter 21. On his own, John sees "the holy city, new Jerusalem, coming down out of heaven from God" in 21:2; assisted by an angel, he is shown "the holy city Jerusalem coming down out of heaven from God" in 21:10. In the first vision, John hears "a great voice from the throne" emphasizing the intimacy of God and his people: "Behold, the dwelling of God is with men. He will dwell with them, and they shall be his people, and God himself will be with them." The emphasis is on the benefits to the people in this communion: "he will wipe away every tear from their eyes, and death shall be no more, neither shall there be mourning nor crying nor pain any more, for the former things have passed away" (21:3–4). This humanizing and softening of the sharp-edged angelic overview of the city recurs in 21:22 and following, when John reemphasizes his own act of vision: "And I saw no temple in the city, for its temple is the Lord God the Almighty and the Lamb." There are no gradations of sanctity here, as there were in Ezekiel's temple, and the walls of the city are not impenetrable barriers: "the kings of the earth shall bring their glory into it, and its gates shall never be shut by day—and there shall be no night there; they shall bring into it the glory and the honor of the nations." This inclusiveness has its limits; John goes on to insist that "nothing unclean shall enter it, nor anyone who practices abomination or falsehood." But as with the earlier reminder of judgmental restriction in 21:8 ("But as for the cowardly, the faithless, the polluted . . ."), this warning seems addressed back to the readers or hearers of the revelation in the present age rather than referring to any criminal elements who have survived the Last Judgment and are trying to slip into the New Jerusalem. The fact that the leaves on the tree of life are said to be "for the healing of the nations" (22:2), on the other hand, suggests that the redemptive work of the New Jerusalem is ongoing rather than a thing absolutely accomplished.

Although such minor details, symbolic rather than literal, should not be pressed too hard, they are further evidence in support of my earlier contention that this most overtly monologic book of the Bible, centripetal and unifying as it aims to be, nevertheless preserves the biblical ethos of dialogue, at a higher level or in a finer tone. Further signs of these "soft boundaries," as Leonard

Thompson calls them, are the alternative images of the city as a garden or paradise, as in the features of the Garden of Eden (mediated by the last chapter of Ezekiel) that appear at the beginning of chapter 22, and the city as a woman, a "bride" and "wife of the Lamb," that is presented twice in chapter 21. This latter image, also widely used in the Old Testament, especially by the prophets, is particularly significant. As Thompson points out, the image of a woman who is also a city is developed in vivid detail, complete with jewels, earlier in the Book of Revelation itself with the description of the Whore of Babylon, a woman "arrayed in purple and scarlet, and bedecked with gold and jewels and pearls" (17:4).[25] From a theological point of view, one can only see the Whore of Babylon as the deceptive and parodic antithesis of the New Jerusalem bride, similar to the parody of God, the Lamb and John the prophet in the demonic threesome of the dragon, the beast from the sea, and the second beast who prophesies in his name that is sketched out in chapter 13. But from a literary-critical perspective, it is just as accurate to say that the New Jerusalem is a responsive transformation of the Whore of Babylon—not only a transformation of a pompous prostitute into a chaste and humble bride but also a transformation of an individual woman representing an imperial city to the other nations into a communal city representing a corporate woman to the Son of God.

A final instance of the way an apparently unitary structure in the Book of Revelation turns out, on closer examination, to embody a dialogic interaction is provided by the scriptural image of the "book of life." The existence of the book (or scroll) of life is mentioned seven times in the course of Revelation; twice it is described as belonging to the Lamb. As the various references to it make clear, it is a book containing the names of those who are destined "before the foundation of the world" (13:8) to enter into the New Jerusalem (21:27) and live forever. Those whose names are not written in this book are thrown into the lake of fire at the last judgment (20:15). Such an eternal census of the people of God is a quintessentially monologic document and gives powerful expression to the centripetal impulses of Revelation. But in the scene where it figures most prominently, the last judgment before the great white throne, the book of life is not the only text consulted. When John sees "the dead, great and small, standing before the throne," he mentions first that "books were opened," then "another book, . . . which is the book of life" (20:12). It is the absence of a person's name from the book of life that causes him or her to be thrown into the lake of fire, but it is "by what was written in the *books*, by what they had done," (emphasis added) that the dead are first judged before the great white throne. The relationship between a person's deeds and his fate is thus textually indeterminate; a peculiar centrifugal countercurrent appears in the midst of the centripetal vortex.

The two sets of records in this supreme court may be explained theologically in the larger context of the New Testament canon. They appear to express the difference elaborated upon in many of Paul's letters between the works of law by which all are condemned and the gift of grace by which many are saved.[26] But the designation of the book of life as "another book" is destablizing in the literary form of Revelation itself, where the worship by the faithful and the judgment on the faithless have been presented as such separate and distinct operations. Does the behavioral sum in the books recording what people have done produce the same names that are inscribed by divine election from the beginning of the world in the book of life? Indeed, are the logical and rhetorical answers to this question given in Paul's letters identical to the homiletic and parabolic answers provided by Jesus in the Gospels? What we are reminded of through the doubled image of books within the text we are reading (or hearing) is that the Book of Revelation itself is only a scribal redaction of a revelation whose full content transcends its literary form.

III

Thus the sense of an ending provided by the Book of Revelation, the way it brings its own expression of the dialogue of God and his people to a resolution, is a complexly creative rather than a simply repressive use of authoritative discourse, to invoke again Morson and Emerson's reformulation of Bakhtin. The same can be said of the way the Book of Revelation, by virtue of its canonical position, brings the whole Christian Bible to a close. We have looked at some of the creative appropriations of the Hebrew Bible that Revelation sets forth, from the patterns of creation and exodus in the Law to the scenes of theophany in the Prophets. What remains to be considered in our dialogic reading is the way in which Revelation is situated among other New Testament writings, canonical and apocryphal, that attempt to provide the Christian Scriptures with a comprehensive sense of an ending. In this context, Revelation is not unique in its teleological imperative. It may be the last book in the canon, but in a literary criticism according to Bakhtin, it appears as only one of many "last words" in the Christian Bible.

Within the New Testament canon, the canon that took shape in the century or so after the Book of Revelation was written, there are other expressions of the proper "end" to the story of salvation. As we noted in the third chapter, there is a conspicuous apocalyptic dimension to the gospel as a whole, repeated indications that in the advent of his Messiah, God is bringing human history and the physical world to a fiery conclusion. This sense of an imminent end to the story of redemption is first articulated by John the Baptist, most explicitly in the Gospels of Matthew and Luke, where John describes the Messiah coming with "his winnowing fork . . . in his hand, and he will clear his threshing floor and gather his wheat into his granary, but the chaff he will burn with unquenchable fire" (Matt. 3:12; compare Luke 3:17). The expectation of such an ending is also voiced by Jesus himself in the eschatological discourse he delivers on the Mount of Olives at the end of the Synoptic Gospels. In Matthew and Mark, at least, it is clear that the wars, earthquakes, famines, false Christs, and "the Son of man coming in clouds with great power and glory" (Mark 13:26) refer to the end of the world and the last judgment of humanity. The sequence of events in this "little apocalypse," as it is often called, is even roughly parallel to the sequence of judgments in the Book of Revelation.[27]

Even in the Gospels of Mark and Matthew, however, this apocalyptic end of history is presented in the form of inset or inserted speeches, not as the denouement of the narrative plot within these Gospels. The end of history is described, first by John the Baptist and later by Jesus himself, in a condensed, prophetic preview of coming attractions. It is not described by the narrator of either Gospel account in an all-inclusive visionary survey, as it is in the Book of Revelation. In the Gospel of Luke, this same apocalyptic discourse by Jesus has had many of its eschatological references removed and seems to refer primarily to the destruction of Jerusalem in 70 C.E. Luke's story of Jesus' earthly ministry in his Gospel is then continued in his story of the establishment of the Christian church in Acts. The Book of Acts is symbolically structured as a sequel to the Gospel of Luke, shifting the center of the church's missionary activity from Jerusalem at the beginning to Rome at the end and transferring the apostolic initiative from Peter to Paul. The apocalyptic end becomes a more tentative historical conclusion. In the Gospel of John, this displacement of apocalyptic eschatology is taken further, though in another direction. The only reference to Christ's *parousia* in John is a cautionary one, an insistence that Jesus did *not* say that the disciple whom Jesus loved would remain alive until his return (John 21:23). Where Luke provides an extended, historical account of the Christian community as his alternative to an imminent apocalyptic resolution, John offers a deepened, theological vision of an interpersonal afterlife. Instead of the apocalyptic discourse in Matthew and Mark, "de-eschatologized" in Luke, John includes the lengthy farewell discourse of chapters 14–17, an extended teaching in which Jesus describes his followers in heaven, in his "Father's house [with] many rooms"(14:2), in communion with the Father and the Son. The sense of an ending in the Gospel of John is essentially sacramental: the sequence of temporal events mediates a set of eternal relations.

There is a similar containment and transformation of apocalypse in the Pauline letters. The canonical order places Romans at the beginning and the Pastoral Epistles at the end, the former giving Paul's most extended theological analysis of the relation of the gospel to the law and thus looking back to Israel, the latter giving the fullest treatment of the institutional ordering of the church and thus looking ahead to catholic Christianity. In between are the apocalyptic previews of 1 Corinthians 15, focused on the resurrection of the dead; of 2 Corinthians 12, where Paul refers obliquely to his "revelation" of the third heaven, which nevertheless "cannot be told"; of 1 Thessalonians 4, which describes the "Lord himself" descending from heaven and the faithful rising to meet him in the air; and of 2 Thessalonians 2, which describes the coming of the Antichrist or "man of lawlessness." In all these instances, distinctly apocalyptic themes and images are expressed, all of them developed at greater length (and often with different details) in the Book of Revelation. But these pieces of eschatological mosaic, as it were, are used by Paul as elements of the theological exposition and the pastoral exhortation into which he characteristically shapes his letters.

In the non-Pauline epistles, among which the Letter to the Hebrews may be included, there is a similar incorporation of bits and pieces of apocalyptic vision in writings that stress abstract, theological resolution of the Christian gospel on the one hand and concrete, ethical resoluteness in the face of temptation and persecution on the other. 1 John mentions "the spirit of antichrist, of which you heard that it was coming, and now it is in the world already" (4:3), representing opposition to God as an attitude already abroad among people instead of as a single, demonic figure. Jude alludes to the impending judgment of God, but puts its main emphasis on the Old Testament precedents for this ultimate judgment (taking them from the Jewish apocalyptic writings like the Assumption of Moses and the Book of Enoch as well as the canonical books of Genesis, Exodus, and Numbers) instead of on the features of the judgment to come. 2 Peter rehearses Jude's argument, using the single Old Testament judgment of the Flood as a type of the fire next time in which the "elements will be dissolved . . . , and the earth and the works that are upon it will be burned up" (3:10). But in the Petrine explanation of the apparent delay in this judgment—that "with the Lord one day is as a thousand years, and a thousand years as one day"(3:8)—the actuality of the end of the world is kept at a distance.

In the Letter to the Hebrews there are similar apocalyptic references: the heavens being rolled up like garments (1:11–12), Christ putting everything in subjection under his feet (2:8), the word of God as a two-edged sword (4:12), "the heavenly Jerusalem," "innumerable angels in festal gathering" and "the assembly of the first-born who are enrolled in heaven" (12:22–23). There are more general resemblances to the Book of Revelation in the numerous Old Testament types and allusions that the Letter to the Hebrews brings into play. Both Hebrews and Revelation also share a liturgical emphasis, in which Christian worship is pictured as a radical transformation of particular Old Testament rituals. Nevertheless, as Sean Freyne notes in a perceptive "intertextual" reading of the two books, the explicit, spatial allegory of Hebrews, relatively static in its correlation of "copies" on earth and true things in heaven, presents a different image of Christian destiny from the symbolic, temporally dynamic convergence of earth and heaven in Revelation. In Hebrews, pilgrims have already arrived at the "heavenly Jerusalem" (12:22) by virtue of Christ's perfected sacrifice on their behalf. In Revelation, the "new Jerusalem" is seen coming down from heaven in a time that still lies historically ahead and in a space that collapses the boundaries between earth and heaven.[28]

The reason that there is more than one sense of an ending, more than one account of the end of salvation history in the New Testament, of course, is that the canon is made up of a number of originally separate books with endings of their own. None of the authors can have anticipated where his contribution would fit in the eventual order of the Christian Scriptures. Indeed, there are only occasional indications that the authors thought of themselves as writing scriptures per se, divinely inspired texts that would come to have, collectively, as much religious authority as the Hebrew Bible on which they drew so heavily. Luke recommends his Gospel as a comprehensive and "orderly account" of events described in more fragmentary fashion by earlier witnesses (1:3). John indicates that he has selected the "signs," acts done and words said, by Jesus, that will best persuade readers to believe he is the Christ (20:30–31). The author of Hebrews sets out to connect the singular way God has spoken to his people "in these last days" by a Son with the "many and various ways" (1:1–2) that he spoke to his people of old in the Hebrew Bible. It is only in the Book of Revelation that the idea of the text itself as sacred comes to the fore. Even so, there is no comprehensively concluding book in the New Testament like the Book of Chronicles at the end of the Hebrew Bible, an extended set of genealogies and narratives that rehearses a major portion of the contents of the Jewish canon from a point of privileged, celebratory retrospection. Like the end of Revelation, the New Testament as a whole and in its various parts continues to strain forward, toward the presence of a person: "He who testifes to these things says, 'Surely I am coming soon.' Amen. Come Lord Jesus" (22:20).

It is instructive, in this regard, to look at some of the other "books of revelation" that were popular in the early Christian church but were eventually excluded from the canon. As the Muratorian Canon List shows, it was with some uncertainty that "apocalypses" like the Apocalypse of Peter and the Shepherd of Hermas were excluded from the New Testament. "We accept only the apocalypses of John and Peter, although some of us do not want it [that is, Peter] to be read in the Church," the author or authors of this document write. "But Hermas composed The Shepherd quite recently in our times in the city of Rome, while his brother, Pius, occupied the episcopal seat of the city of Rome. And therefore it should indeed be read, but it cannot be read publicly to the people in church either among the prophets, whose number is complete, nor among the apostles, for it is after their time."[29] The number of the Christian prophets is arguably two, but definitely not three. In the Codex Claromontanus, however, probably from the next century, both the Apocalypse of Peter and the Shepherd of Hermas are still listed as accepted books of the New Testament, even though the Apocalypse of John would soon be the only survivor as far as the orthodox were concerned.[30]

What is interesting about these particular New Testament apocalypses, eventually deemed apocryphal, is that their sense of Christian ending is noticeably different from the one presented in the Revelation of John. The Apocalypse of Peter is presented as a post-resurrection reprise of the eschatological discourse or "little apocalypse" in the Gospels of Matthew and Mark. Jesus is seated on the Mount of Olives, and the disciples reiterate their request to know "the signs of thy Parousia and of the end of the world" (1).[31] Jesus obliges Peter by showing him an image on the palm of his right hand, a sequence that begins with familiar events like the resurrection of the dead, the fiery end of the world, and Jesus himself coming on a cloud to judge humanity. But the vision then shifts to the eternal punishments of the damned, where hideous tortures appropriate to the offense are visited upon sinners, "torment for every one . . . for ever according to his deeds" (13). The ones who are punished are not people who have worshiped the demonic powers and persecuted the saints, as in Revelation, but "those who have fallen away from faith in God and have committed sin" (5). Seven chapters describing the torments of those who have fallen away and sinned are followed by one chapter describing the paradise inhabited by the "elect and righteous" (14). The apocalypse concludes with a postresurrection reprise of another episode from the Synoptic Gospels, the scene of the Transfiguration. Instead of accompanying the disciples back down from the mountain, Jesus disappears into heaven with Moses and Elijah.

The Apocalypse of Peter thus replaces the heavily temporal eschatology of the Book of Revelation with a spatialized and moralized vision of heaven and hell that was to dominate Christian apocalyptic writing thereafter, from the Apocalypse of Paul to Dante's *Divine Comedy*. Such "tours of hell" were popular in subsequent Jewish apocalypses as well.[32] They differ from the Book of Revelation not only in the way they turn from a temporal end of the world to an eternal world situated above and below the space of human existence, a place to which a visionary traveler can go and from which he can return. They also shift the emphasis from the destiny of the people of God as a whole (and the collective people of God's enemies) to the fate of individual or representative saints and sinners. The corporate deliverance of Revelation, presented as a new Exodus of God's chosen, is transformed into a concern with the salvation, and even more with the damnation, of individual souls.

The transformation of Christian apocalyptic is even more striking in the Shepherd of Hermas. Mixing Jewish apocalyptic images with the Greco-Roman form of the sibylline oracle, this series of visions and supernatural instructions turns away not only from the eschatological future dramatized in the Book of Revelation but also from the other world of heaven and hell presented in the Apocalypse of Peter. The main concern is with the repentance of the individual under the institutional authority of the Church. The Shepherd of Hermas is mindful of the precedent of Revelation in its fourth vision, where the author reports seeing "a huge beast like some sea-monster" with "fiery locusts" coming out of its mouth.[33] Juxtaposed with this figure of evil is his encounter with "a virgin adorned like a bride going forth from a bride-chamber, all in white." This double vision is a composite of the demonic beasts and godly women of Revelation 12 and following: the "great red dragon" (12:3), "the beast rising out of the sea" (13:1), and the second beast (13:11) on the one hand; the "woman clothed with the sun" (12:1) and the Bride of the Lamb, "clothed with fine linen, bright and pure" (19:8) on the other. But the beast of the Shepherd of Hermas is hardly a cosmic adversary. He is immobilized simply by the firm faith of the author, who remembers a word he has been given earlier by "a kind voice" not to doubt God. "As I came near to it, the huge monster stretched itself on the ground and did no more than put forth its tongue and did not stir at all till I had passed by," he reports. And the heavenly woman, far from being threatened by the beast as she is in chapter 12 of Revelation, serves merely as confident expositor of its spiritual significance to the faithful Hermas:

> Thou hast escaped a great tribulation because thou hast believed and at the sight of such a huge beast hast not doubted. Go therefore and declare to the elect of the Lord his mighty deeds and say to them that this beast is a type of the great tribulation which is to come. If ye therefore prepare yourselves and with your whole heart turn to the Lord in repentance, then shall ye be able to escape it, if your heart be pure and blameless and if, for the future days of your life, ye serve the Lord without blame.

The corporate, communal "bride" of Revelation, into whom all the saints are gathered at the end of time, has become the institutional "church," as Hermas immediately identifies her, who deals with her charges on an individual basis.

This is not to say that the Book of Revelation is "more dialogic" and thus of higher literary quality than the later apocalypses that continue to revoice its themes and images in new religious utterances. It is, after all, through the Apocalypse of Peter and its

close successor the Apocalypse of Paul that Dante's literary masterpiece, the *Divine Comedy*, makes its most comprehensive
generic connection with the Bible. And the apocalypses of Gnostic and Manichean sects transformed the orchestration of an ending in Revelation into still other kinds of resolution.[34] As Bakhtin
wrote in the passage quoted at the end of the previous chapter, from
a literary-critical perspective "there is neither a first nor a last word
and there are no limits to the dialogic context." The closing of the
canon of the Bible, Christian and Jewish, was a theological act,
even though, as I have argued throughout this study, it was a theological act with distinctive literary dimensions.

On the other hand, there is a theological dimension that can
be observed in much literary criticism, particularly in the literary
criticism of Mikhail Bakhtin. The supposed open-endedness of
secular literature, in which new utterances, texts, and genres create an ever-expanding universe of significance, is often subject to
a practical closure in the act of literary interpretation. A centripetal tendency to limit the number of utterances that can meaningfully be brought into play in a given reading counterbalances
the centrifugal tendency to consider any utterance in history as fair
game for the interpreter. Such a theologizing closure can be
observed in the very passage cited above, taken from some revisionary notations Bakhtin made toward the end of his life on an
essay he had begun some forty years earlier. In a concluding metaphor that I omitted from the quotation at the end of Chapter 4,
Bakhtin reverses his field. "Nothing is absolutely dead," he writes;
"every meaning will have its homecoming festival."[35] It is with
such a faith—an inevitably communal rather than a merely personal conviction, Bakhtin insists—that the work of literary criticism must proceed, whatever meanings it tries to resurrect and
whatever festival it tries to organize on their behalf.

Afterword

"The Bible . . . according to Bakhtin." The reader of the preceding chapters has been invited to listen in on a variety of dialogues formally encoded in the Jewish and Christian Scriptures in their canonical state. The view has been taken, influenced by Bakhtin's model of a historical poetics, that this canonical state is itself a historical creation. But this study has also assumed that the meanings the canon generates are unavoidably theological, concerned with a communication that takes place between God and his people. The literary criticism developed here in the light of Bakhtin's ideas about the ubiquity of dialogue in verbal communication thus stands in a dialogical position itself, between what Bakhtin would call the centrifugal tendencies of historical analysis and the centripetal tendencies of theological interpretation. To read the Bible as history is to attend first and foremost to the multiple sources and layers of redaction that have been packed together in the canonical text, to separate the different elements and sediments accumulated and deposited over the centuries by the many different human authors and editors who have put the Bible together. To read the Bible as Scripture is to focus primarily on the unity of revelation that these different witnesses, in their totality, produce. It is to hear "the voice of the same God through historically dissimilar traditions," as Gerald Sheppard has put it;[1] it is also to discover one's own identity—for better and for worse— with the ongoing people of God in their historical formation. To read the Bible as literature, according to the view of literature espoused by Bakhtin, is to focus on the negotiation between unity and multiplicity itself, in particular on the formation of paradigms, genres, and intratextual cross-talk that mediate between histori- cal claims for the uniqueness of each and every part and theologi- cal or scriptural claims for the ultimately harmonious identity of the whole. It is to discern recurrent forms and coherent patterns in the conversations between God and his people that have been assembled in the received text, rather than looking behind this text to a broader historical record or looking above it to a higher theo- logical truth.

Of course these divisions of interpretive labor are ideal and abstract. Jewish and Christian theology are vitally concerned with the history in which God has acted, and most historical scholar- ship is quick to acknowledge that the biblical writers were preoc- cupied with discerning the person and presence of God in the midst of his people. Furthermore, both biblical history and biblical the- ology have made significant contributions to what I am here iden- tifying as the aim of literary criticism: the perception of stabiliz- ing forms and adaptable patterns of discourse in the Bible on the many different levels of its communication. And this is to say nothing of liturgical and devotional uses of the Bible, which as James Barr has well observed, frequently treat the text in the same formally synthetic manner, correlating widely separated passages and images with one another, that literary criticism does.[2]

What might be more accurate is to distinguish the type of text that each enterprise imagines the Bible—whichever canon and whatever books—to be. Historical scholarship conceives of the Bible as a set of documents belonging to a much larger archive. For the historian, the Bible is a distinctive set of documents, but it must be understood as a partisan collection of records, written and revised by a particular group of people and deposited in the midst of other collections written by other groups, some only recently recovered and others still waiting to be unearthed. The archive of history is by definition open-ended and in theory all- inclusive. The partial records, preserved by accident as well as design, are to be read for clues to a larger record that has disap- peared. Theological scholarship, on the other hand, reads the Bible as Scripture (the capital letter is necessary), as "containing all things necessary to salvation," as *The Book of Common Prayer* puts it. The Bible may be supplemented with other sources of information and must be read according to hermeneutic principles established by recognized authorities within the worshiping community. But what is written in the Bible is the first word, if not the last word, in any conversation about religious faith and practice, and what it says is ultimately self-consistent.

Literary criticism, in its intermediate activity, can only regard the Bible as an anthology, a selection of pieces or passages of writing of special aesthetic integrity. It does not (or should not) claim that the Bible is nothing but literature—that it has no reference to historical persons and events or is empty of theological significance. But it treats the text as a collection of writings with imaginative purpose and design. The current debates among literary and cultural critics about the virtues and vices of "the canon" of literature are mislabeled. They are concerned not with a canon in the proper theological sense of the word, a definitive rule of faith or fixed list of divinely inspired books. Rather they are concerned with an ideal anthology, a bibliographic museum without walls in which texts considered worthy of inclusion in the permanent collection are always divided between "old masters" and "brave new works" and in which it is understood that the art on display will be subject to considerable change from one show to the next as the tastes and convictions of the viewing public change. There are neoclassical anthologies that favor the ancients and restrict the range of offerings, and there are romantic anthologies that promote modern or contemporary achievements and expand artistic representation. But the literary canon is always open to the addition of new works and the deletion of old ones. Unlike the historical archive, however, it professes to contain the best—not everything—that has been thought and said.

What this means for a literary criticism of the Bible is that the "Battle of the Books," as Swift called the essentially contested character of literary judgment, must be seen as part and parcel of the text. Historical criticism attends to the voices that have been excluded from the Bible or traditions whose distinctive characters have been obscured within it; theological interpretation focuses on the principles by which the voices included in the Bible have been or may be orchestrated into a single chorus. Literary criticism (according to Bakhtin) notes the tension between the assertions of concord and the assertions of discord that the Bible has meaningfully, whether or not intentionally, preserved. It also reminds absolutists of the centripetal or centrifugal tendencies that one reason a book is included in an anthology is that it can be classified as a certain kind of writing, as a "flower" of a certain species. To be accepted and preserved beyond its first appearance, a piece of writing must have a recognizable form.

To read the Bible as literature, therefore, according to Bakhtin or according to any other literary guide, is to observe its coherence as an anthology. This coherence will seem more compelling in some parts of the canon and on some levels of its organization than on others. The particular sites of coherence emphasized in this study are only some of the many places where the Bible reveals its internal articulation. But from the lowest levels of style to the highest levels of genre, the impression of intentional order will always be stronger, from the literary critic's perspective, than the impression of accidental preservation that the historian's ideal of the archive inevitably evokes. Quiller-Couch's comparison of the Bible to a badly scrambled collection of literature cited at the beginning of Chapter 2 simply pits the ideal of the archive and the ideal of the anthology against each other. On the other hand, the Bible read as literature will always seem more various, in content as well as in form, than the theological model of Scripture can allow it to be. Coherence is not the same as unity, and the diversity of the anthology and the testimony of texts outside the collection are always an embarrassment to the theologian, even the "biblical" theologian.

The idea of literary criticism being proposed here, as those familiar with contemporary literary theory will have noticed long before this Afterword, is humanistic as well as formalistic, when all is said and done. I do believe that literary form is ultimately the expression—or the discovery—of persons and voices, however elusive these vital entities may be. This has not been a criticism dedicated to the "hermeneutics of suspicion," as Paul Ricoeur calls the contrary assumption, widespread in literary theory today, that literary form is a mask of false consciousness, concealing libidinous desires, political wills to power, or the metaphysical hoax of language itself.[3] It has rather been a criticism persuaded of the ultimate inseparability of form and content and the interdependence of author and audience in the phenomenon of the literary message. In solidarity with Bakhtin, I would argue that the programmatic suspicion of literature and the literary (which has its religious forms as well as its philosophical and political ones at present) does not lead beyond formalism in any constructive sense. It rather leads back to the old ideologies, of the left and of the right, from which formalism once proposed to set us free. No formalism is ever completely free of ideological agendas, but the programmatic suspicion of literature has ironically given ideologies that have lost their broad social and political appeal a new lease on life in the university.

What Bakhtin's more deeply formal advance beyond Russian Formalism offers literary interpretation, biblical and otherwise, is what I would call a poetics of responsiblity, an approach to the written word in which form is recognized as a reliable revelation rather than a deceptive disguise, but in which the process of its formation is conceived to be social as well as individual and ethical as well as aesthetic. One of the most brilliant practitioners of the hermeneutics of suspicion in recent times, Paul de Man (now under suspicion himself) complained that Bakhtin never distinguished the truth-claims of hermeneutics from the form-claims of poetics.[4] But it was Bakhtin's respect for the capacity of language to represent multiple intentions that made him wary of the demand of theory that language deliver a single truth. This transcendental demand and its inevitable, concomitant defeat have energized the interpretive programs of deconstruction and other poststructuralisms in the last two decades, but deconstruction's "double-play of sense," as Derrida has punningly called it, has contributed to a severe identity crisis within literary criticism itself and has less to offer the art of reading of the Bible, in my opinion, than the more expansive and more generous dialogism of Bakhtin. In his earliest writings, Bakhtin pursued a philosophical project to which Michael Holquist and Katerina Clark have given the title "The Architectonics of Answerability."[5] This suggestive phrase may serve as the ultimate designation of what Bakhtin leads us to see and hear in the Bible.

Notes

Preface

1. *Labyrinths: Selected Stories and Other Writings*, ed. Donald A. Yates and James E. Irby (New York: New Directions, 1964), 42, 44.

Chapter 1

1. *The Literary Guide to the Bible*, ed. Robert Alter and Frank Kermode (Cambridge: Belknap Press / Harvard University Press, 1987), 6.

2. Important literary-critical studies include Robert Alter's *The Art of Biblical Narrative* (New York: Basic Books, 1981) and *The Art of Biblical Poetry* (New York: Basic Books, 1985); Frank Kermode's *The Genesis of Secrecy: On the Interpretation of Narrative* (Cambridge: Harvard University Press, 1979) and several essays in *The Art of Telling: Essays on Fiction* (Cambridge: Harvard University Press, 1983); Northrop Frye's *The Great Code: The Bible and Literature* (New York: Harcourt Brace Jovanovich, 1982) and *Words with Power: Being a Second Study of "The Bible and Literature"* (San Diego, Calif.: Harcourt Brace Jovanovich, 1990); Meir Sternberg's *The Poetics of Biblical Narrative: Ideological Literature and the Drama of Reading* (Bloomington: Indiana University Press, 1985); and Gabriel Josipovici's *The Book of God: A Response to the Bible* (New Haven: Yale University Press, 1988). Literary approaches on the part of biblical scholars include David Robertson, *The Old Testament and the Literary Critic* (Phildelphia: Fortress, 1977); John Barton, *Reading the Old Testament: Method in Biblical Study* (Philadelphia: Westminster, 1984); Edgar V. McKnight, *The Bible and the Reader: An Introduction to Literary Criticism* (Phildelphia: Fortress, 1985); Gordon Fee and Donald Stuart, *How to Read the Bible for All Its Worth* (Grand Rapids, Mich.: Zondervan, 1982); and Stephen D. Moore,

Literary Criticism and the Gospels: The Theoretical Challenge (New Haven: Yale University Press, 1989).

3. *The Eclipse of Biblical Narative: A Study of Eighteenth and Nineteenth Century Hermeneutics* (New Haven: Yale University Press, 1974).

4. "The Struggle for the Text," in *Midrash and Literature*, ed. Geoffrey H. Hartman and Sanford Budick (New Haven: Yale University Press, 1986). In Barry N. Olshen and Yael S. Feldman's *Approaches to Teaching the Hebrew Bible as Literature in Translation* (New York: Modern Language Association, 1989), 12, the editors report that among the academics they surveyed who teach courses in the Bible as literature, the first chapter of *Mimesis* was the literary study of the Bible most often recommended to students.

5. *Lectures on the Sacred Poetry of the Hebrews*, trans. G. Gregory, 3d edition (London: Thomas Tegg, 1835), viii.

6. For a history of this discussion, in England and on the Continent, see the comprehensive account in Stephen Prickett's *Words and The Word: Language, Poetics, and Biblical Interpretation* (New York: Cambridge University Press, 1986). Prickett notes C. S. Lewis's indignant recommendation of Auerbach's *Mimesis* to German biblical critics like Rudolf Bultmann, who claimed that the Gospel of John was poetry rather than a history (80–81).

7. Alter and Kermode, *The Literary Guide*, 454; Josipovici, *The Book of God*, passim. Alter's *Art of Biblical Narrative* and Sternberg's *Poetics of Biblical Narrative* make considerable use of this analogy as well.

8. See Jakobson, "Concluding Statement: Linguistics and Poetics," in *Style in Language*, ed. Thomas A. Sebeok (New York: Technology Press of M.I.T. / London: John Wiley and Sons, 1960), 353ff. for a model that situates the verbal "message" in the midst of four primary determinants: sender, receiver, context, and code. This widely invoked scheme of analytic orientations has been intriguingly elaborated upon by Paul Hernadi in "A Compass for Critics," *Critical Inquiry* 3 (1976): 369–386.

9. *Mimesis: The Representation of Reality in Western Literature*, trans. Willard R. Trask (Princeton: Princeton University Press, 1953), 5; Auerbach quotes the phrase from Goethe and Schiller. Further quotations from *Mimesis* give page numbers in parentheses in the text.

10. See chapter 6 of *Formula, Character, and Context: Studies in Homeric, Old English, and Old Testament Poetry* (Washington, D.C.: Center for Hellenic Studies / Cambridge: Harvard University Press, 1969).

11. The Revised Standard Version follows the Septuagint text—"the child lifted up his voice and wept"—in an example of what Sternberg calls the Septuagint's "*fore*-smoothing and/or *back*-smoothing," its ironing out of contradictions in the Masoretic text (*Poetics of Biblical Narrative*, 371). Unless otherwise noted, all biblical quotations are from the RSV.

12. *The Art of Biblical Narrative*, 181–82. Alter also observes the way a "buffer passage between the two stories" (Gen. 21:22–34) brings further elements of connection to the fore. Regina Schwartz discusses the parallel at greater length and in greater detail in "Free Will and Character

Autonomy in the Bible," *Notre Dame English Journal* 51 (1983): 65–67, noting the numerous *Leitwörter* or recurring key words in both episodes.

13. See chapter 4 of Havelock's *Preface to Plato* (Cambridge: Harvard University Press, 1963).

14. "Free Will and Character Autonomy"; Schwartz compares the relationship of God and his human creatures in the Bible to the relationship of authors like Thackeray and Flaubert to their characters, stressing the complex rhetorical effect rather than simple didacticism. I elaborate upon such an idea at the end of this chapter.

15. Such a typological reading might appeal to Paul's probable allusion to the sacrifice of Isaac in Romans 4:16–25, to his explicit allegory of the birth of Ishmael and Isaac in Galatians 4:21–31, and to the clear allusion to the resurrection of Christ in the rehearsal of Abraham's sacrifice of Isaac in Hebrews 11:17–19.

16. Ricoeur, *The Conflict of Interpretations: Essays in Hermeneutics,* ed. Don Ihde (Evanston, Ill.: Northwestern University Press, 1974); Schneidau, *Sacred Discontent: The Bible and Western Tradition* (Baton Rouge: Louisiana State University Press, 1976).

17. "On the Bible and Literary Criticism," *Prooftexts* 1 (1981): 233.

18. See John Russiano Miles, "Radical Editing: *Redaktionsgeschichte* and the Aesthetic of Willed Confusion," in *The Creation of Sacred Literature: Composition and Redaction of the Biblical Text,* ed. Richard Elliott Friedman, University of California Publications: Near Eastern Studies, vol. 22 (Berkeley and Los Angeles: University of California Press, 1981).

19. The term "abstract objectivism" is first used in V. N. Voloshinov's *Marxism of the Philosophy of Language,* trans. Ladislav Matejka and I. R. Titunik (Cambridge: Harvard University Press, 1986) which some Bakhtin scholars believe was primarily written by Bakhtin himself, though Bakhtin's authorship is disputed by others, including the translators of Voloshinov's book. The opposing trend, represented for Voloshinov by Auerbach's associates Vossler and Spitzer, is termed "individualistic subjectivism."

20. *The Dialogic Imagination: Four Essays,* ed. Michael Holquist, trans. Caryl Emerson and Michael Holquist (Austin: University of Texas Press, 1981), 276. Further quotations from this volume give page numbers in parentheses in the text.

21. Katerina Clark and Michael Holquist, *Mikhail Bakhtin* (Cambridge: Belknap Press / Harvard University Press, 1984), 120.

22. For different assessments of this issue, see Clark and Holquist, *Mikhail Bakhtin,* chap. 5; Ann Shukman, "Bakhtin's Tolstoy Prefaces," in *Rethinking Bakhtin: Extensions and Challenges,* ed. Gary Saul Morson and Caryl Emerson (Evanston, Ill.: Northwestern University Press, 1989); and Gary Saul Morson and Caryl Emerson, *Mikhail Bakhtin: Creation of a Prosaics* (Stanford: Stanford University Press, 1990), passim.

23. *Words and The Word,* 214. Harold Fisch makes a similar observation in "Bakhtin's Misreadings of the Bible," *Hebrew University Studies in Literature and the Arts* 16 (1988): 130–49, which applies Bakhtin's

concept of dialogue to passages of Isaiah and the Psalms. Robert Polzin uses Bakhtin's (or Voloshinov's) more specific concept of "reported speech" to interpret the Deuteronomic history in two books, *Moses and the Deuteronomist: A Literary Study of the Deuteronomic History* (New York: Seabury, 1980) and *Samuel and the Deuteronomist* (New York: Harper and Row, 1989). And I offer a preliminary version of my argument in Chapter 2, pointing out the relevance of Bakhtin for biblical criticism, in "A Poetics of the Bible: Problems and Possibilities," *Literature and Theology* 1 (1987): 154–66.

24. Alter and Kermode use both of these last two terms to describe the common denominator of the essays in their *Literary Guide to the Bible*. The biblical hermeneutics of Paul Ricoeur, although concerned to some extent with the rhetorical or poetic model of metaphor, is also heavily invested in notions of narrative, which Ricoeur derives from Aristotle's *Poetics*, as well as other sources, in volume 1 of his *Time and Narrative*, trans. Kathleen McLaughlin and David Pellauer (Chicago: University of Chicago Press, 1984). The term *dialogics* is used by Don Bialostosky in his essay "Dialogic Criticism," in *Contemporary Literary Theory*, ed. G. Douglas Atkins and Laura Morrow (Amherst: University of Massachusetts Press, 1989), where he usefully distinguishes the concerns of this type of criticism from the concerns of Aristotelian and structuralist conceptions narrative.

25. Pointed out by Isaac M. Kikawada and Arthur Quinn in *Before Abraham Was: A Provocative Challenge to the Documentary Hypothesis* (Nashville, Tenn.: Abingdon, 1985), 92. Kikawada and Quinn provide an interesting analysis of the structure of Genesis based on the five-part rhetorical structure of the *Atrahasis Epic*.

26. *From Sacred Story to Sacred Text* (Philadelphia: Fortress, 1987), 187.

27. *Introducing Biblical Literature: A More Fantastic Country* (Englewood Cliffs, N.J.: Prentice-Hall, 1978), 13.

28. "Inner Biblical Exegesis: Types and Strategies of Interpretation in Ancient Israel," in Hartman and Budick, *Midrash and Literature*. Fishbane has developed this analysis at much greater length in his *Biblical Interpretation in Ancient Israel* (Oxford: Clarendon, 1985). On a more purely formal level, the use of associated words and phrases to link together individual units of law, prophetic oracles, psalms, and wisdom sayings, is noted by Umberto Cassuto ("The Sequence and Arrangement of the Biblical Sections," in *Biblical and Oriental Studies,* trans. Israel Abrahams [Jerusalem: Magnes, 1973], vol. 1). Cassuto argues that this linking was made by editors mainly for purposes of the reader memorizing the text.

29. See chapter 5 of *The Art of Biblical Narrative*.

30. Adele Berlin, *The Dynamics of Biblical Parallelism* (Bloomington: Indiana University Press, 1985), 6. James Kugel's *The Idea of Biblical Poetry: Parallelism and Its History* (New Haven: Yale University Press,

1981) convincingly challenges the traditional idea, revived by Lowth in the eighteenth century, that there is a distinction between poetry and prose in the Hebrew Bible, but Berlin recuperates the notion of a poetic *function* of parallelism by drawing on the descriptive poetics of Roman Jakobson.

31. Francis Landy, "Poetics and Parallelism: Some Comments on James Kugel's *The Idea of Biblical Poetry*," *Journal for the Study of the Old Testament* 28 (1984): 81.

32. David Damrosch's *The Narrative Covenant: Transformations of Genre in the Growth of Biblical Literature* (San Francisco, Calif.: Harper and Row, 1987) is a notably dialogic study of the relationship of narrative in the Old Testament, primarily in Genesis, 1 and 2 Samuel, and Leviticus, to the Mesopotamian genres of poetic epic and prose chronicle. In New Testament studies, Vernon Robbins has developed a sophisticated rhetorical reading of the interdependence of the gospels and classical literary forms; see his *Jesus the Teacher: A Socio-Rhetorical Interpretation of Mark* (Philadelphia: Fortress, 1984).

33. Damrosch, *Narrative Covenant*, 118–35, notes the extended parallels between Genesis, the *Atrahasis Epic*, and the *Epic of Gilgamesh*.

34. See Brevard Childs, *An Introduction to the Old Testament as Scripture* (Philadelphia: Fortress, 1979), 145–46.

35. Robert L. Cohen offers a persuasive and thorough account of this five-part scheme in "Narrative Structure and Canonical Perspective in Genesis," *Journal for the Study of the Old Testament* 25 (1983): 3–16.

36. See in particular J. P. Fokkelman, *Narrative Art in Genesis: Specimens of Stylistic and Structural Analysis* (Assen: Van Gorcum, 1975); Michael Fishbane, "The Sacred Center: The Symbolic Structure of the Bible," *Texts and Responses: Studies Presented to Nahum N. Glatzer*, ed. Michael A. Fishbane and Paul R. Flohr (Leiden: Brill, 1975); Robert C. Culley, *Studies in the Structure of Hebrew Narrative* (Philadelphia: Fortress / Missoula, Mont.: Scholars Press, 1976); and Terry J. Prewitt, *The Elusive Covenant: A Structuralist-Semiotic Reading of Genesis* (Bloomington: Indiana University Press, 1990).

37. "Narrative Structure and Canonical Perspective in Genesis."

38. *Narrative Covenant*, 119–20. The close resemblances between Noah and Utnapishtim have been long noted and variously explained, but Damrosch is arguing for a larger generic influence.

39. "The Problem of Speech Genres," in *Speech Genres and Other Late Essays*, trans. Vern W. McGee, ed. Caryl Emerson and Michael Holquist (Austin: University of Texas Press, 1986), 60.

40. Later rabbinic commentary, seized on by Milton in *Paradise Lost*, insisted that Adam was well out of earshot during the temptation, but the KJV and the NIV render the Hebrew *ima* by noting that Adam was "with her," a detail omitted in the RSV.

41. See Isaac Rabinowitz, "'Word' and Literature in Ancient Israel," *New Literary History* 4 (1972): 127: "Man is here shown participating

with God in creating the vitality and the various natures of animals and birds." God's ten words to Abraham are linked in rabbinic tradition with his Ten Commandments to Moses.

42. See *The Voice of Jacob: On the Composition of Genesis* (Bloomington: Indiana University Press, 1990), 91–92. Brisman interprets Genesis as a struggle between two authors or "voices," combining the Documentary Hypothesis concerning historical sources with Harold Bloom's agonistic theory of literary influence. Brisman's reading is a brilliant literary-critical alternative to my own Bakhtinian interpretation in this chapter.

43. See pages 3–12 of *The Art of Biblical Narrative*. The drunkenness and nakedness of Noah recur earlier in more degrading form in the incestuous seduction of Lot by his two daughters, a seduction motivated by their belief that "there is not a man on earth to come in to us after the manner of all the earth" and give them offspring other than their father (Gen. 19:31).

44. "Bakhtin, Sociolinguistics and Deconstruction," in *The Theory of Reading*, ed. Frank Gloversmith (Brighton, Sussex: Harvester / Totowa, N.J.: Barnes and Noble, 1984), 128.

45. Damrosch, *Narrative Covenant*, 132–34. E. A. Speiser suggests an allusion to the building of Babylon described in the earlier creation epic *Enuma Elish*; see the commentary in his Anchor Bible *Genesis* (Garden City, N.Y.: Doubleday, 1964), 75–76.

46. *Irony in the Old Testament*, 2d edition (Sheffield: Almond, 1981), 88; Good cites earlier remarks by A. J. Heschel and Walther Zimmerli to this effect.

47. "The Shape of Genesis 11:1–9," in *Rhetorical Criticism: Essays in Honor of James Muilenberg*, ed. Jared J. Jackson and Martin Kessler (Pittsburgh: Pickwick, 1974).

48. Josipovici, *Book of God*, 294. A full discussion of "Gospel Criticism as Narrative Criticism" is provided in the first part of Stephen D. Moore's *Literary Criticism and the Gospels*.

49. Timothy Bahti argues that *Mimesis* employs the same kind of typological pattern of fulfillment that Auerbach analyzes in his essay "Figura," thus requiring that "history" continually transcend and cancel itself as it moves from one textual example to another. See Bahti, "Auerbach's *Mimesis*: Figural Structure and Historical Narrative," in *After Strange Texts: The Role of Theory in the Study of Literature*, ed. Gregory S. Jay and David L. Miller (University: University of Alabama Press, 1985).

50. *The Genesis of Secrecy*, 115. Kermode notes several of the repetitions I describe here, but he uses a narratological scheme of motifs, "Betrayal, Flight, and Denial" (62), which obscures the dialogic resemblances between the different types of testimony.

51. Cited in Robert Coles, *Flannery O'Connor's South* (Baton Rouge: Louisiana State University Press, 1980), 105. René Girard notes the connection between Peter's denial of Christ in chapter 14 and his rebuke of

Jesus in chapter 8, but he does not believe that Mark or any of the other gospel writers perceived this relationship; see *The Scapegoat*, trans, Yvonne Freccero (Baltimore: Johns Hopkins University Press, 1986), 149–164, for Girard's reading of this episode according to his theory of mimetic desire.

52. For an alternative account of Judas that considers Matthew's and John's portraits of his character as developing Mark's version but without reference to Peter, see Kermode, *Genesis of Secrecy*, 84–99.

53. In "John Come Lately: The Belated Evangelist," in *The Bible and the Narrative Tradition*, ed. Frank McConnell (New York: Oxford University Press, 1986), Donald Foster argues that an opposition between Johannine and Petrine Christianity is represented in the rivalry of the two disciples in the Fourth Gospel. His idea that John the evangelist feels himself in competition with the earlier Synoptic writers, even in competition with Jesus himself, treats the author of the Fourth Gospel as if he were the Jacob of Genesis, trying to steal the blessing.

54. See *Art and Answerability: Early Philosophical Essays by M. M. Bakhtin*, ed. Michael Holquist and Vadim Liapunov, trans. and notes by Vadim Liapunov, supplement trans. Kenneth Brostrom (Austin: University of Texas Press, 1990), passim; and Michael Holquist, *Dialogism: Bakhtin and His World* (London: Routledge, 1990), 32–33.

Chapter 2

1. "On Reading the Bible (II)," *On the Art of Reading* (New York: Putnam, 1920), 174–76.

2. *The Modern Reader's Bible* (New York: Macmillan, 1895); *The Bible Designed to be Read as Living Literature* (New York: Simon and Schuster, 1936), xii; *The Book of J* (New York: Grove Weidenfeld, 1990).

3. Lou H. Silberman, "Listening to the Text," *Journal of Biblical Literature* 102 (1983): 6. As an example of an alternative, literary analysis, Silberman applies some of the categories of the Russian Formalists to a reading of the Book of Genesis.

4. See especially Sanders, *Torah and Canon* (Philadelphia: Fortress, 1972) and *From Sacred Story to Sacred Text*; Childs, *Introduction to the Old Testament as Scripture* and *The New Testament as Canon: An Introduction* (Philadelphia: Fortress, 1984). J. F. A. Sawyer's *From Moses to Patmos* (London: SPCK, 1977) gives a synthetic view of the Christian Old Testament that balances historical and theological perspectives. Walter Brueggemann's *The Creative Word: Canon as a Model for Biblical Education* (Phildelphia: Fortress, 1982) is the most comprehensive of a number of synoptic Old Testament studies by this author. The historical subdiscipline of "form criticism," although concerned with questions of literary genre, has concentrated on reconstructing small units of an oral stage of composition and has not dealt extensively with the question of a larger system of comprehensive genres that a poetics addresses; see Gene M.

Tucker, *Form Criticism of the Old Testament* (Philadelphia: Fortress, 1971). Tucker notes that the founder of form criticsm, Hermann Gunkel, derived many of his generic categories and attitudes toward the biblical text from the folklore studies of the Grimm brothers in the early nineteenth century.

5. *The Literary Guide*, 595, 597. A notably synthetic and comprehensive literary reading that antedates all of these is Leonard L. Thompson's *Introducing Biblical Literature*. Gabriel Josipovici's *The Book of God* is less systematic but ranges widely over the Hebrew Bible and the New Testament and locates the connectedness of the Bible's parts in the "rhythm" of the reader's response. Adele Berlin's *Poetics and Interpretation of Biblical Narrative* (Sheffield: Almond, 1983) is a preliminary but suggestive discussion of characterization and point of view in the Hebrew Bible.

6. "A Poetics of the Bible," 156–59.

7. *The Great Code*, 175.

8. *The Literary Guide*, 7; Olshen and Feldman, *Approaches to Teaching the Hebrew Bible as Literature*; Roger Brooks and John J. Collins, eds., *Hebrew Bible or Old Testament? Studying the Bible in Judaism and Christianity* (Notre Dame: Notre Dame University Press, 1990). A thoughtful treatment of the difference from a Christian perspective is provided by Sawyer's *From Moses to Patmos*.

9. *The Book of J*, 14.

10. Early dating for the closing of canon of the Hebrew Bible is argued by Sid Z. Leiman, *The Canonization of Hebrew Scripture: The Talmudic and Midrashic Evidence* (Hamden, Conn.: Archon Books, 1976) and by Roger Beckwith, *The Old Testament Canon of the New Testament Church* (Grand Rapids, Mich.: Eerdmans, 1985). The case against the Alexandrian-canon hypothesis is made by Albert C. Sundberg, *The Old Testament of the Early Church*, Harvard Theological Studies 20 (Cambridge: Harvard University Press, 1964), while late dating for the closing of the Jewish canon has been proposed by J. N. Lightstone, "The Formation of the Biblical Canon in Judaism of Late Antiquity: Prolegomenon to a General Reassessment," *Studies in Religion* 8 (1979): 135–42, and by John Barton, *The Oracles of God: Perceptions of Ancient Prophecy in Israel after the Exile* (New York: Oxford University Press, 1986).

11. See the article by Nahum Sarna, "The Bible: Canon, Text and Tradition" in the *Encyclopedia Judaica* (Jerusalem: Keter, 1971), vol. 4, cols. 815–32 on this point.

12. The Samaritan canon, limited to the Pentateuch, was not so much an alternative canon as a restrictive version of the Hebrew Bible; in any case, it was not historically influential beyond the first century C.E.

13. "The Bible," col. 821. In his doctoral dissertation, "The Closing of the Collection of Holy Scriptures: A Study in the History of the Canonization of the Old Testament," (Diss., Vanderbilt University, 1970),

Theodore Norman Swanson argues that the formal division of the books beyond the Law into the two sections of the Prophets (*Nebi'im*) and the Writings (*Ketubim*) did not occur until the end of the second century C.E. within the Babylonian Jewish community and was only formally accepted by Jews in Palestine in the fourth century. But Swanson believes the content of the Hebrew Bible canon was essentially fixed by 50 C.E., as far as the Pharisees were concerned, and he acknowledges that different genres were perceived among the books beyond the Pentateuch well before the formal separation of the Prophets and the Writings.

14. "Canonization: Hearing the Voice of the Same God through Historically Dissimilar Traditions," *Interpretation* 36 (1982): 25. More detailed discussion of this phenomenon can be found in Sheppard's earlier book *Wisdom as a Hermeneutical Construct* (Berlin: de Gruyter, 1980).

15. James L. Crenshaw, *Old Testament Wisdom: An Introduction* (Atlanta, Ga.: John Knox, 1981), 41.

16. Frye, *Anatomy of Criticism* (Princeton: Princeton University Press, 1957), 246–47; Guillén, "On the Uses of Literary Genre," *Literature as System* (Princeton: Princeton University Press, 1971), 117–21. In the first chapter of his *Reading the Old Testament* (Philadelphia: Westminster, 1984), John Barton offers a useful analysis of "literary competence and genre-recognition" as defined by traditional biblical criticism.

17. P. N. Medvedev / M. M. Bakhtin, *The Formal Method in Literary Scholarship: A Critical Introduction to Sociological Poetics*, trans. Albert J. Wehrle (Baltimore: Johns Hopkins University Press, 1978), 129, 136.

18. *Problems of Dostoevsky's Poetics*, ed. and trans. Caryl Emerson, intro. Wayne C. Booth, Theory and History of Literature, vol. 8 (Minneapolis: University of Minnesota Press, 1984), 106, 142.

19. *Speech Genres*, 107. For a full discussion of Bakhtin's theory of genre, see chapter 7 of Morson and Emerson's *Mikhail Bakhtin*.

20. *Dialogic Imagination*, 84–85.

21. See "Adaptable for Life: The Nature and Function of the Canon" in Sanders's *From Sacred Story to Sacred Texts*, which nevertheless seems to me to underestimate the importance of the "stable, 'eternal'" aspirations of the biblical canon.

22. Brueggemann, *The Creative Word*, 8; Childs, *Introduction to the Old Testament as Scripture*, 53.

23. On the rabbinic ideas of the canon, see Sarna, "The Bible," and Jacob Neusner, *From Testament to Torah: An Introduction to Judaism in Its Formative Age* (Englewood Cliffs, N.J.: Prentice-Hall, 1988). On the canon-formation of the Hebrew Bible, see Sarna, "The Bible"; Leiman, *Canonization of Hebrew Scripture*; Beckwith, *The Old Testament Canon of the New Testament Church*; and Barton, *Oracles of God*.

24. See Joseph Blenkinsopp, *Wisdom and Law in the Old Testament: The Ordering of Life in Israel and Early Judaism* (Oxford: Oxford University Press, 1983); Gerald Bruns, "Canon and Power in the Hebrew Scrip-

tures," in *Canons,* ed. Robert von Hallberg (Chicago: University of Chicago Press, 1984); and Gerald Sheppard, "True and False Prophecy Within Scripture," in *Canon, Theology and Old Testament Interpretation: Essays in Honor of Brevard Childs,* ed. Gene M. Tucker, David L. Petersen, and Robert R. Wilson (Philadelphia: Fortress, 1988) for persuasive formulations of these claims. The historicist maxim of Julius Wellhausen that "the Law is later than the Prophets," along with other positivist assertions of priority, may be countered with the idealist maxim of Jorge Luis Borges that "each writer *creates* his precursors" ("Kafka and His Precursors," in *Other Inquisitions, 1937–1952,* trans. Ruth L. C. Simms [Austin: University of Texas Press, 1964], 108).

25. "The Problem of Speech Genres," in *Speech Genres,* 91.

26. For a shrewd discussion of this latter poetics, see "Genre and Countergenre: The Discovery of the Picaresque," in Claudio Guillén's *Literature as System* (Princeton: Princeton University Press, 1971). Guillén borrows the term "unwritten poetics" from Renato Poggioli, and develops his historical view of genre in other valuable essays in this book.

27. "Averroes' Search," in *Labyrinths,* 149.

28. Sarna, in "The Bible," explains the order of books at this stage as a function of the shelving of individual scrolls in archives and houses of study.

29. See Mendenhall, "Covenant Forms in Israelite Tradition," in *Biblical Archeologist Reader,* ed. E. F. Campbell and D. N. Freedman (Garden City, N.Y.: Doubleday, 1970), 3:25–53; Hillers, *Covenant: The History of a Biblical Idea* (Baltimore: Johns Hopkins University Press, 1969); and chapter 4 of John H. Walton's useful survey, *Ancient Israelite Literature in Its Cultural Context* (Grand Rapids, Mich.: Zondervan, 1989). "The striking formal characteristic of this section," Mendenhall observes of the historical prologue, "is the 'I-Thou' form of address" (32).

30. *The Narrative Covenant,* 166.

31. Nohrnberg, "Moses," in *Images of God and Man: Old Testament Short Stories in Literary Focus,* ed. Burke O. Long (Sheffield: Almond, 1981).

32. On the treaty form of Deuteronomy itself, see Meredith G. Kline, *Treaty of the Great King: The Covenant Structure of Deuteronomy* (Grand Rapids, Mich.: Eerdmans, 1963); and Moshe Weinfeld, *Deuteronomy and the Deuteronomic School* (Oxford: Clarendon, 1972).

33. *The Book of the Torah: The Narrative Integrity of the Pentateuch* (Atlanta, Ga.: John Knox, 1988), 117, 118. This the most informative study of law and the Law as a whole that I am aware of, as well as the most congenial to the kind of literary approach I am developing here. But see also David Clines, *The Theme of the Pentateuch, Journal for the Study of the Old Testament* Supplement Series no. 10 (Sheffield, 1978); Sawyer, *From Moses to Patmos;* and Brueggeman, *The Creative Word,* for useful analyses of this part of the canon.

34. *Torah and Canon,* 34.

35. See *Moses and the Deuteronomist* and Polzin's summary of this analysis in his essay on Deuteronomy in Alter and Kermode's *Literary Guide.*

36. In *Torah and Canon* James Sanders gives a plausible historical rationale for the creation of a five-book Law, a collection of sacred writings that ends with Israel before the land of Palestine rather than within it. The Pentateuch was given its definitive form by Jews in Babylon during the Exile, he argues, and reflects their sense of Israel's need to replace its loss of political and territorial identity with the constitution for a new type of religious community.

37. *The Book of God,* 114–115. Josipovici makes the interesting observation that "we seem everywhere to be asked to read Judges as a parody of Genesis and Exodus" (121). On the representation of women in this episode, see Mieke Bal, *Death and Dissymmetry: The Politics of Coherence in the Book of Judges* (Chicago: University of Chicago Press, 1988), 80–93.

38. Nohrnberg, "Moses," 37. Compare Paul D. Hanson, *The Diversity of Scripture: A Theological Interpretation* (Philadelphia: Fortress, 1982), 27: "in Israel prophecy was born with the emergence of kingship and died with its demise."

39. See in particular two essays, Paul D. Hanson, "Israelite Religion in the Early Postexilic Period," and Eric M. Meyers, "The Persian Period and the Judean Restoration," both in *Ancient Israelite Religion: Essays in Honor of Frank Moore Cross,* ed. Patrick D. Miller, Jr., Paul D. Hanson, and S. Dean McBride (Philadelphia: Fortress, 1987).

40. *The Prophetic Existence,* trans. William Wolf (South Brunswick, N.J.: Barnes, 1969), 114.

41. *The Creative Word,* 65.

42. "1 and 2 Chronicles," *The Literary Guide,* 365.

43. "The Joseph Narrative and Ancient Wisdom," in *The Problem of the Hexateuch and Other Essays,* trans. E. W. Trueman Dicken (Edinburgh: Oliver and Boyd, 1966). On Jonah as a wisdom-based satire of prophecy, see Bruce Vawter, C.M., *Job and Jonah: Questioning the Hidden God* (New York: Paulist Press, 1983). In addition to the ironically moralized narrative of the book itself, there is also the creational psalm of thanksgiving that Jonah utters while he is in the belly of the fish.

44. See Sawyer, *From Moses to Patmos,* 74–75.

45. "Psalms," *The Literary Guide,* 250.

46. "The Place and Limit of Wisdom in the Framework of the Old Testament Theology," in *Studies in Ancient Israelite Wisdom,* ed. James L. Crenshaw (New York: KTAV, 1976), 323.

47. John L. McKenzie, S.J., "Reflections on Wisdom," *Journal of Biblical Literature* 86 (1967): 5.

48. *The Creative Word,* 68.

49. "Author and Hero in Aesthetic Activity," *Art and Answerability*, 191.

50. "Canonization," 25. See also Sheppard's *Wisdom as a Hermeneutical Construct* for further analysis of the way biblical wisdom underwrites the formation of the canon.

51. In *Temples and Temple-Service in Ancient Israel* (Oxford: Clarendon, 1978), 2 Menachem Haran distinguishes between the "tent of meeting" described in Exodus 33, which Moses pitches "outside the camp" and at whose entrance the pillar of cloud stands while Yahweh speaks with Moses, and the tabernacle itself, also called "the tent of meeting" in Exodus 40 and elsewhere, which is at the center of the camp and which Moses cannot enter "because the cloud abode upon it, and the glory of the LORD filled the tabernacle" (40:35). Nevertheless, a generic analysis may choose to emphasize the similarity of these historically diverse representations, as Thomas W. Mann does in calling the tent in Exodus 33 "a temporary substitute for the tabernacle," erected by Moses when it appears that God will abandon his original plan for dwelling among his people after they have rejected him in their idolatry of the Golden Calf (*The Book of the Torah*, 110).

52. Carol Meyers notes that "the relationship between God, king, and temple in the ancient Near East was an intimate and essential one," and suggests that David's plan for a temple was in part a "propaganda measure" to reach the non-Israelite elements in David's expanded empire with the message of his royal authority, elements for whom the symbolism of the ark of the covenant would have no great appeal ("David as Temple Builder," in Miller, *Ancient Israelite Religion*).

53. See Haran, *Temples and Temple-Service*, 48–57 on this subject.

54. *Temples and Temple-Service*, 3–4, 45.

55. Marvin Pope gives a modern, historical version of the traditional allegorical readings in "Metastases in Canonical Shapes of the Super Song," in *Canon, Theology and Old Testament Interpretation* ed. Tucker et al.; he finds traces of a Canaanite goddess behind the figure of the bride in the Song of Songs. It is only in the paradigm of wisdom, I would argue, with its cosmopolitan and somewhat syncretistic outlook, that such an alien theology could be so directly appropriated by the Hebrew Bible.

56. Among the many interpretations of the puzzling secularity of the Book of Esther, where God is never mentioned, see Stan Goldman's reading of the story as "an example of Jewish self-criticism" in the context of the Diaspora, "a bold questioning of the Jewish self image" ("Narrative and Ethical Ironies in Esther," *Journal for the Study of the Old Testament* 47 [1990]: 15–31). Since Daniel is believed to have been composed later than Esther, it might be seen as an "answer" to Esther, a more pious and straightforward presentation of exemplary exilic behavior designed to counter Esther's ambiguous secularity.

57. *Palestinian Parties and Politics that Shaped the Old Testament* (London: SCM, 1987; first published 1971), 121–22. Smith attributes the

collection of these materials to an "assimilationist" Judean aristocracy from the end of Nehemiah's govenorship to the Maccabean revolt, but he does not address the question of whether these biblical books were directly influenced by the Greek writings.

Chapter 3

1. *Problems of Dostoevsky's Poetics,* 132, 135.

2. The quotation from *Problems of Dostoevsky's Poetics* given above is from a chapter that Bakhtin added to his monograph of 1929 in a revised edition published in 1963. In this later edition, Bakhtin modifies his earlier claim that Dostoevsky's novels are unprecedented and unique in their dialogic character with observations about earlier manifestations of dialogism in the novel from his essays of the 1930s.

3. "From the Prehistory of Novelistic Discourse," *The Dialogic Imagination,* 61. Recent sociolinguistics would call this a "creolization" of a dominant language.

4. Helen Elsom, "The New Testament and Greco-Roman Writing," in Alter and Kermode, *The Literary Guide,* 570.

5. There is a brief survey of this literature in Elsom and an extended one in chapters 5 and 6 of David E. Aune, *The New Testament in Its Literary Environment* (Philadelphia: Westminster, 1987). James Barr criticizes a "modern purist theology" among biblical scholars in the twentieth century which "in drawing up a fierce alignment against the categories and mental patterns of the Greeks . . . has radically departed from the position of the New Testament itself" (*Old and New in Interpretation: A Study of the Two Testaments* [London: SCM, 1966], 58).

6. See "Parable of Cervantes and the *Quixote,*" *Labyrinths,* 242.

7. *Parables and Paradoxes* (New York: Schocken, 1958), 93.

8. "Discourse in the Novel," *The Dialogic Imagination,* 342.

9. In *Rediscovering the Teaching of Jesus* (New York: Harper and Row, 1967), Norman Perrin calls Jesus' practice of eating with social outcasts a symbol of "the central feature" of his ministry (107). On the importance of dietary regulations in rabbinic Judaism, Jacob Neusner remarks, "the rabbis believe exactly this: The ordinary meal of an ordinary person in his own home has to be eaten *as if* he were a priest, as if his home were the Temple, and as if he were engaged in the act of sacrifice to God. It is not merely that his food has to conform to the biblical laws of what may or may not be eaten" (*Invitation to the Talmud,* revised and expanded edition [San Francisco, Calif.: Harper and Row, 1984], 19).

10. One of the most sophisticated recent discussions of the ancient novel is John J. Winkler's *Auctor & Actor: A Narratological Reading of Apuleius's The Golden Ass* (Berkeley and Los Angeles: University of California Press, 1985); a survey of the various narrative genres is provided by P. G. Walsh, *The Roman Novel* (Cambridge: Cambridge University Press, 1970), Chapter 2. In an unpublished essay, R. Bracht Branham draws

on Bakhtin to make a distinction between the idealizing Greek romances and the parodic Roman novels that begin with Petronius's *Satyricon*. And in an argument that parallels Bakhtin's but does not mention his writings, Mary Ann Tolbert argues that the strongest affinities between the New Testament and Greco-Roman literature lie with "popular" forms like the novel rather than "classical" forms like historiography and biography ("Gospel in Greco-Roman Culture," in *The Book and the Text: The Bible and Literary Theory*, ed. Regina Schwartz [Oxford: Oxford University Press, 1990]).

11. "The Beginnings of Christian Theology," *Journal for Theology and the Church* 6 (1969): 40.

12. Collins, *The Apocalyptic Imagination: An Introduction to the Jewish Matrix of Christianity* (New York, Crossroad, 1984), 3; Hanson, *The Dawn of Apocalyptic* (Philadelphia: Fortress, 1975); von Rad, *Old Testament Theology*, trans. D. M. G. Stalker (New York: Harper and Row, 1965), 2:301–15.

13. *The Apocalyptic Imagination*, 4. This helpful definition is a collective formulation of the Society for Biblical Literature Genres Project and was first published in *Semeia* 14 (1979).

14. See Chapter 2, note 10. Barton's recent *Oracles of God* argues the extreme liberal position; Beckwith's *The Old Testament Canon of the New Testament Church* argues the most conservative one.

15. *Messianic Exegesis: Christological Interpretation of the Old Testament in Early Christianity* (Philadelphia: Fortress, 1988), 14.

16. *The Formation of the Christian Bible*, trans. J. A. Baker (Philadelphia: Fortress, 1972), 27.

17. Wilder, *Early Christian Rhetoric: The Language of the Gospel* (London: SCM, 1964), 86; Barr, *Old and New in Interpretation*, 57.

18. *Messianic Exegesis*, 177.

19. *The Canon of Scripture* (Downers Grove, Ill: InterVarsity, 1988), 56.

20. See J. D. G. Dunn, *Unity and Diversity in the New Testament* (Philadelphia: Westminster, 1977), 223, on the difference between the christology of the later creeds, centered on the idea of incarnation, and the christology of the New Testament, centered on death, resurrection, and ascension.

21. Alan F. Segal's *Two Powers in Heaven: Early Rabbinic Reports about Christianity and Gnosticism* (Leiden: Brill, 1977) notes that "the figure of Jesus begin[s] to take over divine titles in the Pauline and Johannine corpora" and that in Revelation "the identification of the Christ with the tetragrammaton is even more obvious" (210, 212). In *Jesus the Teacher*, Vernon Robbins notes that even in the Gospel of Mark, "Jesus' call to individuals is reminiscent of the action of Yahweh in the biblical tradition" rather than of the way rabbis call their disciples in Pharisaic practice (115).

22. The Greek words used by both writers include *sophos* and *phronesis* and their derivatives.

23. Bacon, *Studies in Matthew* (New York: Henry Holt, 1930), passim, a view reflected in the introductory notes and editorial division of Matthew in *The Jerusalem Bible*; Childs, *The New Testament as Canon*, 71.

24. See Herbert Marks, "Pauline Typology and Revisionary Criticism," *Journal of the American Academy of Religion* 52 (1984): 71–92, on the radically revisionary nature of Paul's hermeneutic, the way he undermines the central authority of the Law in Moses by appealing to the earlier precedent of Abraham, for example. James Sanders argues that while the Pharisees stressed ethical stipulations of the Law and Christians stressed the soteriological narrative in it, neither sect completely ignored the other aspect; see "Torah and Christ," in *From Sacred Story to Sacred Text.*

25. It is possible that this double denunciation of Eli and the priestly status quo was perceived by Luke as a specific precedent for the double proclamation of the gospel by John the Baptist and Jesus, already a firm part of the Christian tradition, though I would not want to insist on this connection.

26. *The New Testament as Canon*, 137; compare James M. Reese, "Christ as Wisdom Incarnate: Wiser than Solomon, Loftier than Lady Wisdom," *Biblical Theology Bulletin* 11 (1981): 44–47.

27. Beckett, *Murphy* (New York: Grove, 1957), 65.

28. See, for example, Augustine's interpolation of the Gospel of John into the doctrines of the Platonists he tells of learning in book 7 of his *Confessions.*

29. "The Epistle to the Hebrew and the Catholic Epistles," in Alter and Kermode, *The Literary Guide*, 521.

30. *The Book of J*, 3.

31. *The Origins of the Gospel Traditions* (Philadelphia: Fortress, 1979), 71.

32. See R. W. Funk, "The Apostolic *Parousia:* Form and Significance," in *Christian History and Interpretation: Studies Presented to John Knox* (Cambridge: Cambridge University Press, 1967), 265, on the "eschatological overtones" of Paul's presence, physical and epistolary, within the early churches. It would seem that in this earliest letter, the association of the apostolic and messianic *parousias* was most explicit.

33. *The Eerdmans Bible Dictionary* (Grand Rapids, Mich.: Eerdmans, 1987), 647.

34. *The Other Bible*, ed. Willis Barnstone (San Francisco, Calif.: Harper and Row, 1984).

35. This point is made convincingly by Childs in *The New Testament as Canon*, 94–95.

36. Childs, *The New Testament as Canon*, 387ff. A similar distinction between the "historical Paul" and the "canonical Paul" is made by Harry Y. Gamble in *The New Testament Canon: Its Making and Meaning* (Philadelphia: Fortress, 1985), 77.

37. *Jesus the Teacher*, 65–67.

38. These canon catalogues appear in *New Testament Apocrypha*, 2 vols., ed. Edgar Hennecke and Wilhelm Schneemelcher, trans. R. McL. Wilson (Philadelphia: Westminster, 1963, 1965), 1:43–45 and 1:47–49.

39. *New Testament Apocrypha*, 1:43–44.

40. This has been most influentially argued by Sundberg, *The Old Testament of the Early Church*. A cogent statement of the older Alexandrian-canon hypothesis can be found in the article "Canon of the OT" by R. H. Pfeiffer in *The Interpreter's Dictionary of the Bible* (New York: Abingdon, 1962), 4:510–11. One recent reinterpretation of the vexed issue of the Old Testament canon even argues that the tripartite structure of the Hebrew Bible of Judaism was itself a late conception, arrived at in Babylonia at the end of the second century C.E. and only widely accepted in Palestine in the fourth century; see Swanson, "The Closing of the Collection of Holy Scriptures."

41. *The Cambridge History of the Bible*, ed. P. R. Ackroyd and C. F. Evans (Cambridge: Cambridge University Press, 1970), 1:140. The canon lists are printed in convenient synoptic form by Sundberg, 58–59.

42. This "permanent basic assumption of the Christian Bible" is traced back to Paul himself by Campenhausen, *The Formation of the Christian Bible*, 37.

43. I am paraphrasing Campenhausen's conclusion to *The Formation of the Christian Bible*, 328.

44. *On Christian Doctrine*, trans. D. W. Robertson, Jr. (New York: Liberal Arts, 1958), 41–42. Augustine's list of the books of the New Testament is also essentially bipartite. It names "the four evangelical books," Matthew, Mark, Luke, and John, and then twenty-one "epistles" by Paul and other apostles. Acts and Revelation are mentioned together, with no generic classification, at the end of the list (42).

45. *From Moses to Patmos*, 72. Sawyer is one of the few commentators who reflects on the signficance of the structure of the Christian Old Testament as a whole.

46. "The 'Bible as Literature' in Late Antiquity and the Middle Ages," *Hebrew University Studies in Literature and the Arts* 11 (1983): 20–70.

Chapter 4

1. See on these matters James Kugel, *The Idea of Biblical Poetry*, chapters 3 and 4, and "The 'Bible as Literature' in Late Antiquity and the Middle Ages."

2. *A Defence of Poetry, Miscellaneous Prose of Sir Philip Sidney*, ed. Katherine Duncan-Jones and Jan van Dorsten (Oxford: Clarendon, 1973), 80.

3. Carlyle, *On Heroes, Hero-Worship, and the Heroic in History, The Works of Thomas Carlyle* (New York: Scribner: 1898–1901), 5:49; Froude, *The Book of Job* (London: John Chapman, 1851), 3.

4. Sewell, *The Vision of Tragedy* (New Haven: Yale University Press, 1959), 9; Harold Fisch, "Job: Tragedy Is Not Enough," in *Poetry With a*

Purpose: Biblical Poetics and Interpretation (Bloomington: Indiana University Press, 1988); William Whedbee, "The Comedy of Job," *Semeia* 7 (1977): 1–39.

5. See Frost, *A Masque of Reason* (New York: Henry Holt, 1945), MacLeish, *J. B.* (Boston: Houghton Mifflin, 1958), and Simon, *God's Favorite* (New York: Random House, 1975). In fiction, Stanley Elkin's *The Living End* (New York: Dutton, 1979) and Robert A. Heinlein's *Job: A Comedy of Justice* (New York: Ballantine, 1984) are recent additions. Robert Gordis in *The Book of God and Man: A Study of Job* (Chicago: University of Chicago Press, 1965) is one of those who claims of Job that "it is literally the only book of its kind" (4).

6. *The Literary Study of the Bible: An Account of the Leading Forms of Literature Represented in the Sacred Writings* (Boston: Heath, 1896).

7. Job 12:9 refers to God as "Yahweh," but in his Anchor Bible *Book of Job*, Marvin Pope suggests that the phrase in which the name occurs, "the hand of the LORD has done this," has been transposed from Isaiah 41:20 (*Job* [Garden City, N.Y.: Doubleday, 1965], 88).

8. See Pope's introduction to the Anchor Bible *Job*, l–lxvi, for a useful summary of this "parallel literature." Translations of the Babylonian texts and commentary on them are provided in W. G. Lambert, *Babylonian Wisdom Literature* (Oxford: Clarendon, 1960); translations of all potentially relevant materials can be found in James B. Pritchard, ed., *Ancient Near Eastern Texts Relating to the Old Testament*, 3d edition (Princeton: Princeton University Press, 1969).

9. *Babylonian Wisdom Literature*, 26.

10. *Torah and Canon*, 103.

11. "The Place of the Book of Job in the History of Israel's Religion," *Ancient Israelite Religion*, 523, 526. This argument is developed in greater detail in Janzen's commentary on Job in the *Interpretation: A Bible Commentary for Teaching and Preaching* series, ed. James Luther Mays, Patrick D. Miller, and Paul J. Achtmeier (Atlanta, Ga.: John Knox, 1985), a commentary that offers many good literary-critical observations. In *Torah and Canon*, James Sanders argues similarly: "The question the Book of Job poses is how to relate the Mosaic-prophetic theology of the God of Israel as a nation to the situation of Israel's dispersion, where covenant responsibility has dramatically shifted to the individual, wherever he may be" (107).

12. Moshe Greenberg, "Job," *The Literary Guide to the Bible*, 294. Historical critics usually claim that the speeches in these chapters have been "thoroughly scrambled" (Pope, *Job*, xviii), with the lines assigned to the wrong speakers. But Greenberg, Gordis (*The Book of God and Man*), and others more attuned to the literary features of the book argue convincingly that the received text may be read here as irony on Job's part.

13. *Job*, 169.

14. Alter and Kermode, *Literary Guide*, 296.

15. *Job*, 134.

16. *The Book of God and Man*, 67.

17. Janzen, *Job*, 218

18. *The Art of Biblical Poetry*, 91–92.

19. Even in the Prologue and Epilogue, as Janzen points out, the terse conversational exchanges that Robert Alter singles out as a distinctive feature of the narrative parts of the Hebrew Bible are prominent; see Alter's *Art of Biblical Narrative*, chapter 4, "Between Narration and Dialogue," and Janzen's *Job*, 31–34.

20. *Problems of Dostoevsky's Poetics*, 40.

21. Bruce Zuckerman, *Job the Silent: A Study in Historical Counterpoint* (New York: Oxford University Press, 1991). Although it makes only passing reference to Bakhtin, this is a challenging dialogical study of the Book of Job based on the assumption of the historical variousness and formal incoherence of its component parts.

22. *Theological Wordbook of the Old Testament*, ed. R. Laird Harris, Gleason L. Archer, Jr. and Bruce K. Waltke (Chicago: Moody, 1980), 1:417; 2:621.

23. "Blake's Reading of the Book of Job," in *Spiritus Mundi: Essays on Literature, Myth, and Society* (Bloomington: Indiana University Press, 1976), 229.

24. *Job: The Victim of His People*, trans. Yvonne Freccero (Stanford: Stanford University Press, 1987), 142.

25. *The Art of Biblical Poetry*, 87, 96.

26. *The Art of Biblical Poetry*, 104.

27. Janzen, *Job*, 248–49; Pope, *Job*, 289. Pope himself puts the lines in brackets in his translation.

28. *The Testament of Job*, ed. and trans. Robert A. Kraft (Missoula, Mont.: Society of Biblical Literature / Scholars' Press, 1974), 77.

29. The point is made by Alter in *The Art of Biblical Poetry*, 99. One might add that the designation of the ruler of Babylon as the "Day Star, son of Dawn" who tried to "set his throne on high" "above the stars of God" in Isaiah 14:12ff. was later understood as a description of Satan's abortive rebellion against God.

30. See Frye, *The Great Code*, 194–95, for an account of the way Satan is "metaphorically identified" with Leviathan and Behemoth.

31. Janzen, *Job*, 23; Greenberg, *The Literary Guide*, 300. David Clines interprets the epilogue similarly in "Deconstructing the Book of Job," in *The Bible as Rhetoric: Studies in Biblical Persuasion and Credibility*, ed. Martin Warner (London: Routledge, 1990), as does Whedbee in "The Comedy of Job." Zuckerman reverses the argument, claiming that the poetic body of the book is a parodic critique of a traditionally pious prologue and epilogue.

32. *Job and Jonah*, 1.

33. See the Anchor Bible *Psalms, III: 101–150*, ed. and trans. Mitchell Dahood (Garden City, N.Y.: Doubleday, 1970), 286. Details of the parallels with Psalm 8 (including the Hebrew word *behemot* in verse 7) are given by Janzen in "The Place of the Book of Job in the History of Israel's

Religion"; Janzen and Gordis (*The Book of God and Man*, 144–45) also elaborate on the parallels with Second Isaiah.

34. See Elias Bickerman, *Four Strange Books of the Bible: Jonah, Daniel, Koheleth, Esther* (New York: Schocken, 1967).

35. Morton Smith, *Palestinian Parties and Politics*, 121.

36. *Testament of Job*, 61.

37. See chapter 1 of Judith R. Baskin's *Pharaoh's Counsellors: Job, Jethro, and Balaam in Rabbinic and Patristic Tradition*, Brown Judaic Studies 47 (Chico, Calif.: Scholars, 1983).

38. *Speech Genres*, 170.

Chapter 5

1. "Preface to the Revelation of St. John [I]," *Luther's Works*, ed. Jaroslav Pelikan and Helmut T. Lehmann (Philadelphia: Muhlenberg Press / Concordia Publishing House, 1955–86), 35:399.

2. Hal Lindsey, with C. C. Carlson, *The Late Great Planet Earth* (Grand Rapids, Mich.: Zondervan, 1970). According to the April 1991 issue of *Bookstore Journal*, Zondervan has printed almost 11 million copies of this book; figures for the Bantam Books edition, first published in 1972, are not available.

3. M. Eugene Boring, *Revelation, Interpretation: A Bible Commentary for Teaching and Preaching* (Louisville, Ky.: John Knox, 1989), 4.

4. *Apocalypse and the Writings on Revelation*, ed. Mara Kalnins, *The Works of D. H. Lawrence* (Cambridge: Cambridge University Press, 1980), 63.

5. *The Great Code*, 137. Frank Kermode's *The Sense of an Ending: Studies in the Theory of Fiction* (New York: Oxford University Press, 1967), in contrast, which also uses Revelation as a literary model, insists on the crucial difference between religious myth and literary fiction.

6. *Literary Criticism of the New Testament* (Philadelphia: Fortress, 1970), 53.

7. *A Rebirth of Images: The Making of St. John's Apocalypse* (Westminster: Dacre, 1949), 49. This seems not a direct allusion to Job so much as the reflection of a family resemblance between Israelite wisdom literature and later Jewish apocalyptic; see Janzen, *Job*, 110ff. Job was read through the lens of Jewish apocalyptic in the Testament of Job and in the Dead Sea Scrolls, however.

8. Collins, *The Apocalyptic Imagination*, 211.

9. For an account of these Greco-Roman revelations, see Aune, *The New Testament in Its Literary Environment*, 226–38. Aune adds the consideration of the "function" of apocalyptic writing to Collins's attention to the form and the content of the genre. Dante's *Divine Comedy* has the pilgrim-poet protest, "I am not Aeneas, I am not Paul" when he is invited by Virgil in canto 2 to visit Hell, alluding to the *Aeneid* and the Apocalypse of Paul.

10. Adela Yarbro Collins, *Crisis and Catharsis: The Power of the Apocalypse* (Philadelphia: Westminster, 1984), 47; Beardslee, *Literary Criticism of the New Testament*, 59. Yarbro Collins compares the linguistic effect with the deliberate cultivation of "Black English" in American speech.

11. See Merrill C. Tenney, *Interpreting Revelation* (Grand Rapids, Mich.: Eerdmans, 1957), 101–5, for these tabulations.

12. *The Dialogic Imagination*, 341–42.

13. I agree with G. R. Beasley-Murray and others who argue against the common view that these martyrs are the only ones who are resurrected and reign in the Millennium. It is more likely that the martyrs are singled out for mention from the larger group of "those to whom judgment was committed" (20:4). See Beasley-Murray, *The Book of Revelation, New Century Bible Commentary*, rev. ed. (Grand Rapids, Mich.: Eerdmans, 1978), 294–95.

14. Nohrnberg explores the typological relationship between circumcision and the Passover in Exodus in his essay "Moses," 53–54.

15. *The New Testament in Its Literary Environment*, 241; *A Rebirth of Images*, 36.

16. *The Book of Revelation: Apocalypse and Empire* (New York: Oxford University Press, 1990), 42.

17. *A Rebirth of Images*, 85.

18. *Mikhail Bakhtin*, 132, 220

19. *Mikhail Bakhtin*, 220.

20. Paul Minear points out that in the New Testament writings "the native habitat of prophecy was the gathering of believers for worship, instruction, mutual aid, and guidance on their mission in the world. This gathering formed a highly charged magnetic field in which unusual spiritual powers operated" (*New Testament Apocalyptic* [Nashville, Tenn.: Abingdon, 1981], 21).

21. *The Combat Myth in the Book of Revelation*, Harvard Theological Review / Harvard Dissertations in Religion (Missoula, Mont.: Scholars, 1976), 27–28.

22. In his essay on Revelation in *The Literary Guide*, Bernard McGinn credits Victor of Pettau (c. 300) with the first statement of the popular recapitulation theory of the three sevenfold judgements.

23. See, for example, Beasley-Murray's commentary and Jaques Ellul, *Apocalypse: The Book of Revelation*, trans. George W. Schreiner (New York: Seabury, 1977).

24. See Minear's chapter 3, "The Gift to the Congregation." Leonard Thompson provides an excellent formal analysis of "Unity through the Language of Worship" in chapter 4 of his *Book of Revelation*.

25. *The Book of Revelation*, 81–82.

26. Thus, for example, M. Eugene Boring in *Revelation*, 212.

27. Farrer, *The Revelation of St. John the Divine*, (Oxford: Clarendon, 1964), 10; for a discussion of John the Baptist as apocalypticist, see Aune, 238–39.

28. "Reading Hebrews and Revelation Intertextually," in *Intertextuality in Biblical Writings: Essays in Honour of Bas van Iersel*, ed. Sipke Draisma (Kampen, Neth.: J. H. Kok, 1989). It is also worth noting that Hebrews quotes the Old Testament directly instead of "retelling in its own words," as Bakhtin would say.

29. Quoted from the "Appendix: The Full Text of the Muratorian Canon List" in Gamble, *The New Testament Canon*, 95.

30. See *New Testament Apocrypha*, 1:45–46.

31. Quotations are from the translation by Hugo Duensing in *New Testament Apocrypha*, 2:668–83 and give paragraph numbers in parentheses.

32. See Martha Himmelfarb, *Tours of Hell: An Apocalyptic Form in Jewish and Christian Literature* (Philadelphia: University of Pennsylvania Press, 1983).

33. Quotations are from *New Testament Apocrypha*, 2:636–37.

34. The Apocalypse of Thomas, for example, reorganizes the various septenary judgements of Revelation into a single, seven-day week in which the physical universe is progressively destroyed (*New Testament Apocrypha*, 2:799–803).

35. "Toward a Methodology for the Human Sciences," *Speech Genres*, 170.

Afterword

1. *Interpretation* 36 (1987): 21–33.

2. *The Bible in the Modern World* (New York: Harper and Row, 1973), 58–59.

3. See "The Critique of Religion" and "The Language of Faith" in *The Philosophy of Paul Ricoeur*, ed. Charles E. Reagan and David Stewart (Boston: Beacon, 1978).

4. "Dialogue and Dialogism," *Poetics Today* 4 (1983): 107.

5. *Mikhail Bakhtin*, 54, 63.

Index

Abraham: dialogues with God, 22, 23; plea for Sodom, 22; and sacrifice of Isaac, 5–6, 7–10, 11, 12, 26; and sacrifice of Ishmael, compared with sacrifice of Isaac, 7–10, 11–12; and Sarah, compared with Adam and Eve, 19, 20, 22; treaty between Abimelech and, 26

"Abstract objectivism," 13, 175 n.19

Acts of the Apostles, 87, 111; and canonization of New Testament, 107, 108; compared with 1 and 2 Kings, 96; contrasting images of Paul in, 17; Day of Pentecost in, 92; and genre criticism, 106; and Greco-Roman writings, 79, 96; on David as prophet, 63; and redemption, 103

Adam and Eve, story of, 22; compared with Abraham and Sarah, 20; compared with *Epic of Gilgamesh*, 21; and concern with clothing and nakedness in Genesis, 26; verbal exchange with God in, 18, 19

Aeneid (Virgil), revelatory writing in, 143

Aesthetic activity, Bakhtin on, 66

Aesthetic appreciation of Bible, differences between paradigms of communication and, 65–67

Alexandrian canon hypothesis, 42, 109

Alexandrian Judaism, and interpretation of canonical Old Testament, 85, 86

Alter, Robert, 3, 4, 6, 25–26, 40, 41, 63, 124, 129–130, 173 n.2, 174 n.12, 176 n.24, 190 nn.19, 29

Amadis of Gaul, 80

Ancient Near Eastern literature: and apocalyptic writings, 83; epic, compared with Genesis, 21–22; influence on Bible, 17, 49, 50; and origins of Book of Job, 117, 118, 143; and Tower of Babel story, 27; wisdom writings of, compared with wisdom literature of Hebrew Bible, 64

Anthology, Bible as, 39, 40, 41, 170

Antichrist, figure of, 160–161

Apocalypse of John. *See* Revelation, Book of

Apocalypse of Paul, 143, 165

Feldman, Yael S., 174 *n*.4, 180
  n.8
Fisch, Harold, 175 *n*.23, 188 *n*.4
Fishbane, Michael, 16, 176 *n*.28,
  177 *n*.36
Flaubert, Gustave, 32–33, 175
  n.14
Flood: in *Epic of Gilgamesh*, 21;
  in Hebrew Bible, 20, 21, 25
Fokkelman, J. P., 177 *n*.36
*Formal Method in Literary
  Scholarship, The* (Medvedev/
  Bakhtin), 45
Formalism: and dialogical
  poetics of Bible, 41; and
  literary criticism, viii, 170–
  171
Former Prophets: prophetic
  character of narrative history
  of, 58; recapitulation in
  Chronicles, 62
"Forms of Time and of the
  Chronotope in the Novel"
  (Bakhtin), 46–47
Foster, Donald, 179 *n*.53
Frei, Hans, 4
Freyne, Sean, 161
Frost, Robert, 189 *n*.5
Froude, J. A., 115
Frye, Northrop, 40, 41, 129, 140,
  173 *n*.1, 181 *n*.16, 190 *n*.30
Funk, R. W., 187 *n*.35

Galatians, Letter to the, and
  Law, 94
Gamble, Harry Y., 187 *n*.36, 193
  n.29
Generic conventions. *See* Genre
  criticism
Genesis, Book of, 41; appearances of God in, 53; Auerbach's interpretation of, 4, 32;
  Cain and Abel story compared
  with stories of sacrifices of
  Ishmael and Isaac, 8; circumcision as sign of God's covenant with man in, 148;
  communication between God
  and his people in, 36; com-

pared with *Atrahasis Epic*, 176
  n.25; compared with *Epic of
  Gilgamesh*, 21–22; compared
  with the *Odyssey*, 4, 9;
  comparison of sacrifices of
  Ishmael and Isaac in, 7–11;
  dating of Book of Job and, 119;
  and Job's curses upon the day
  of his birth, 126; and Job's
  testing as test of creation as a
  whole in Book of Job, 135;
  Joseph story in, and interpolation of biblical wisdom in
  Law, 62; narrative character
  of, 12–13; on Hagar's exile into
  wilderness, 7; preamble and
  historical prologue, Exodus
  and, 51–52; sacrifice of Isaac
  in, *see* Isaac, sacrifice of;
  sacrifice of Ishmael in, *see*
  Ishmael, sacrifice of; structure
  of, 18; types of verbal exchange
  between God and humanity in,
  18–20. *See also* Dialogic
  interpretation of Genesis; God,
  dialogue with his people
Genre criticism, 11; and apocalyptic literature as extracanonical genre of religious
  literature, 83; Auerbach and,
  6; and Auerbach's interpretation of Gospel of Mark, 31;
  and Bakhtin's concept of "the
  novel," 78–79; and Bakhtin's
  theory of dialogue, 15; and
  canonical divisions of Hebrew
  Bible, 45–49; and canonization
  of New Testament, 106;
  and classification of Book of
  Job, 115–116; and earliest
  Christian writings compared
  with Greco-Roman novels,
  77–84; of Genesis, 6; and
  heterogeneity of paradigm
  of gospel, 90; and influence
  of apocalyptic literature on
  New Testament, 83–84;
  stylistic criticism and, 7. *See
  also* Genre(s)

of the Bible. In addition, literary critics especially concerned with Bakhtin's theory and its potential application to different texts will find this study illuminating.

About the Author

Walter L. Reed has taught English at Yale University and the University of Texas, where he was Director of Comparative Literature. He is currently Chair of the English Department at Emory University. He is the author of *Meditations on the Hero: A Study of the Romantic Hero in Nineteenth-Century Fiction* (1974) and *An Exemplary History of the Novel: the Quixotic versus the Picaresque* (1981).